GREENING THE PSYCHOLOGICAL POLLUTION OF HUMAN

DR. VALER GABRIAN
DR. CORNEL FLOREA-GABRIAN

authorHOUSE®

AuthorHouse™
1663 Liberty Drive
Bloomington, IN 47403
www.authorhouse.com
Phone: 1-800-839-8640

First published by AuthorHouse   10/04/2011

ISBN: 978-1-4670-0203-5 (sc)
ISBN: 978-1-4670-0204-2 (ebk)

Printed in the United States of America

ABSTRACT

Thousands of years, many intellectuals, big thinkers you time historical, were anxious to find ways and means necessary normalization life and work of the human species in consensus with laws of Nature. Sentence and views designed by the time historical high thinkers, designed to normalize life and work human species, have endorsed "effectual cause", the remaining an unknown for thousands of years.

Following the way of thinking of some great intellective of historical time, concerned about the influence of human society going to normalization of relations between people and people and nature (environment), we found that their way of thinking, although always evolved dialectically, however perceived world state by the time they lived by "causal effect", because thousands of years the cause remain unknown.

We lived in a historical period with many and miscellaneous changes economic, social and political, some of which formal and content at the dimension of "socio-economic order ": transition of some countries from the capitalist socio-economic order to the socialism socio-economic order.

Favored by older, I participated actively and very hard to build socialism in Romania, a country whose citizens have been and I been, the country, until the age of 19, I met in a capitalist socio—economic order and between the age 19 to age 64, I met in the process of building the socialist socio-economic order, and after the age of 64 years, until the age of 83 years, I write this, I have lived and continue to live in a period of transition from socialism to capitalism.

This historical period in my life gave me enough information to know and perceive what was good and evil in a socio-economic capitalist and socialist orders, under the construction period, again, to the capitalist socio-economic order.

Meditating on those written by historians about what characterized the primitive commune, slavery, feudalism, capitalism and socialism, and knowing some of the concerns of many great intellectuals of historical time, to influence the theses and their views of society going to normalization life and work of the human species in line with the laws of nature surprised by what happens in Romania after 1989 and so far in 2009, I began to perceive that a socio-economic order witch is characterized not by itself but by the time people, which, by nature and their nature, shape and content state of the world in time and space.

I began to perceive that in order to normalize life and activity of the human species in line with the laws of nature, human society should be seen in the form of socio-economic order, as a "general form" whose "particular form" is "practical man". Practical man, particular of General and "living cell" of the General must know in detail, as "kind and nature." To know man as kind and nature, we developed a characterization of the man who provides the information necessary to enable to help the perception of "nature and human nature."

"Man is a being endowed with social and biological species with thinking and articulate speech, is owner of four forces: physical strength, intellectual strength, the force of good and evil force and is dominated by a series of laws: the law of accumulation of wealth (wealth) to any price and by any means, without limits law, the law of lust, the lust for power, without limit law, law of selfishness, and many other laws (see Democracy and justice books).

Through imagination and contemplation on how my being as nature and temperament, using me to characterize of every man me have formulated a series of thesis, and from these I formulated the these that: "The Human Forces acting shared with the laws of man throughout his life", generating the nature and temperament process. The conjugate action between the Human rip tides with/and laws that it dominates works independently beyond him.

Through imagination and by contemplation on me and on many of my fellow men whom I knew, I deduced that the law of nature and human flesh generates three processes, which define the nature and human nature:

1) Process of a psychological "compass" imaginary invisible and hardly discernible, which directs how to be human in his relations with his fellows and in dealing with the environment;

2) The process of "imaginary invisible nets" and hardly discernible, "belt" by the conjugate action of human forces with/and human laws which it dominates, "lace" witch enchaining him "psychological", as a nature and temperament, breaking and even stranding him evolve dialectics from what is normal and should be used judiciously;

3) Psychological pollution of thought process with many and various nuisances generated by the conjugate actions between human forces with/and human laws which it dominates.

The laws of nature and human flesh, with the processes that it generates, shall, by induction from private to general, the laws of human society, giving shape and content of human society in time and space.

As a result of scientific discoveries, we concluded that: "the source and engine" which give form and content of the world in time and space is the "law of nature and human flesh", with the three processes it generates. Hence the conclusion that the conclusions that change the world with many bad condition and various social wrongs in a straight world, beneficial to each class of social dialectic, as assumed human nature and of nature, from what is normal and should be used judiciously.

Man, human society and the environment, as organic unit, viewed through the prism of the law of nature and human flesh, and highlight the leading role in the process of determining the human movement and auto-moving of organic unity, as the form and content, in time and space. Organic unity between humans, human society and the environment is an issue that concerns the quality of life of the human species as a whole.

The man is General and cell particularly of general human society as a whole. By man, that nature and temperament, depends on the State of the world in time and space as the form and content.

The environment is so "common house" of the entire human species, and the "basis" on which acts, through work, the man in order to ensure the primary needs and social and spiritual. Environment, the common house of the entire human species, quality and his laws, is the premise of man on Earth; is the premise, as a factor in primary production and passive, in which the man, through work, primary production factor and active, can act to produce the goods needed in his life.

The man, "individual of General" and "cell" of general human society as a whole, tenant in common house of the entire human species, through work, which is primary and active protection due to the law of nature and nature's Act when beneficial, when the mischievous fellows and its impact on the environment. The work is specifically human activity and, depending on how it works depends on both the quality of life, as well as functional quality of the House of his environment.

Particular-man, "General" and "cell" of general human society as a whole, hosted in the House of common, does not know and do not perceive the role and importance of its historic to the House and lives that he built it.

The man turns out to be an exception to the force that created it. The House where he lives, "environment", by its forces and laws, is an environment optimal for human survival, and the action of human immunoglobulin and human laws forces which it dominates, not consistent with the laws of nature. The man turns out to be "a being biologic-social" with "thinking and articulated language", owner of four forces: physical strength, intellectual force, the force of good and evil force and dominated by a series of laws: the law of accumulation of wealth (wealth) at any cost and by any means, without limitation, law regulations appetite, thirst for power, law, law of selfishness without limit and many other laws.

Life Experiences reveals that human forces acting shared with the laws of man throughout his life, independent of his will and desire.

Conjugate actions between human action with forces and human laws which it dominates his proved direct it as a nature and temperament, sometimes enemy of his fellows and, in many cases, and a factor harmful to the environment.

The discovery of the law of nature and human flesh is the premise of a peaceful world, started revolutionary beneficial human, like nature and fire, and, through him, beneficial human society as a whole and the environment.

The man, knowing and perceiving himself, as a kind and threads, begin to produce a work containing only beneficial to human society as a whole and on the environment. So that the environment of the common house of the entire human species, it becomes equally for each tenant, optimum work environment and life, and the inhabitants, in the knowledge of the facts, acts generally only beneficial influence on the environment, whilst through their work and some negative effects generated periodically by forces of nature, which, by the Frost and thaw, torrential and others causes "wounds" of the environment, degraded it qualitatively and quantitatively.

The man, knowing and perceived himself as kind and threads, begin a process of radical change, as kind and fire, becoming its own "enemy" a "friend" of his and the environment. Man, human society and its environment, the organic, beneficial influence each other, and only the environment, the common house of the entire human species evolves dialectal to "the garden of Eden", imagination of man that would have been sometime.

This "dream" is not a utopia, but it is a matter of social conscience, which comes with the auto-knowledge, auto-perception man, as nature and temperament, is a "dialectical law". The man, knowing it and perceiving it, as a nature and temperament, by the conjugate action between its forces and its laws which it dominates, begin a process of influencing beneficial joint action.

The process is profoundly revolutionary and beneficial organic unity: man, human society and environment, and is organized and run by representatives of a triad» psyche—politics, religious and scientific—a body which I've "named" **Supreme Forum of the human species.**

INTRODUCTION

The man, human society and environment must be known and perceived both separately and that an organic unit. The man is known and perceived as "o being fitted with social thinking and language articulated". (Characterization fever man). Human society is known and perceived as an organization of the people in time and space that one has been moved and was auto-moved dialectical passing through forms of organization always superior.

Once the man broke away from the Animal Kingdom (scientific hypothesis of the emergence of man), humanity through several historic eras, the oldest of which was prehistory and protohystory.

Prehistory lasted a few hundred thousand years and was the Stone Age, then hewn Stone Age where the living conditions of peoples were very heavy and the man was subjected to continuous different perils.

He followed Proto—History ERA is characterized by great progress towards its being the age of metals. Heavy conditions of life of those times removed, which were subjected to dangers continuously, he has led people to live together and to defend himself together. People, based on relationships of relatedness, had cooperation relations and mutual aid. In the course of history, man progresses continuously, so that as far back as the Stone Age, discovered the fire and, later, the bow with arrows, discovery that marked a qualitative leap in the way of life. Start a new way to prepare feeding stuffs, it may be easier to defend animals, hunting is practiced and starts gradually and then domesticating of animals in farming, and fishing is intensified.

Using stone tools from the start, and then rudely carved stone and, later, of base metal, bronze, iron, and subsequently, procurement feed gradually begins to relieve and to diversify, which has caused some changes in social life. The first change in social life is represented by the "primitive" commune, which was characterized by an extremely low level of productive forces, which resulted in joint work, the property of the means of production, and the egalitarian effects.

Gradually, over time, changes occur in the way of thinking and mode of work, so that more families come together to form races, which is the first form of social organization of the primitive commune. Races, in turn, begin to unite, while addressing tribe weather for thousands of years of human skill increases continuously, while perfecting your metal tools, starts to develop agriculture and to increase continuously the volume of agricultural products. Begin to appear as new occupations, handcrafts and metalworking. Gradually social division arises.

The gradual development of production forces has resulted in increasing production and productivity of work, which led to the ongoing development of the Exchange and, eventually, to the emergence of factors that have led to the dissolution of the social system of the primitive commune.

Is born the possibility for people to differentiate into landowners, tools and cattle, it causes the phenomenon of enrichment of some families and pauperization of others, the poor being forced to work for the rich. Those who held public office in the races or tribe, like those of military chiefs, priests, and had mastered a great part of the municipality, achieving a dominant economic role.

The riches of some fighting between the tribes grow, exacerbating the estate of the losers is taken and wealth are monetizing slaves; in this historic process, the place of the primitive commune, taking it first human divided society into antagonistic classes, namely the slave society.

At the end of the Millennium III, IV Millennium BC takes ownership of the primitive commune that lasts thousands of years.

Since the primitive commune period highlight that man once detached from among animals, used to **work.**

The work is a fundamental feature of man, which distinguishes it from the animals from which it originated, forged by the ability and tools to act using their influence on the environment, to produce the goods required to meet the necessities (food, clothing and housing) and supporting him and his family. Other human specific abilities such as: language and thinking, drifting in the upshot, from his work.

Scientific hypothesis of human encroachment in the animal world was made by the great biologist Charles Darwin (1809-1882), which demonstrated for the first time the human origin of the animal world, in his origin of species, published in 1859, and the Descent of man and sexual selection, which appeared in 1871, and materialist philosopher German F. Engels (1820-1895) supported the thesis that the Darwinian theory of man from animals is just a prerequisite and that the monkey role in man transformation has had work. The hand work form, "a body of work and, at the same time, the product." The work has had a decisive role in the development and continuous improvement of the brain and the emergence of consciousness; it led to the emergence of language, means of communication is essential in the management of social activity, which has influenced, in turn, the development of thought and conscience. At the same time, the work had its leading role in the emergence of human society and in the evolution of human society, dialectic which passed historical through several socio-economic orders (municipality of primitive, slavery, feudalism, capitalism and the emergence of socialism which, after World War II, the global co-extensive with the disposition of capitalist social-economic development in an atmosphere known as the "cold war", and at the end of the Millennium II has entered into a process of crisis in which a number of former socialist countries have gone through a process of "revolutionary" to capitalism, which had been). In the labor process of have formed social relations of production, the foundation of all other social relationships and decisive further development of both human and human society as a whole.

The environment is 'House "man and the human society as a whole. The organic unity of man,

Human society and the environment is that man cannot exist outside human society, and society cannot exist outside the environment.

And what is particularly important is the fact that man is "individual of General" and at the same time, it is "cell", i.e. the general human society as a whole; "cell" that "rattled" nature and give them form and content, "the State of the world" in time and space and affect the environment.

The man and human society were moved and were auto moving dialectics in time and space, but as "kind and fire", man has always remained the same. Nature and human nature have been known and collected thousands of years, although the Greek philosopher Socrates (469-399 BC) made the famous maximum: "know thyself!" From Socrates, maxima "know thyself!" have a double purpose, aimed, on the one hand, logical thinking, on the other hand, moral notions . . . (Encyclopedic Dictionary, (4), Editor Political, Bucharest, 1966, p. 442).

Knowing thyself, that nature and that the fire, you start getting to know and to "distinguish" State of the world in time and space, and to discover the "absolute truth", "source and engine" which gives the State of the world in time and space form and content, and you start the perception of its historic role in changing the world of what is normal and should be used judiciously; start your historic role in distinguish of environmental protection, "House of the entire family of human species."

CHAPTER 1
MAN AS NATURE AND TEMPERAMENT
(HUMAN NATURE AND GREENING OF THE FLESH)

The man, from the anthropological point of view, it is known with luxury details. From the viewpoint of nature and his flesh was known and seen thousands of years, and if we call the classical characterization of man: "man is a social being equipped with thought and articulated language", we note that, although it expresses a truth absolutely, however do not provide the information needed to assist in the perception of human" as nature and temperament".

Dialectical thinking and rationing, being influenced by the German philosopher's idealistic theses of Hegel (1770-1831)-modernized theory claiming knowledge of the world through the formulation of cognoscibility laws and the principles of dialectic, and that he had the wisdom to demonstrate scientifically that 'things, phenomena and dialectical thinking evolves and progressively thinking that leads to the dialectic of the knowledge of the absolute truth "(laws of dialectic: quantitative collections lead to a new quality internal forces, fight and denying negate)—put a couple of issues and questions: what a cause, secret, enigma that although human thinking dialectics, always evolving, however, that beneficiaries of people thinking, have failed to be auto knowledge and auto perception, as a nature and temperament? Why the man did not know and does not charge for what he's doing what he does with his fellows and in relation to the environment and why not do what normal and sensible should do since it comes with thinking?

Subscriptions to and from the famous Max made by Socrates (469-399 BC): "know thyself!" we take the next, without reservations, characterizing human made it below is from the book democracy and social justice—the future of humanity: man is a being in possession of biologic-social four forces: 1. physical force; 2. force intellectual; 3. the force of good and 4. force of evil, and dominated by a series of laws: the law of accumulation of wealth (wealth) by any means and at any price, Bill without limit; appetite, thirst law breakers, law no limit; law of selfishness, individualism law; argument law and non-reasoning dualism; vim and idleness dualism law; pregnancy and superficiality dualism law; optimism and pessimism dualism law; Cossette's and forgiveness dualism law; concern and disregard dualism law; the law differentiated facilities (equipment to paint, sculpt, the Endowment is to organize and lead, and so on; the law differentiated the pleasures (the pleasure of being the head, the pleasure of being welcomed, listened to) and so on.

This man does not preclude the characterization of the classical characterization of man; instead she gives all the information needed to be able to discover the cause, the secret of why the man, the kind and nature, is:

a) "Man to man) when compared to man";
b) When "man Fox devious manipulation and fox-like to man";
c) When "man versus man" crook;
d) When "man versus man killer".

This way of being human, nature and fire, it should be perceived as a "PSYCHOLOGICAL" POLLUTION, pollution of thinking which is the latest known to man. "Pollution", as a kind of psychological and fire, it is more harmful than environmental pollution of chemical, physical and pollution generated by man through human activities. This psychological pollution of human thinking is beginning to be felt, with the characterization of human as a biological being, in possession of four forces and dominated by a series of laws, "imaginary" thinking and "imaginary" rationing.

Human forces acting shared human laws throughout his lifetime, generating process of nature and his flesh to be perceived as a "psychological pollution of human thinking". Physical and intellectual strength force of man is like a "living" human capital, the prerequisite for the creation of all forms of capital, and the force of good and evil force is constituted as a dualism of good and evil, the prerequisite for the creation of things good and bad. According to the report ("R") between the forces of good (**F.G**) and share of evil forces (**E.F.**), this report ("R") can be ("imaginary" thinking) of the form:

$$R= FG/EF = 1; >1; <1.$$

I stated that this characterization made man offers all the elements, or sufficient, to know and perceive why "nature and human nature" is what it is and why it is beneficial for the dialectical man and human society, since man is endowed with thought? Or dialectical thinking evolves.

The German philosopher Hegel, the thesis that "things, phenomena and dialectical thinking evolves and progressively thinking that leads to the dialectic of knowing the truth essential" must be understood and perceived by the source and engine which gives the dialectical evolution.

Scientific demonstration made in Democracy and social justice books-the future of humanity, and other books on the spring and dialectic thinking engine as the dialectic of human intellectual labor, which, through the process of speaking and writing, sometimes accumulate part of the total, from man to man, from generation to generation, with the trend of evolution partial to infinity (∞) indicates that it generates and the process of dialectic "live" of human capital from the "physical force and intellectual force". Physical and intellectual force of human force that is in the "capital live" man premise of creation of all forms of capital must be perceived as generating "capital live", dialectical evolves. Motivation: the human's physical strength is **relatively constant = "A"** and locate the muscular system. This force, physical force, is characterized by the fact that in addition to the fact that it is relatively constant, it cannot be transmitted from human to human. Intellectual force of man is located in the central nervous system in the human brain, is radically different from man to man, from generation to generation, with the trend of evolution dialectical as potentially to infinity (∞), the process taking place through speech and writing, hence the conclusion that intellectual force **"B"** is always in motion and dialectic auto-moving: „B1" $\rightarrow$ "B2" $\rightarrow$ „B3" . . . $\rightarrow$ „Bn"; „Bn" > „B_{n-1}" > „B_{n-2}" > . . . . „B3" > „B2" > „B1".

Hence the conclusion that the sum of physical stretch A and intellectual force B (form) = "live capital" of the human which is in the process of moving and always auto moving with the dialectical evolutionary potential trend to infinite (∞).

Intellectual force of man is the first spring and the first engine of dialectic thinking, another source and engine of the practical experience of dialectic thinking is of life and human activity.

Pursuant to the first principle of the dialectic, movement and auto moving, and, according to the law of dialectic, quantitative treasure up lead to a new quality, such that:

Dialectic of intellectual labor + practical experience generates dialectic thinking. So always evolving thinking and dialectical thinking leads progressively to the dialectic of knowing "truth absolutely".

Want to be "absolute truth", because "nature and temperament" of man did not evolve dialectal, beneficial human society and as a whole? In order to give an answer to this question should be charged "the human nature and temperament" as a "laws" generated by the action of the conjugate base of human laws human forces that dominate it. Or, the man, in addition to the fact that thousands of years has been able to know and to charge the secret nature of the cause, and his flesh, must also bear in mind that the action by forces and laws which it dominates operates independently of the desire and the will of his.

The human nature and temperament is generated by the action of the conjugate base of the force of good and evil with force with/and human laws that it dominates.

Force of good and evil force is finding themselves in a process of internal struggle continues, beating when one when the other, with minimal breaks tie, hence the report ("R") between the forces of good **(F.G)** and share of evil forces **(E.F.)**, this report ("R") can be ("imaginary" thinking) of the form:

$$R= FG/EF = 1; >1; <1.$$

Meditating on this report ("R") we can conclude that when:

   a) **R= FG/EF > 1 "the man like nature and spirit is man for all the people"**
   b) **R= FG/EF < 1 "the man like nature and spirit is:**
      ⏰ **"man Fox devious manipulation and likely to man";**
      ⏰ **"man versus man" crook;**
      ⏰ **"man versus man killer";**
   c) **R= FG/EF = 1 "the man like nature and spirit not do any good, nor bad for all the people.**

By accepting this principle, the imaginary thought, giving rise to the nature and human nature, and in view of the fact that the action by the human forces and laws with which man/it dominates works independent of human will and desire, we can formulate **this thesis**:

The conjugated actions between the human forces and laws which it dominates generates, "imaginary thinking", the following processes that define the human nature and temperament: a) Process of "psychological" imaginary compasses, invisible and hardly discernible, which directs nature and human nature, causing him to be what is in its relations with his fellows and in relation to the environment (nature); b) the come into being process of a "net" imaginary invisible and poorly discernible, which "enchain psychologically" man as kind and threads, trig and even stranding him to evolve as a dialectical and fire, in what once was, what is the normal and rational should be since the man is endowed with thought; c) Psychological pollution process "thinking" with many and various nuisances arising from co-operations between human action with forces and laws of human/it dominates.

The human nature and temperament **polluted** with many and various nuisances generated by the conjugate action between human forces and laws with/and it dominates stifles and even blocking the dialectical thinking **to develop** the laws and principles that give rise to any process of change the human nature and temperament from what is normal and should be used judiciously.

If this is the "ultimate truth", it once it is known, can man on their own power to improve its psychological "compass" invisible and hardly perceptible which directs nature and rattled?; Maybe the man with the power to auto freedom itself from the "place" invisible and perceptible that it hardly "enchain psychologically", lock it and even stranding him to evolve as a dialectical and threads?; man on their own power to "ecologies" polluted thinking psychologically pollutants generated by the action of the conjugate base of the human forces and laws with which man/it dominate?

Our answer is definitely "can't!" Can't because "psychological" compass and hardly perceptible invisible which directs the human nature and temperament, is generated by the action of the conjugate base of the human forces and laws with which man/it dominates and which operate independently of the will and desire of man; can't because "psychological" enchain of man, the human nature and temperament, in a "mesh" invisible and perceptible, "hard strapped" by the action of human immunoglobulin with forces and laws of human/it dominates works independently of the will and desire of man.

For improving psychological "invisible" compass and hardly discernible, which directs nature and human nature, training leading to the human dialectic as kind and fire, in what it is:

When "man versus man";

When "man Fox devious manipulation and likely to man";
When "man versus man" crook;
When "man versus man killer"

The normal and rational should be to always be only: "man versus man" man should be helped by his fellows.

This is possible through the improvement of "means" by acting "compass psychological" invisible and hardly perceptible which directs the human nature and temperament of **labor in general and in particular the work of the Organization and management at the level of State administration.**

As for the issue of the human nature and temperament "wire netting" invisible and hardly perceptible that it "enchain psychologically", should be helped by his fellows. Or, "meshes" invisible and perceptible that it hardly "enchain psychologically" on nature and man, that is, threads of action strapped conjugate of human forces and laws with which man/it dominates, action that works independently of the will and desire of man. The aid may be given by his fellows by the means by which act as "psychological" compass of human, i.e. WORK in general. In this respect, it is very important work of the ORGANIZATION and MANAGEMENT at the level of State administration, which must be reconciled with the dialectic of human intellectual labor and inputs must be harmonized, the nature of work and accumulated capital according to capital live "dialectic" of man. This task was f. f. complex, requires that it be subject to the priority of a triad» psyche: politics, religious and scientific.

Only the conjugate actions of human laws human forces that dominate thinking it pollutes with many and various nuisances, so dialectic of dialectical thinking, though evolving, yet she remains always polluted psychologically; pollution that functions as a sinusoidal magnetic wave form due to the report ("R") which takes place between **F.G** and **E.F.**

$$R= FG/EF = 1; >1; <1.$$

Psychological pollution of human thought from the "special", "practical man", and makes the level of a triad» psyche (politics, religious and scientific) the work carried out is always the same as efficiency because political leaders, people being, no matter how eager we were to change the "State of the world", in the borders of their country, fail do so because they, people are being "compassing psychologically" that kind of action and between the human forces, conjugated with human laws which it dominates.

The same phenomenon occurs in the religious sector, so that representatives of religious worship "sing" always the same song, which at one time annoys listeners, because it is hitting the maximum sought by the native intelligence of man: "what's too much not healthy . . ."

The help that you need to give the company the humanity of those who are my invested to organize and lead the country? In providing a platform of politics-program of work designed by great intellectuals engaged in work in the institute of scientific research on the knowledge and perception profiled nature and human flesh.

CHAPTER II
HUMAN SOCIETY
(GREENING OF HUMAN SOCIETY BY MANY AND DIVERSE SOCIAL WRONGS)

Human society is a "universal design" in a process of continuous motion and auto movement whose source and engine is "concrete" that man is "particular of General" and "cell" of general human society as a whole.

History of the facts of life and human activity highlights that human society and auto movement in time and space is generated by "practical man", and "cell" of human society and more highlights that between man, "particular of General" and "General" there is a special organic unit currently dialectical in time and space. In this organic unity "concrete" man is "particular of General" (human society as a whole), with emphasis upon explicit request that particular of General, and specifically, the man is "cell" of the General, who by nature and rattled her form and content "world" status in time and space.

Organic unity between concrete human society and man as a whole, considered by the laws of dialectic in which fits perfectly, moves and auto moving in time and space, with emphasis upon explicit dialectical movement and auto movement are the source and the engine in his cell "," in man. Or, specifically, the "cell" by the human nature and temperament, generates State of the world in time and space the form and content, depending on how the "psychological" compass and hardly perceptible invisible, which directs nature and human nature, is influenced by the report ("R") of **G.F.** and **E.F.**, report ("R") of the form:

$$R= FG/EF = 1; >1; <1.$$

And acting shared human laws which it dominates. The bottom line is that: the human nature and temperament, "compassing psychologically" by the conjugate actions of human between human forces and laws which it dominates, the man being and "cell" of society, through the process of generating work organization and leadership at the level of State administration, State of the world in time and space, with all that characterize good and evil.

Sentence: the processes that define the human nature and temperament, the concrete man being particular of General and specific "cell" General has become, processes that determine the State of the world in time and space to what it characterizes good or bad. The main processes from private to general, induction, is achieved through the work of the Organization and management at the level of State administration and thus the psychological "compass" invisible and perceptible targeting hard-to-nature and human nature becomes, through the work of the Organization and management at the level of State administration, "compass" walking human society in time and space, respectively determine the State of the world in time and space. "Enchain Psychological" of man, the kind and nature, in a "mesh" invisible and perceptible "hard strapped" by the conjugate actions between human forces and laws with/and which it dominates, becomes, through the work of the Organization and management at the level of State administration, "enchain" of human society, thereby hindering it and even blocking a dialectical evolve from what is normal and should be used judiciously.

Many thinkers have historical times have been sensitive to the "State of the world" time with many and diverse social wrongs caused by nature and human nature and which were "State of the world", elaborated theses and points of view which would lead to a change in his State of the world "in" what was what he wanted to be. Their work has brought in almost mild improvements "in his State of the world", but the background remains the same problem: the "absolute truth", "source and engine" of the State of the world "polluted" remains a conundrum, because social injustices must be perceived as a "moral-social pollution", being, in my view, the most "harmful pollution". This pollution "moral-social" shall be forwarded to the actual man particular thinking psychologically "polluted" by induction, from private to general, the process taking place through the work of the Organization and management at the level of State administration.—Hence the conclusion: State of the world in time and space, with everything good and evil is characterized by "EFFECT", it is hardly noticeable because it is found in nature and human nature that is all "EFFECT", because the conjugate base of the human forces and laws with which man/it dominates.

Labor dialectics of human intellectual and practical experience in the life and work of the human species, "the source and engine" of dialectic thinking leads to knowing truth progressive "absolutely".

The fact that for thousands of years, the great thinkers have historical times managed to influence by the theses and their points of view to change the State of the world is because potential human intellectual labor and collections of quantitative experience and work of the human species have reached that level that the knowledge of "absolute truth" as "spring and engine" that gives motion and auto movement of human society in time and space that gives the form and content in time and space.

The history of the facts along the way of the human species, highlights that "the human nature and temperament is a law" unknown and not collected thus far by man at the beginning of the Millennium III. It works independently from the Law will and desire of man and which is transmitted, by induction, as a magnetic wave from "particular", "practical man" at "General" human society as a whole, the particular man concrete being also the "live cell" of the general phenomenon taking place through the work of the Organization and management at the level of State administration, particular. The particular concret man being also a "live cell" of general (human society as a whole), it appears that between particular concrete man of General and human society as a whole there is an "organic unity" that moves and auto moving dialectic in time and space, but **uneven**. The source and the engine of movement of the "organic unit "is "cell vineyards", which by its nature and temperament generates State of the world in time and space with everything good and bad characterized. This "absolute truth" was not known and it was perceived by all the great thinkers of the time, although historical were concerned about the changing state of the world, the theses and their points of view on "the effect of the case", the cause remains a conundrum.

This way of thinking of the great intellectual figures of historical times, big thinkers, since the slave era and until now, at the beginning of the Millennium III, was and is a common feature.

Some examples that confirm that the great thinkers of the historical times have benefited from such a potential of the intellectual and labor sufficient quantitative accumulation of human life to enable knowledge and perception of the world State "given time" (live) by causes that it generates:

1. Lao-Tzi), great Chinese thinker of the 20th century VI BC, living in an age of historic slave, where the wealthy lived in a kind of "paradise" on Earth, and the poor (the majority) were living in a sort of "hell"; having done him under psychiatric care on their peers (poor) worse than on some animals, it connected in chains, he struggled and iron red were forcing to work up to total exhaustion, and if it were, were killed. The rich, slave owners, slaves were held on the link in the chain, they were selling at fairs like any other tool, the slave being considered by owners of slaves "speaking" tool.

Lao-tzi, unknowing and not perceived the cause its time of the State of the world, proposed changing the State of the world and perceptions by returning to the primitive commune.

2. Pythagoras and Socrates, the Greek philosophers, great thinkers of the 20th century BC, their ignorance of the reason YOU State of the world of time lived, the slave era, he imagine that democracy and freedom to think, you can change the State of the world. However, although democracy and freedom of thinking are

extremely important, yet they are just means to change the State of the world time given, if known the cause that you determine. These two great Greek thinkers have tackled philosophical questions "what is happiness?", "what is good?" philosophical questions for which it was accused that disregard the ancestral faith and have been sanctioned.

3.) Winstanley (1609-1659), English, French ideologue in his Law of liberty held the notion that private property on land is the fount of all evil and social disasters and called for the establishment of common property on Earth and on the products, despite the fact that private property on Earth is "effect".

4.) Mably (1709-1785), French philosopher, regarded as private property, of any kind would have it, as the source of all evil, and social organization based on it unjust and averse to the laws of nature; Mably devised an ideal Republic aimed at restoring "old natural state of mankind", based on the community of goods, by proposing a series of legislative measures in this respect.

5.) Morelly, sec. XVIII, French utopian Communist, criticized private property, considering it "spring of the addictions of moral and social hydras", with the expectation of constructing a social order "true reason and the laws of nature, based on collective property and the obligation of all members of society to work".

6.) Babeuf (1760-1797), French revolutionary theorist utopian communism, was considering the formation of a "society of egalitarian" by means of a provisional revolutionary dictatorship which would lead to the dissolution of private property and to the introduction "egalitarian society", designed by him in the form of a Republic, which was to transform itself into a "big town", in which national assured labor obligation and egalitarian sharing of goods. This thinker of France for his ideas was executed in 1797. France was in the 18th century generation of many great thinkers on changing the status of world thinkers who have made and directions of action of the world change: "liberty, equality, fraternity".

7. Enlightenment 17th-centuries) XVIII, ideological movement of emergent anti-feudal of bourgeoisie, consider irrational rules as "feudal", campaigning for their replacement with a social "rational" order.

Notable exponents of the Enlightenment were: a) In France: Voltaire, Montesquieu, Rousseau, La Mettrie, Holbach, Helvetius, Diderot and others; b) In Germany: Lessing, Herder, Schiller, Goethe, etc; c) In the Netherlands: h. Grobius, Baruch Spinoza; d) In North America: b. Franklin, Th. Jefferson and others.

Historical, spiritual movement of Enlightenment has influenced subsequent philosophical thinking, the Marxian philosophy that rests, and German idealist philosopher's thinking on **Kant (1724-1804), philosopher who criticizes**

speculative philosophy and theology, removing religion from the sphere of knowledge, and on that of Feuerbach (1804-1872), German philosopher, materialist, which develops and defends the materialistic theory of knowledge. After German materialist philosopher Feuerbach, divinity is nothing but fantastic quality restoration the personification of the human being. Feuerbach States and famous sentence: "God is man . . ." hence the Feuerbach's thinking to be envisaged a new "religion without God in the center of the universe to hang the man . . . ."

A great spiritual influence on the occurrence of Marxist philosophy had an idealistic philosophy of the great German philosopher Georg Hegel (1770-1831), which has historic merit to modernize and develop the theory of knowledge, stating the thesis cognoscibility the world through the development of the dialectical thinking. After the German idealist philosopher Hegel, "dialectic thinking leads progressively to knowing truth absolutely . . ."

Marx (1818-1883), German philosopher, materialist, economist and politician, a great thinker, connoisseur of philosophical principles so idealistic and materialistic, promotes a dialectical materialist philosophy—that philosophies and list the phrase "historical times have not made anything other than to interpret the world in all sorts, important is to change it."

In such a conception, Marx develops dialectical materialism and thesis of historical materialism, by extending the principles and laws of the dialectic society and list the thesis that human and social-capitalist economic disposition is limited in terms of history and that she will follow each other. Marx's philosophical thinking i joined and Engels (1820-1895), materialist philosopher. These two philosophers materialistic Germans, big thinkers, thinking dialectics, have stated that the sentence after the disposition of capitalist social-economic development will follow a social economic Socialist order, superior of capitalism.

Lenin, the Russian philosopher and politician, a great thinker, is the co-author of the thesis made by Marx and Engels. Equipped with "the art of being and organization and management", initiates, organizes and leads a revolutionary process in Russia in which appears the first socialist State in the world. Thus is created the principles and conclusions formulated by the many great thinkers of humankind, on the ways and means necessary for the normalization of the life of the human species in line with the laws of nature, to be checked by the practice of life. After World War II, the disposition of social-economic Socialist installed in Russia in 1917 is expanding worldwide, so that at one time there are two orders: one social-economic capitalist private property based on the means of production, and other socialist based on common ownership of the means of production. The existence of these two orders socio-economic situation worldwide, viewed through the knowledge of truth absolutely "dialectic", offers to mankind, the human species sufficient elements to get to know and perceive the cause, the secret, "the source and engine", which gives the State the world form and content. These philosophers, psychologists, historians this, theologians of this and other great thinkers, intellectuals, may avail themselves of the existence of the two orders socio-economic world, as a "huge" laboratory of fundamental scientific research on the knowledge and perception "of the spring and the engine" which gave "State of the world" in time and space form and content, "source" engine and which has been known and perceived large thinking of historical times. For over 70 years after the advent of the Socialist order socio-economic and 45 years of existence of socialism worldwide, those who have practiced an ideology to which they gave the theses and the views of many great thinkers of the time, of which some I have outlined and which they viewed as "private property" on the means of production because of the evil of human society the fount of all social disasters, proposed replacing them with "ownership of the means of production and the obligation of all members of society to work", and so the current Enlightenment of the 17th-19TH centuries influenced the ideology of socialist countries practiced and in many other ways, some of whom believed that religion is a significant brake on the knowledge of the absolute truth.

In Romania, Mihai Eminescu (1850-1889), Romanian poet and one of the most notable of universal literature lyric, Emperor and proletarian poetry, criticized also him the religion:

"Religion-a phrase invented by them

As with her power to destroys the chain,

Because of divest of hearts the hope of reward,

After whole life misery work,

You may wear damnation as vita of the plug?"

Experiencing a global thinking on many large historical personalities, intellectual times great thinkers have revealed that the forms of ownership are "effects of a case", which was known and collected thousands of years.

The existence of "huge" laboratory of fundamental scientific research on the knowledge of the case which gave and continues to give 'State of the world "in time and space form and content through the history of the facts revealed that both capitalism and socialism, as enslavement and realizing they have a common denominator:" cell ", specifically, that man by nature and rattled her/his gives" form and content in his State of the world historical times ". However, thousands of years, thinking human being psychologically "polluted" with the nuisance caused by the action of immunoglobulin of human forces and laws with which man/it dominates, the dialectics in the sense of finding ways and means necessary to grub up "" the way of nature and the human flesh of pollutants generated by the action of the conjugate base of the human forces and laws with which man/it dominates. Big thinkers of the time, concerned about the fate of man, within an order socio-economic data, because of their ignorance, the secret of the underlying State of the world, historical time, have formulated theses and ways to change the form and content of the State of the world from what it was in something like the laws of nature, aimed at "the EFFECT of the CASE", the cause remains an unknown.

The existence of two orders socio-economic situation on the basis of which stood at one, private property over the means of production (social-capitalist economic organization), to another, the property of the means of production (the disposition social-economic Socialist) have been established and that a "huge" laboratory of fundamental scientific research on the knowledge and perception of 'truth' as "absolutely and spring which gave the engine" and gives the State of the world, historical time, form and content.

The history of the facts in the USSR and other socialist countries of the world socialist system reveals that the ownership of the means of production is "EFFECT", that democracy and freedom of thinking are the means which can influence on improving the status of "beneficial"; "absolute truth", "source and engine", which gave his State of the world, and deliver in time and space, the form and content, is still unknown.

"Giant laboratory", consisting of the existence of both social and economic orânduiri, capitalist and Socialist, by the nature of the facts, and one that highlights and other have their advantages and disadvantages and what deserves much attention is that, regardless of the superiority of one over the other, the disposition of Socialist, social-economic thought of Marx and Engels, and existing at any one time worldwide, high capitalism, could not be and cannot be what was thought of Marx and Engels and Lenin. Developments in each country the existing Socialist has shown that a social and economic order is characterized not by itself, that "cell vineyards", "practical man" endowed to lead the country's Affairs is the case, "spokesman secrecy" which give form and content of a socio-economic order. And events at the end of the Millennium II and the beginning of the Millennium III highlights that human society is moving and isn't auto moving in time and space continuum dialectal and uniform. The return of former socialist countries to capitalism, where once had been, it is not beneficial to the human species in general and hence for socialism nor capitalism, nor is dialectical in nature.

I am aware that this perspective captures, which is why I have to explain why this point of view.

The disposition of social-economic capitalist always evolved and continues to evolve dialectics dialectic, but in a highly polluted, which endanger human life on Earth.

Social-economic Socialist Organization, once formed, evolved and she always dialectal, and at one point a "revolutionary" process which gives the world socialist system, for the most part, a direction of movement toward capitalism, where were the countries that have renounced socialism.

Consequences with concrete example: Romania since 1989, the year of change "direction" channel of human society development, Romania 500 billionaires and millions of poor peoples, living in a white-knuckle, and much of the population of the country, of the order of over two million, emigrates to various countries (Spain, Italy, France, England, etc.).

Nothing bad at the first looking, but the existing production facilities in the form of joint ownership shall pass through a sales process in private property. This process of buying-selling is extremely mischievous for the population of the country, because the property is sold to the public of the whole people, ownership (public wealth) gained a lot of work for 45 years without her owners to receive something, and the sale is made, like how a peasant handicapped and would sell steers, cows, sheep, and others on a cock and a hen, perhaps those who sell a substantial fee illegal.

So they appeared to us in Romania most billionaires, not to say all billionaires. Consequences for Romania: billionaires build villas and swimming pools, buying all sorts of modern cars, buy jewelry, wandering abroad, and so on, and most citizens are suffering . . . Basically, the revolutionary process, in terms of economic and social terms, is: "expropriation of the whole people of wealth accumulated by the public a lot of work for about 45 years without even a minimum of compensation".

With all these great social wrongs, which historical improving, the Fund is another problem altogether, which I am determined to say that this process is not beneficial either for capitalism. Discard the humanity of the knowledge and perception of "absolute truth", "source and engine" which gives the form and content of the world, because status and Marx, Engels and Lenin had formulated conclusions and views, and other great thinkers historical times, all on "the EFFECT of the CASE", the cause remains a conundrum."

Neither the Marx, Engels and Lenin had not benefited from such a potential of the intellectual forces and sufficient quantitative accumulation by the life and work of the human species, so as to be sensitized to the organic unity between particular, concrete man and general, human society as a whole, have been not sensitized by the fact that particular of General is also the "cell vineyards", which gives the movement and auto movement to General, human society as a whole, and that what characterizes the particular, particular which is also the "life cell" of general witch is transmitted as a magnetic wave on General. Hence the conclusion that in order to change radically, form and content of existing socio-economic order at a time, as the particular of general compulsory special, action must be taken of the special. Its special nature and temperament must suffer a big revolution.

Being sensitive, these great thinkers of humanity, to the fact that particular, by nature and temperament of him, generates walking of society with everything good and bad, is they haven't seen that human nature and temperament "compassed" the society, held the riding . . . And what is particularly important is the fact that "dialectic thinking" of those historical times, in which they lived, Marx and Engels and Lenin, has led to human knowledge, the human nature and temperament, as a "absolute truth". Thinking human being psychologically "polluted" by the conjugate actions between human forces with/and human laws which it dominates, was not able to know the absolute truth, "the source and engine" which gives the State the world form and content. Marx, although he had the wisdom to make the sentence: "historical times philosophers have done nothing other than to interpret the world, but he doesn't think is important is change the world" and he was not was able to promote a philosophy based on the knowledge of the absolute truth.

This concept arise the idea of a political party to organize and lead a revolutionary process, in which human society can evolve dialectical, thus changing the world from what it was in a world of flooding and the welfare of the whole human species. Marx, Engels and Lenin have imagined that this process of revolutionary change in the world of what was what he wanted to be, can be achieved by a party of the working class and with an ideology that sought to "dictatorship of the proletariat". Said and done, only that the nature and human nature, "compass psychologically" by the action of human immunoglobulin with forces and laws of human/it dominates, have created the "dictatorship of the proletariat, became in the dictatorship of an individual in concrete and its familiar, pollute serious democracy and freedom of thinking". From this point of view, rather than as socialism, as the social economic order, to be superior to capitalism, as it was thought by Marx, Engels and Lenin, history facts reveal that he was inferior. It appears no more political: the cult of Stalin in the USSR, Ceauşescu in Romania, and so on in all existing socialist countries at a time, which is represented worldwide.

The existence of two orders socio-economic one based on an ideology which was based on private property over the means of production, and other public property over the means of production through the history of the facts reveals that the forms of ownership are only "EFFECT", the cause remains unknown.

Dialectical thinking dialectics, rationalized, the existence of these two orders socio-economic situation worldwide, imagined as a "huge" laboratory of fundamental scientific research on the knowledge and perception of absolute truth "," Spring "and" engine "that gives" State of the form and content of the world in time and space is a big "brick" put into "endless column" "KNOWLEDGE".

Knowing the absolute truth "," spring and engine" which gives walking the world in time and space form and historical perspective, open content for human society to evolve dialectics in direct proportion to the dialectic of human intellectual labor; Open the perspective of the life and work of the human species would enter into normality, in conformity with the laws of nature. This is why philosophers, historians, psychologists, biologists, theologians, writers of this genre, all knowing, "absolute truth", "source and engine" which gave and gives the State of the world in time and space form and content are "key" to change the world by placing a where is social justice on the "orbit", with historical perspective as the human species to enter the "era of wisdom and reasoning".

This "key" imaginary human perception is as a social being, licensed biologic-social of the four forces: physical strength, intellectual force, the force of good and evil force and it is dominated by a series of laws: the law of accumulation of wealth (wealth) at any cost and by any means, without limitation, regulations; appetite, thirst law breakers, law no limit; law of selfishness and also this imaginary "key" is the imaginary "perception" of joint action between forces of man with man and the laws that/it dominates.

Knowing the classical characterization and human: "man is a social being equipped with thought and articulated language", confirmed by the practice of life characterize the human species, I think the characterization of man should be: "man is a being biologic, equipped with thought and articulated language", and is in possession of four forces: physical strength, intellectual force, the force of good and evil force and dominated by a series of laws: the law of accumulation of wealth (wealth) at any cost and by any means, without limitation, regulations; appetite, thirst law breakers, law no limit; law of selfishness and so on.

This imaginary "key" is based on knowledge and perception of nature and human flesh, why he is in relation to his fellows: "when man to man to man":

When "man Fox devious manipulation and likes to man";
When humans duffer to man ";
When "man versus man killer"

May only be only "man versus man"; It is based on the perception of "imaginary" joint action between forces of man with man and the laws that/it dominates.

Using this characterization of the human, perceive "dreamy" that human forces acting shared with the laws of man throughout his life, generating nature and nature's process. So nature and human nature is a law unknown and not collected by humans thousands of years.

"Imaginary" thinking and "imaginary" rationing, co-operations between human action with forces and laws of human/it dominates is constituted into a "psychological" compass and hardly perceptible invisible, which directs nature and human nature, causing him to be what it is in relation to his fellows, and in relation to the environment.

The action of immunoglobulin of human forces and laws with which man/it dominates, "imaginary" thinking, which defines the nature of the processes that generate and human nature:

a) process of a psychological "compasses" invisible and hardly discernible, which directs nature and human nature, "the invisible psychological compass and hard perceptible" that works independent of human will and desire, creating relationships between people and between people and nature (environment);

b) process of a "net" invisible and poorly identified that "enchain psychologically" on man as kind and threads, decelerate him and even stranding him to evolve the nature dialectics and wires, from what is normal and should be used judiciously, since it is packed with thought.

These two processes generate and process pollution psychological thinking, with many and various nuisances generated by the action of immunoglobulin of human forces and laws with which man/it dominates, on the other hand, "psychological causes" long-range thinking, what makes nature and human nature to be polluted, and decelerating under, and even blocked to evolve dialectics.

The human nature and temperament, man is "particular" of General and "live cell" of general (human society as a whole), is transmitted as a magnetic wave through induction, from private to general phenomenon taking place through the work of the Organization and management at the level of State administration. "Psychological compass so that" blind and hardly perceptible, generated by the conjugated actions between human forces and human laws which it dominates and which directs the human nature and temperament, it becomes, through the organization and management work at the level of State administration, "compass" targeting human society development in time and space, creating the "State of the world" with everything good and bad characterize!. Enchaining Psychological of man, the kind and nature, in a "mesh" invisible and perceptible, "hard strapped", "imaginary" thinking, conjugate actions between human forces and human laws which it dominates, becomes the work of the Organization and management at the level of State administration: "enchain" of human society to evolve from what is dialectic, "severely polluted" with particulate matter generated by the conjugate actions between the man forcer which it dominates, in what is intended as, in conformity with the laws of nature.

Dialectical thinking dialectics, rationing, knowing the absolute truth, "the source" of the movement and motor and auto movement of human society in time and space, and taking into account the concrete situation of the State of this world, we can conclude that: the dialectic of human society, by violent social revolution, organized by a social class against other social classes, becomes out of date (it is out of date), dialectical social revolutions, that violent organized by a social class against another social classes, are evolving towards peaceful social revolution, beneficial social classes, each of which is platform independent-program: "GREENING" of NATURE and HUMAN FLESH, and by man, "cell" of society, "GREENING" of HUMAN SOCIETY, social injustices.

"The ECOLOGY of THE HUMAN NATURE and TEMPERAMENT" implies "GREENING PSYCHOLOGICAL THINKING of THE MAN" by POLLUTANTS GENERATED by the ACTION of the CONJUGATE BETWEEN the HUMAN FORCES and HUMAN LAWS which it DOMINATES.

"ECOLOGIZATION OF THE PSYCHOLOGICAL POLLUTED THINKING" on the human BY POLLUTANTS GENERATED by the CONJUGATE ACTIONS BETWEEN HUMAN FORCES / HUMAN LAWS and that it opens the perspective that DOMINATES the lives of the human species to normalcy and to operate in conformity with the laws of nature, humanity is entering a new historical era: "the ERA of WISDOM and REASONING", HISTORICAL ERA in which "HATRED and REVENGE", "apish gun", remains of history and unjust wars and terrorism will disappear in the life of the human species, getting into the OPOZITE.

Organic unity between particular, concrete man, and general human society as a whole, shall be grubbed up on a "new road" without by the brakes and obstacles, which may evolve dialectics in direct proportion to the dialectic of human intellectual labor, and thinking "psychological polluted" with pollutants generated by the action of the conjugate base of the human forces and laws of man with/in purgatory, and may develop dialectal ecologisation of all points of view.

Organic unity between humans, human society and the environment by "greening" psychological pollution of thinking, deeply revolutionary process will result in the dialectic of the environment to "the garden of Eden", shadowy to be "sometime".

CHAPTER III
ENVIRONMENT PROTECTION

Environment-air, water and soil—is a medium who through composition and quality of the life . . .

Nature (environment) is a primary factor of production and liabilities that provides all the necessary elements that work, primary production factor and active, the man can produce the goods needed in his life and his family.

Man, human society and its environment, viewed as "organic unity" in the time factor, have degraded quality, so that the life and work of the human species is seriously affected, meaning that some people cannot benefit from primary production factor and passive Earth.

The man, the particular of general and life cell of general human society as a whole, due to the law of nature and his flesh, which generates the three processes, of which, and the "psychological pollution of thinking", began a process of malevolent influence on organic unity "man, human society and the environment", so that some people have appropriated some of the production factor—Earth the primary factor of production, and liabilities, any pre-existing human element and wrongfully appropriated certain families as private property. This process, once appeared, has evolved over time so that some families, owners of vast expanses of land, caused, for other families, unable to practice because of the factor of production ", in the interests of his family.

This process, at a time, it has proved to be the source of the engine and all social disasters, and those who have noticed this phenomenon, they could influence the spiritual return of "organic unity: man, human society and environment" to normality.

The process resulted in "abnormal and irrational "relationships between people and between people and nature.

Thousands of years, many great intellectuals, thinkers of the time of history, have sought ways and means necessary to ensure that the life and work of the human species to enter the normality and in line with the laws of nature. Their desire, although he had a moral and rational, could not catch life because, thousands of years, intellectuals, thinkers of the time of great historical, perceived state of the world of her time lived by "effect" of the case; the cause remains unknown and many thousands of years not levied by human thinking. The man, be he and great scholar in certain areas of activity, he managed to discover the secret of nature and human flesh, and the spring and engine, which gave his State of the world and give form and content in time and space.

THE ROLE OF A TRIAD SOCIAL CONSCIENCE: POLITICS, RELIGIOSUL AND SCIENTIFIC, IN THE ORGANIZATION AND LEADERSHIP OF THE REVOLUTIONARY PROCESS "GREENING OF NATURE AND HUMAN FLESH, HUMAN SOCIETY AND THE ENVIRONMENT"

"The ecologic process of human nature and temperament" by the pollutants generated by the conjugate actions between the human forces with/and human laws which it dominates, to "ecologic process of human society caused by the social-historical injustices" and "ecologic process of environment polluted by physical and chemical pollutant" caused by human activities, is extremely complex and long-lasting, perhaps eternal, which is why this revolutionary process should be organized and led by representatives of a triad» psyche: politics, religious and scientific.

The role and the rationale behind a triad» psyche, social division of labor, history, which should be normalization and harmonization of relations between people and between people and nature, so that human life, on Earth, would enter into normality in line with the laws of nature.

Representatives of a triad» psyche: politics, religious and scientific, have a common denominator that gives movement and auto movement at world status in time and space", "living cell", "man concrete ". However, this "living" cell, the common denominator of politics, religious and scientific, and orders of any socio-economic situation in which it was moved and auto moved human society, "hosts" and "source" engine which gave and gives State of the world in time and space, the form and content. Knowing and perception of the source and engine which gave and gives the world moving and auto moving dialectic, as "hosted" by "concrete man" which is "particular of General" "and" living cell "of general human society as a whole," concrete "as a human being biologic-social thinking and language provided with articulated, owner of four forces: physical strength, intellectual force, the force of good and evil force and dominated by a series of laws: the law of accumulation of wealth (wealth) at any cost and by any means, without limitation, the Regulations Act of selfishness and so on, we understand that human forces acting shared human laws which it dominates, throughout his life, generating the "nature and human flesh". Also, perceive, "imagination", which the action by the human forces and laws with which man/it dominates is constituted into a "psychological" compass and hardly perceptible invisible, which directs "man step" as "kind", and fire are:

When "man versus man";
When "man Fox devious manipulation and likely to man";
When "man versus man" crook;
When "man versus man killer"

The conjugate actions between human forces with/and human laws which it dominates, "enchain psychologically" man in a "mesh" invisible and perceptible, that hard it braking and even dialectical locks to evolve, as kind and fire, and may only be as kind and nature, being always only "man to man" in its relations with his fellows.

Therefore, if we perceived the man, like a "particular of General" and "living cell" of "general human society as a whole", we realize that General, human society as a whole, as moving and auto moving dialectic, is dependent on the function of the cell its dialectic "live", "practical man", as wild and fire.

Between "particular", "concrete man", and "general", "human society as a whole", there is an organic unit, which moves and auto moves in time and space, dialectic, but discontinuous due to the nature and the flesh of the "living cell "of General." Knowing and perceived the organic unity between "particular", "concrete man" and "general", "human society as a whole", which are in a dialectic process of discontinuous movement, whose "spring and engine" is the conjugate action of the human forces and laws with/and which it dominates, it can be concluded that the dialectic of human society, without barriers and without brakes, assumes "its live cell "dialectic, as wild and temperament. However, the human nature and temperament are "psychological compass" by the conjugate actions between human with forces and laws of human which it dominates and which operate independently of the will and desire of man. And then what is to do that yet "concrete man", as "nature and temperament", able to develop into dialectal? The improved "psychological compass" and hardly perceptible invisible, generated by the conjugate action between human forces with/and laws which it dominates on man and which operate independently of the will and desire of man.

Resolution: "Compass psychological ", invisible and hardly perceptible, which channel the man, as nature and temperament becomes, through the work of the Organization and management at the level of State administration, "compass" targeting human societies in development time and space.

The secret that human society cannot develop dialectal continuously, in direct proportion to the dialectic of human intellectual force is because the work of the Organization and management at the level of State administration progressing dialectics in direct proportion to the dialectic of human intellectual labor. Dialectical continuously progressing because it is made of "concrete man", "compassing psychologically" by the conjugate action between the human forces with /and laws of human which it dominates and operate independently of the will and desire of man. Or the work of the Organization and management of the human society is made by the leaders of the political class that people are being "compassing psychologically", as nature and temperament, by the conjugate action between human forces with/ and laws which it dominates, being what they are.

Conflict resolution: work organization and leadership at the level of State administration, practiced by leaders of the political class in order to develop dialectal, direct proportion the dialectic of human intellectual labor, and should be based on fundamental scientific research studies, institute of scientific research. They will be profiled on knowledge and perception of nature and human flesh, the condition of the world in time and space, generated by "his" cell, specifically endowed man lead at one point, the country's Affairs. Also, knowing the man, who by his physical and intellectual strength, built up as a "capital live", the generator of all forms of capital gives the State of the world, a movement in time and space, dialectic, and by the force of good and evil force set up in a dualism of good and evil, by human action combined with laws which it dominates, gives State of the world in time and space and a "polluted with many and diverse social wrongs".

Politics, social consciousness form, through its leaders, no matter how willing they would be to change the world from what it is, with many and diverse social wrongs, as normal and should be used judiciously, can do it, because they are "people" and they, and people are being "compassing psychologically" like nature and temperament, by the conjugate action between human forces with/and laws which it dominates what makes their work through the Organization and management at the level of State administration, based on their way of thinking and of acting, human society, "State of the world" remain polluted with many and diverse social wrongs.

Democracy and freedom of thinking, means of action of utmost importance, since the slave era conceived of the great thinkers of the time, for enhanced social injustices and democracy general elections, political parties shall be rotated in the direction of the country, led historically to the continued improvement of the status of the world of social injustices. History of the facts of life and work of the human species reveals that at one time, the means for improving the social injustices are insufficient for the State of the world to enter the "orbit" social justice. The struggle between political parties and alternate their leadership, beyond their importance, it begins to lose efficiency due to the fact that political parties are "compass psychological" by the conjugate action between human forces with/and laws which it dominates. The common denominator of the people in the case of politics, social consciousness, the form generates the type of business organization and management at the level of State administration, always with the same content, which can no longer perform dialectics at a time when leadership. Alternating the leadership of political parties can no longer be effective for human life. To overcome this "critical point" is an absolute need to find ways and means necessary to ensure that the work of the Organization and management at the level of State administration can evolve without obstacles and dialectic, without brakes and in direct proportion to the dialectic of human intellectual labor.

Religious, a form of social consciousness, whatever its nature, through the work carried out by representatives of religious worship, generates a very beneficial influence on humans, nature and fire, but that representatives of a religious practice, always the same job with same content. The dialectic of human intellectual labor, benefiting from full, religious leaders, and collections in his life and work of quantitative human species, sources of dialectic thinking, paradoxically, not in dialectic thinking of religious worship to practice a work always in line with the overall progress of human society. Representatives of the religious affairs religious fail to about is the way to work and to make a contribution on the role and always creative joint on the change of religion, as human nature and threads, and therefore not sufficient political support to the practice of organizing work and always driving, based on dialectic human intellectual labor.

Attainments, a form of social conscience, his work, and the representatives of its labor force of dialectic process generates intellectual man and all they are the ones who have the greatest potential of the intellectual force of man, the greatest source of dialectic thinking.

Attainments, pyramid peaks of attainments, knows very well the evolution of human thought in time and space; knows very well the concern of many intellectual personalities of the time historical truth "about the knowledge of the absolute", "spring and engine", which gives the form and content of the world in time and space.

Attainments, pyramid peaks of attainments known and perceive things, phenomena and dialectic thinking through the specifics of physical laws, they discover, chemical, biological, and others who experienced some generalized, go to the dialectic of State of the world.

What he managed to make attainments, pyramid peaks of attainments is that it gave philosophical answer to the question: "If the man is thinking, why do what they do in relation to his fellows, and in relation to the environment; Why man is doing what it does and why not do what normal and sensible should do, since it is packed with thought?"

Attainments, a form of social consciousness, the representatives of its pyramid peaks of attainments, people having a common denominator and religious, with the political forms of the psyche: "the HUMAN NATURE and TEMPERAMENT", generated by the action of the conjugate base of the human forces with/and laws which it dominates. It is, "imaginary thinking", in a "psychological compass" and hardly perceptible invisible, which directs nature and human nature, and by a "net" and hardly perceptible invisible that it "psychological" on enchain, as a kind man and threads, locked him and even stranding him evolve dialectics from what is normal and should be used judiciously. Intellectual force, through the process of human speech and writing, sometimes accumulate part of the total, from man to man, from generation to generation, with the potential of evolving trends to infinity (∞), and collections of quantitative experience and the life of the human species grow continuously. Knowledge and perception of dialectic human intellectual labor, collections of quantitative and business experiences of life as 'the human species and the source of dialectic thinking engines ", go to the knowledge of the absolute truth and perception", "Spring" and "engine which gives the State of the world in time and space, the form and content. This "absolute truth", "source and engine" which gives the State of the world in time and space, the form and content is: "the action of immunoglobulin of human forces and laws with which man/it dominates and which operate independently of the will and desire of man". This conjugate action between human forces with/and the laws of man which it dominates, as I demonstrated scientifically, "imaginary thinking", generates two processes: a) the process "psychological compass "of man, that nature and temperament; b) the process "enchain psychological" of man, like nature and temperament, in a "mesh" invisible and perceptible, "hard strapped" by the conjugate actions between human forces with/and the laws of man which it dominates. Or, "concrete man" is "particular" of General "and" living cell of general, "human society as a whole", hence the conclusion, "imagination", that the two processes, induction from private to general, becomes "compass" movement processes and auto movement of the world State in time and space, with all that characterize good and evil, and human society "enchaining", thereby hindering it and even blocking a dialectical to evolve from the viewpoint of social right.

Knowing the ABSOLUTE TRUTH and perceived this, concluding that the dialectic society, turning it from what it is, with many and diverse social wrongs, in a society of abundance and general well-being is dependent on the function of the cell its dialectic "live", "like kind and fire". This means that violent revolutionary processes in the life and work of the human species, which have given moving and auto moving of human society, which gave shape and content of the world in time and space, with everything that has characterized it good or bad, become, dialectal, peaceful revolutionary processes each beneficial social classes whose platform-program is: human nature, as a dialectic and fire, in what is:

When "man versus man";
When "man Fox devious manipulation and likely to man";
When "man versus man" crook;
When "man versus man killer "

The normal and rational should be, to be always only:

"Man to man".

The revolutionary world-rational and peaceful and beneficial to every social class, will generate the historical perspective that humanity, life of the human species, to enter into normality, in conformity with the laws of nature, historical perspective will generate as human society and live to enter into a new historical era:

"THE WISDOM AND REASONING".

This revolutionary process peacefully must be organized and led by the triad psyche: politics, religious and attainments.

The leaders of a triad» social consciousness, the peaks of the pyramid, religious and attainments of politics, informed choices, to be able to generate a peaceful revolutionary process beneficial to each class, must find ways and means to carry out the work of the Organization and management at the level of State administration to evolve constantly and sensitively approached dialectics dialectic of human intellectual labor. For this reason, the political religious and attainments, the tips of their pyramid will form a collective of major intellectual personalities, big thinkers: philosophers, theologians, historians, psychologists, biologists, writers of all genres, great connoisseurs of the law of dialectic which to charge the company perfectly framed in human law of dialectic thinking, things and phenomena. Those perceived the society dialectic by human his "living cell", "concrete man", "particular" of General and living cell of general human society as a whole, "the law of nature and human flesh", which is in a "psychological compass" and hardly perceptible, invisible that directs how to be human in its relations with his fellows and the environment, and knowing that "concrete man", "particular" and "living cell" of general human society as a whole "by human nature and his temperament, transfuse, through the work of the Organization and management at the level of State administration, as a magnetic wave, what characterizes it, human society, thus walking human society directs, generating the status of the world in time and space.

To get into normality, in conformity with the laws of nature, human society should be organized and managed on the basis of fundamental scientific research studies made in the scientific research institute profiled on knowledge and perception of man, that nature and human society thread, as the most advanced building in the world, incorporating any other achievement in itself. This, due to its "live cell ", moves and auto moves in time and space non-uniform-dialectical-and-continuous as the content is extremely polluted "psychological" pollution that is generated by "nature and temperament" of its "living cell", "concrete man" found at the level of social and economic order in social injustices.

In the institutes of scientific research on the knowledge of the nature and profile of the flesh of man, "living cell" of society, will develop tactics and strategies that govern the work of the Organization and management of human society. Tactics and strategies designed in scientific research institutes, profiled on "knowledge of the law of nature and human flesh," by the great intellectual figures (philosophers, psychologists, theologians, historians, biologists, writers of all genres), will be approved by the team formed by the leaders of a triad» psyche, and the contractor shall, in the work of the Organization and management of human society, as tactics and strategies designed to walking the world in line with the laws of nature be complied with strictly.

Why this view? Because experience shows that although political life by its leaders that are my invested to organize and lead the human society, no matter how eager we were to change the course of the world, can do it, although many of them are recipients of a high intellectual potential of the labor force. It may be due to "their psychological compass" generated by the law of nature and human flesh, which directs him to do what he does. All the experience of life in the work of the human species highlights that, although there is democracy and freedom to think, where they exist, many demanding and critical intellectuals, the press freedom and free broadcasting, how to work of those who organize and conduct the Affairs of the country, and the results are like saying "water passes, the stones remain". And what deserves much attention is the fact that although political parties are rotated through a general election, at the head of State, political leaders of my invested to organize and conduct the Affairs of the country are "psychological compass" by conjugate action between the human forces with/and laws of human it dominates, as their predecessors.

Attainments, pyramid peaks of attainments the owner of the largest potential of intellectual labor, there should be political organizations summoned Moldovan authorities that, through its leaders, no human society can lead based their own ideas, because they become "electoral slogans" during the performance, and power is "evaporated" and work for the Organization and management at the level of State Administration has always the same content, regardless of which party holds power and what you need to bring it to the attainments is that: the action of human immunoglobulin and human laws forces which read "enchaining psychologically", the man politically, causes him to be conservative, to be always the same.

Design of tactics and strategies of the great intellectual personalities, big thinkers, which govern the work of the Organization and management of human society, which must be perceived as the most advanced building in the world, "universal design" and in the process of moving and auto moving continues, necessarily requires that the Organization and its leadership to stand for the fundamental scientific research studies that is the basis of design of tactics and strategies on the Organization and management "located on modernization of universal construction."

Attainments, through its pyramid peaks, can and should support both the political and religious, as to the practical work of the Organization and management who are always in line with the dialectic of human intellectual labor, but this implies fundamental scientific research on the causes of the State of the world in time and space; assume that the fundamental scientific research on the State of the world in time and space, researchers in the field, "big thinkers" and with "a lot of mind" to design tactics and strategies that generate work organization and leadership of "universal" construction site that the company always human to evolve in all dialectical viewpoints, which means human society and the "greening of social injustices".

Attainments, a form of social consciousness, owner of a considerable potential of the intellectual force of the connoisseur society, human development in time and space, of the theses and the views expressed by the many great thinkers of the time of historical change of the world, the visa of what was in their time in what is hoped to be, so that human lives in normalcy and consensus with the laws of nature and social injustices to be removed. Those theses and ways they have inspired many violent revolutionary processes have led to some improvements social injustice because theses and the views of the great thinkers of the time of historical change, concerned about the world, were made in "the effect of the case", the cause remains unknown.

Attainments of the present era, taking cognizance of the conclusions and views expressed in the books social justice and Democracy-the future of humanity; The dialectic of human society; Dude, let's change the world; Nature and human nature-"the compass" targeting human society development, theses and ways in which the joins and continue to respond with "Yes" to the call made by the author of the books: "man, wherever you are and whoever you are, let's change the world" (the book man, let's change the world, page 356). These theses and views very synthetic said, aims: knowing the "absolute truth," Spring and motor" which give form and content of the world in time and space, as well as ways and means of changing the world of what is normal and should be used judiciously.

Attainments, through its pyramid peaks, taking informed conclusions and views expressed in the aforementioned books and theses outlined in this, that may be organizations summoned Moldovan authorities: politics and religious, forms of social consciousness, cannot make step dialectics to practice work in consensus with the dialectic of human intellectual labor; not only can practice a rational and creative work for the benefit of human society, because the conjugate of the human forces and laws with which man/it dominates it stifles, and even the locks to be about is the way to work. This conclusion is confirmed by the fact that, although in some countries, democracy and freedom of thinking works, however, the political struggle between political parties and their alternation in power, would lead to the normalization of the life of the human species in line with the laws of nature and what do you have this many intellectuals, including some great thinkers, under the action of immunoglobulin of human forces and laws with which man/it dominates continue to provide political viewpoints that confuses him.

Furthermore, it directs to "beat up on the spot" as regards work organization and leadership at the State level, and administration for extremely negative, not contributing their work to put a "new brick column knowledge of the infinite ", and some ground, alter some bricks made in the knowledge of truth absolutely endless column.

This state of facts is highly negative and is intended both to present and future of human society.

Attainments, a form of social consciousness, the holder of the intellectual potential of the new force, besides that failed, for thousands of years, to know and to charge the "absolute truth", "source and engine" which gives the State of the world in time and space, the form and content, by which a practice, generate process of dialectic human intellectual labor, the main source and engine of dialectic thinking whose "antennas" extend "and the" psychological pollution of human thinking, thereby hindering it and even blocking a dialectical, i.e. to evolve to "ecologies the pollutants they pollute".

Attainments, through its pyramid peaks, should be organizations summoned Moldovan authorities that this state of facts in the history of the human species has a "Spring", and an engine, attainments, that he may discover this spring "and" engine, as "absolute truth". The fact that I have done thousands of years is the result of the case that attainments is made up of people, and they, people are being "compass psychologically" that kind of action yarn, and conjugate of human forces and laws of nature with/that it cannot dominate, nor her representatives, attainments, auto freedom of "place" invisible and perceptible that hard "enchaining psychologically", hence the conclusion that the nature of their nature and could not generate the knowledge and perception of "absolute truth "Spring, "and" engine, which gives the world a direction course-keeping of many and various social wrongs.

If attainments will succeed through the tips of his pyramid to auto freedom of "place" invisible and perceptible that it hardly "enchaining psychologically", then you will begin to formulate sentences and ways to influence the politics of spiritual practice work only rational and creative, only for the benefit of all social classes. It will also influence the spiritual representatives of religious worship to practice work in line with what I say through songs and sermons, and saying: "do what said the priest, not do what do priest" becomes "do what it says and what does priest".

Attainments, its pyramid peaks, must be auto notify that political has the most needed his help, to be able to get out of this psychological condition which undermines its historic role to organize and lead the company, and to place it on the "orbit" social injustice that is found for thousands of years, on "social rights" orbit with historical perspective going into the "wisdom and reasoning".

CHAPTER IV

HARMONIZATION OF THE FACTORS OF PRODUCTION

Inputs to the work, the nature and the accumulated capital-must be known and perceived as an organic unit, which, in time and space, find themselves in a process of internal contradiction and continuously generated by nature and content of each factor of production.

Thus, the primary factor of production and is active in a process of continuous change, in terms of both form and content. This process is explained by the fact that work is a human activity without which man and human society cannot be, and practicing certain assumed energy consumption, on which man possesses a form of physical force and intellectual force. These two forces of man is "live" human capital, the prerequisite for the creation of all forms of capital known to man. "Living Capital" of the man, whose source is the physical and intellectual strength, force, currently dialectal in time and space, because human intellectual dialectic of force, which, through the process of speaking and writing, sometimes accumulate part total of man-to-man, from generation to generation, with the trend of development potential to infinity, making it live as "capital" of humans to tend to infinity (∞).

"Live" Human Capital, looked perfectly within the law of dialectic thinking things, phenomena and accumulates in quantity, and periodically turns into a new quality, so that old as composed of "A" + "B", where "A" is the physical force, and "B" is intellectual force, becomes, through quantitative accumulations, a new quality "of" + (B + b) ", where" b "is intellectual force accumulated rise from man to man from generation to generation. "A" being constant (physical force being constant), "B—Variable (variable intellectual force is through the process of dialectic), it appears that live inside the "capital" of human grounds of contradictions of infighting between "A" and "(B + b)" (from physical force constant and variable intellectual strength).

"Live" Human Capital, the premise of the accumulation of all forms of capital known to man, through work, primary production factor and actively joins the primary production factor and passive "nature", and by a factor of production "," the capital accumulated in the form of fine and circulating capital.

The factor of production "NATURE", the "EARTH" is that side on which the Act is limited by WORK area, and over time is subject to degradation and in terms of quality, which makes the work production factor and factor of production nature (Earth) to show a contradiction, which generates a process lock braking, part of the "capital live "the holders of a certain "capital live" and it may not draw upon the WORK.

Derived production factor, "the capital accumulated", evolving and dialectical, but he cannot influence beneficially on "capital live". Between these three factors of production: LABOR, nature and CAPITAL ACCUMULATED contradictions appear that generates a very negative influence on the "live" human capital, in terms of the use of both intensive and extensive; the phenomenon occurs due to the fact that the dialectic of human intellectual labor generates a process of growth of labor productivity, which causes as required to meet the needs and necessities of social-spiritual people should be performed in a dynamic situation, without the need to use the full "live" capital available to human society at a time to perceive this phenomenon that actually is beneficial to human society as a whole, in the book democracy and social justice—the future of humanity, are presented in a graphical form "imaginative" economic goods produced on account of the different forms of work carried out by man: the physical, intellectual, organizational and managerial. Thus, in Figure 1, is a graph share economic goods produced in primitive when goods required meeting the man produces necessities, only through physical work. Gradually, in his history, along the way, yet man starts from the primitive commune, to practice and a minimum of intellectual work which gives rise to thinking and confection tools as: stone, stone carved stone, and, later, of bronze, iron tools and so on.

Historical, this phenomenon entails a process of change in the weighting of the goods produced on behalf of the economic laws practiced in the sense that the share of goods on account of economic products decreases physical labor, and the share of ongoing economic intellectual work product on account grows continuously. Also, at one point, the man, in addition to the physical and intellectual work, employment and work organization and management, which means that goods produced economic is carried out in different proportions on account of both the physical labor, intellectual and labor organizing and leadership. The imaginary, the share of these products on behalf of the economic work in slavery is presented in Figure 2.

In Figure 2, item 3, which is the weight of economic intellectual work product on account, last work listed because it is the accumulation of both physical labor, intellectual and organizational and managerial.

In Figure 2, graph and highlight that in the slave society, the share of economic goods, in their great majority, are produced on account of physical labor.

In feudalism, Figure 3, the share of goods on account of economic products decreases in physical labor, and the community produced on account of intellectual and organizational work and driving increases continuously, but in percentage terms, the vast majority of economic assets is carried out on account of physical labor.

In capitalism, figures 4-6, the disposition of social-economic development that is developing dialectics from primitive capitalism, capitalism, capitalism to the environment, the capitalism advanced capitalism to capitalism developed, advanced capitalism developed from modern capitalism, the share of economic goods made on different work charged radical changes, so that at one point, the intellectual work is one that produces the vast majority of their and, in addition to the physical work that is continuously due to modernization makes technical and manufacturing technologies, participating in all with a share of less than their production (figures 7 and 8).

Graph with the share of the economic laws of those products is shown in figures 1-8.

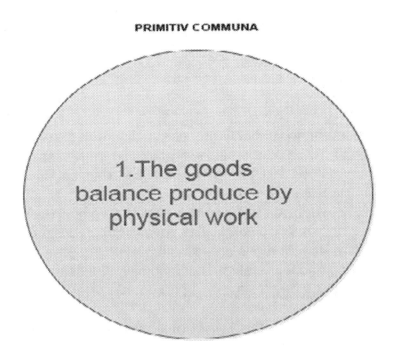

Figure no.1

Slavery

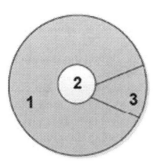

Legend
1- goods balance produce by physical works
2.- goods balance produce by work set up and Management
3.- goods balance produce by intellectual and past works

Figure no.2

Feudalism

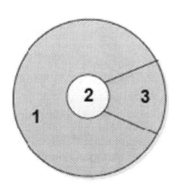

Legend
1- goods balance produce by physical works
2.- goods balance produce by work set up and Management
3.- goods balance produce by intellectual and past works

Figure no.3

Barbaric capitalism

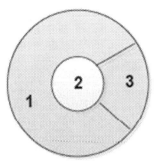

Legend
1- goods balance produce by physical works
2.- goods balance produce by work set up and Management
3.- goods balance produce by intellectual and past works

Figure no.4

Midle capitalism

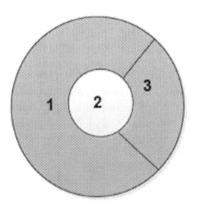

Legend
1- goods balance produce by physical works
2.- goods balance produce by work set up and Management
3.- goods balance produce by intellectual and past works

Figure no.5

Advances capitalism

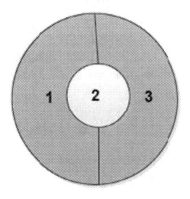

Legend
1- goods balance produce by physical works
2.- goods balance produce by work set up and Management
3.- goods balance produce by intellectual and past works

Figure no.6

Developed capitalism

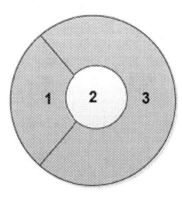

Legend
1- goods balance produce by physical works
2.- goods balance produce by work set up and Management
3.- goods balance produce by intellectual and past works

Figure no.7

Modern capitalism

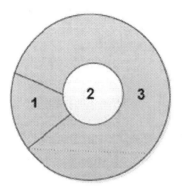

Legend
1- goods balance produce by physical works
2.- goods balance produce by work set up and Management
3.- goods balance produce by intellectual and past works

Figure no.8

Intellectual force, through the process of human speech and writing, sometimes accumulate part of the total, from man to man, from generation to generation, with the trend of development potential to infinity (∞) and through the process of processing them in techniques and technologies always upgraded stretches "aerials" in all activities of the human species, "beneficial" for economic and social progress of human society in general. In addition to the benefit of the transformation of intellectual labor in a continuous process of modernization of the economy, appear and some evil. The "evil" is that a greater proportion, always, "capital live" available to the company, shall not be recovered. A number always increased people become unemployed, being marginalized on the fringes of human society; they are generally lives in poverty and misery.

The dialectic of human intellectual labor, technical and scientific progress, also in a continuous movement, embodied in the dialectic, mechanization and automation of technological processes, sometimes using the robots remains and grows the number of those who do not find a job, and at one point, the production process can no longer continue at the level of technical possibilities, technological and organizational. As a result, a number appears, for some people, involuntary unemployment, times, and a volunteer force of human intellectual dialectic stretches "aerials" in all branches of the economy of a country, what generates the impossibilities that persons who become unemployed to find and take up a job.

Unemployment, of any kind would have it, is extremely malevolent influence on unemployed and on the economy: a) Loss of income, health problems, social status, etc; and b) For society in general, through the aid for the unemployed, the State's use of the growing resources for helping the unemployed, etc.

The problem of unemployment was and is a major concern of many great intellectual personalities of the time, so that unemployment is at a time is characterized as a combination of several forms of unemployment:

1) Unemployment by insufficiency of the application;
2) Unemployment through insufficiency of production;
3) Adaptive Unemployment;
4) Unemployment by the expenses;
5) Unemployment frictional;
6) Unemployment randomly;
7) Structural Unemployment.

Unemployment, which at one point is a combination of several forms of unemployment:

1) Unemployment by demand insufficiency manifests itself when an undertaking or more must reduce the production and sales volumes, which means more unemployment and less demand. This is for Keynesian unemployment, since the economist J.M. Keynes (1883-1946) described at length this time unemployment in two situations:

When prices are considered "rigid"; the adjustment between the labor market, the market of consumer goods and money market may take place only in quantities, in particular by the level of employment. Hence the probable appearance of involuntary unemployment, which means that individuals do not find jobs at current rates.

If it is assumed that prices "flexible" achieve an overall balance, then the change of employment resulting from the Monetary Authority intervention. In this case, it should be assumed that the nominal variations (and real) of wage and price influences the behavior of employees, i.e. they suffer from "monetary illusion".

If, for example, monetary authorities, creates additional currency, causing a corresponding rise in price and wage earners will believe then that the real wage (the purchasing power of wages) increased nonobservant rising prices; they will want to provide more work, because they think that it is better remunerated. Those who do not want a job at current rates of unemployment support volunteer.

The two explanations Keynesian of unemployment differs radically:

* The first focuses on a malfunction of the system of markets (price rigidity), hence the character in-voluntary unemployment;
* The second appeal to irrational behavior of individuals (monetary illusion), hence the voluntary character of the resulting unemployment.

2) Unemployment through insufficiency of production manifests itself when the request exists, and it is greater than is supply. Enterprises will not or cannot produce any more and to hire additional workforce: unemployment also appears in the conditions of the shortage of a good, or because of the lack of production equipment, which does not enable the undertaking to produce more. The unemployment rate of this type occurs especially in times of transition or reconstruction, but also where the undertakings deemed not production conditions enabling them to achieve sufficient profits. As a result, demand is there, but there are shortages and rising prices and unemployment persists.

3) Adaptive Unemployment, due to the effect of interference of monetary creation. Authors who have made this theory, in which the best known is Milton Friedman, have resulted in start-up unemployment rising in conditions of prolonged inflation. Described as "monetarist", the explanation of unemployment Adaptive focuses on the postulate that the market, thanks to information data through prices, allows the optimal allocation of resources. The emphasis on monetary creation stems from the fact that it is the means available to the authorities to act on the economy and that can be a source of disruption of the functioning of the system. If there is inflation, monetary authorities because it creates too much "currency", citing it as a stimulant of the economy, but in reality they are causing in particular an increase in the price level, which does not reduce, but speeds up unemployment.

4) Unemployment by expenses to work. Inadequacy may have several causes: poor working conditions, low level of wages for young people, etc.

5) Unemployment frictional is determined by insufficient labor mobility or gaps exist between the professions available and required. Job seekers may not respond to the offer of employment, because either does not possess the requisite qualifications or not residing in the town where there are jobs.

6) Unemployment randomly designates unemployment tied to short-term fluctuations in economic activities, so being reversible. It concerns the number of unemployed, resulting from declining real P.N.B. during periods of recession or contraction in economic activity, when the economy operates below its potential.

7) Unemployment structural appears in a situation where you cannot create jobs as you increase the offer of employment. He may have because changes in economic structures (for example, the decline of production in the mining sector) generated by changes in the demand for goods and services or technological changes that affect the likelihood of employment.

In any economy, interest is shifting to stop authorities of unemployment and to achieve full employment.

Full employment is the volume of employment which makes it possible to obtain with the aid of production factors most important volume of production in relation to the needs of individuals and the community. Thus, full employment does not mean that everyone has a job, but the fact that existing workplaces give maximum yields.

Concrete modalities of action for the achievement of full employment and unemployment alleviation differ from country to country and from one period to another. In general, the measures of decrease of unemployment are integrated in the general economic policy of fostering long-term economic growth.

Fiscal pressure and unemployment

Among the best known terror explaining unemployment and provides solutions for reducing is the theory of the offer. The authors of the theory of supply, particularly a. Laffer, explain the tax pressure decay. Lafter's curve in the employment relationship so put pressure for tax and tax receipts. To do this, Laffer uses a function of production where the capital and work are interchangeable, and are paid to the factors their marginal productivity.

$$Q=K^{\alpha}L^{1-\alpha} \text{ where:}$$

Q—production
L—capital
and $0< \alpha <1$

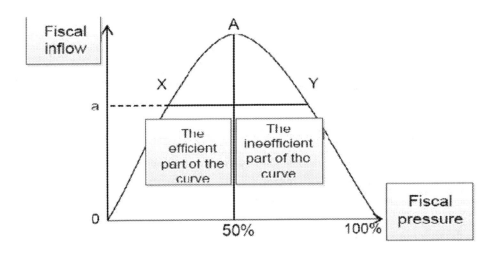

Figure no.9 Laffer Curve

The curve is easily interpreted and understood: If the tax rate is 0%, tax receipts are clearly invalid, and if the tax rate is 100% tax receipts will be obviously all null and void, because businesses will opt out of such work formally rejecting a confiscatory attitude.

One can imagine, however, that the tax rate is 50% and that it is the psychological level at which it is more difficult to work, because symbolically it is working more for less and State for itself (see Figure 9).

Laffer demonstrates that the situation is theoretical, and point to the rate of tax to which the yield is high. This allows the demarcation point up to the two parties: the efficient (the normal values) of the inefficient (excessive values). The authorities have a choice between these two, it provides for the same tax receipts, but the point X is Y because X is more employment than employment in Y.

It may get a lower level of earnings (see Figure 9), making it easier for the tasks of administrations, citizens and economic agents. This allows obtaining a level of public funding in a growing economy and a high level of employment.

Laffer's curve can be used to illustrate examples of countries with fiscal tolerance or fiscal pressure. (See Fig.10 and 11).

Figure no.9 Laffer Curve

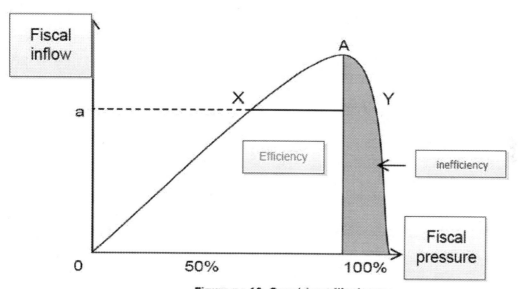

Figure no.10- Countries with strong fiscal tolerance

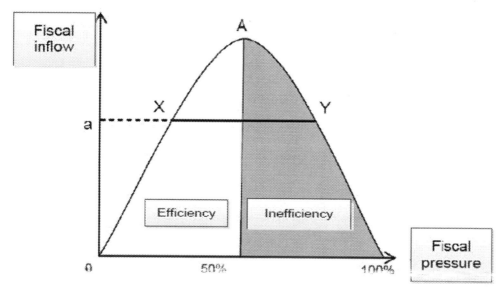

Figure no.11 – Countries with poor fiscal tolerance

Laffer's theory, applied in such a liberal, gave the yields on short to medium term. Suggesting an economic issue and a social issue, normally its application requires continuous adjustments and corrections.

Inflation: causes and forms

Researching the problem starts from empirical evidence—exclusive relationship between currency and inflation-mediated through one middleman—the general level of prices—and the independence of that relationship to employment.

According to some definitions, inflation is increasing regularly and supported prices.

Being a global phenomenon of increase in the level of prices, inflation is usually deducted from the general price index. Although the general price index generates some controversy of principle, he highlights the direct relationship between the growth of production measured by indicator type GDP or GNP growth and monetary expansion, as measured by the stock of currency. Price index takes into account, in principle, all prices and by catching the products in the budget of an average family. Not always increase price index is a good landmark to allow deduction of inflation, especially when it is transferred mechanically raising prices relative to absolute prices. The view that inflation is unavoidable in countries seeking a strong pressure on the resources available (which means an increase in demand accompanied by a rise in prices) are founded in fact on the confusion between physical aggregates and monetary aggregates. In essence, the pressure on national resources in the relative prices affect the development process; It creates the image of higher prices on goods for which demand is stronger in this period, relative to other goods, but does not affect the absolute prices.

In general, the inflation rate can be determined as the ratio between the change of the price and the price in the period concerned.

$$Ri = (P_1-P_0)100/P_0, \text{ where:}$$

Ri-inflation rate
P_1-current price
P_0—is price in the period concerned.

Economists disagree about the immediate cause of the inflation that you identified in the economic and financial imbalances due to the faster growth of the money in circulation than production growth, which means the creation of a power purchase (application solvent) supply of goods. Amid various opinions relating to the definition of inflation, to identify the causes and remedies of inflation, there is a common element: creation of currency.

Among **the causes of inflation** are often invoked as follows:

- ⊕ **Budget deficit**: where the State is spending more than your current income, to cover the difference, it borrows from the Central Bank. Consequently, money in circulation will increase the movement needs to be increased, because the State borrow to consume it and not to produce extra goods.
- ⊕ **Credit Bank**: when banks granted loans without a serious analysis of their destinations, it is possible that the money of account inflationary effect similar cash money.

The forms under which can be seen in inflation can be structured in two categories:

A. After the order of magnitude, you can distinguish the following types of inflation:

- ▓ **Creeping Inflation**, with prices falling between 3-4% per year;
- ▓ **Open Inflation**, where price rises, currently between 5-10% per year;
- ▓ **Galloping inflation**, prices increase by more than 15 percent, provoking strong economic and social imbalances;
- ▓ **Hyperinflation**, where the monthly inflation rate exceeds 50%, reduced confidence in the local currency, and relative prices are determined by bartering.

B. **The causes that produce**, inflation may refer to:

🌑 **Inflation by request**:

The monetarist approach, inflation in the application itself has a number of causes, some immediate, others more distant.

Between the immediate causes, the most relevant are:

- ❖ Increased abnormally rapid amount of currency in relation to volume production. The imbalance between the very strong solvent demands in relation to the offer at a price given cannot be alleviated only by rising prices.
- ❖ Increased costs to operate the State without a tax increase, by applying the tax Fund indirectly by inflation. Inflation occurs so as the only form of taxation

that can be applied without requiring the consent of the person (or, how do you say m. Friedman, inflation is the tax policy).

Causes more distant attached errors on Government policy on employment and the Central Bank, which takes decisions based on erroneous theories (if you have to deal with the interest rates, then the task is to control the amount of currency).

In Keynesian economics, inflation through global demand appears when costs grow rigid in relation to the offer, and this State, the economy is not able to respond rapidly, requiring a period of time for adjustment. To create a difference arises between the supply and demand, prices are increasing, which leads to an intensification of price, because the price among of price would be an increase in consumer's increasingly higher prices. Accordingly, the phenomenon of inflation is auto maintenance and is expanding.

❖ Inflation through costs. This means higher prices brought about by rising prices on items like raw materials, materials, generally to factors of production. The rising cost is inflationary when she persists. Causes and phenomena of inflation shall register the many divergent interpretations arising mainly from how it is portrayed in the context of economic mechanisms.

Inflation mitigation policies

Deflationary measures are claimed by the two major concepts:

⬥ The first (represented by Mises, Hayek, Friedman, and Barro) considers the freedom essential for the proper functioning of the relationship between individuals; and to preserve this freedom, must limit the role of Government, with a frozen private property, freedom of the market and voluntary agreements. The acceptance of such terms leads to a policy based on free competition. If all the difficulties of which hit economic policies are linked to unemployment-inflation relationship and economic growth, then what is fixed in the short-stop growth of expenditure related to the reduction of costs and printing a quantity less than currency-is supplemented by two other long-term actions: renunciation by the State to the pursuit of full employment and sustained economic growth as economic policy objectives and the relaxation of monetary market by lifting the State monopoly on monetary creation.

The first action consists in the recognition that all concepts that unemployment must be maintained at the lowest level possible, and sustained economic growth must be encouraged at any cost; they have no economic motivation and are just plain superstitions. They have their roots in the old days when it was believed that the purpose of economy is increasing wealth (wealth) of countries and to its sovereign and survived the revolution Keynesian due to faith in the natural instability of markets.

The other measure will contribute to lessening the economic fluctuations of the currency and spreading through the privatization of the decision. Basically, Gresham's law will reverse: good currency will banish bad currency from circulation.

- The Second (represented by Keynes and neo—Keynes) considers the welfare or social security objectives, which have the chance to be achieved by Government actions intended to control and to regulate private activity. The appropriations of such visions were born guideless economic policies. Mainly, the followers of this concept argue control salaries.

No matter and anyway how well would give labor economists to restrict to the minimum points of divergence against inflation, its cures arise from what apparently wants the electorate.

If there is a cancer that fray ruthless economy, it is inflation. Most often described as a persistent increase in the level of prices, whose revenue is declining purchasing power, inflation has to devaluate origin following a change in the relationship between supply and demand of money. Such an increase in the money supply can be achieved only through the State—represented by the Central Bank-which has the monopoly of money creation. What may cause the State to increase the supply of currency? In orthodoxy, there is an inverse proportionality relationship between inflation and unemployment, and the State is obliged to yield a maximum occupancy of the workforce by manipulating the supply of currency, Credit Union and stimulating the growth of investments. Incidentally, there is a union on the opinion that the State must secure full employment, price stability and economic growth. In the background, we are witnessing a change in the public image of the State, from State-to-State arbitrator settles everything, though, because of this posts, seven and eight decades of last century Governments fell because of inflation.

Long regarded as a "necessary evil" to provide a level of employment to ensure so-called "social peace", inflation represented only an alibi for redistributing income after the wishes of the Governments and the escapes parliamentary vote. While inflation, clearly, some WINS that lost others. **The grand winner is the State, together with debtors and creditors and the losers are the people with fixed incomes.**

Relationship inflation-unemployment

If until the early 1970s, inflation was moderating unemployment, starting with the re-launch of the rates of growth was accompanied by a strong inflation and decay.

Coexistence with high inflation, unemployment and collapse of economic activities was called stagflation.

Economist a. w. Phillips in 1958, based on the statistical data on the British economy between the period 1857-1957, he found an inverse relationship between the rate of change of prices and the level of unemployment: the first will be higher, the other will be lower, and each other. Phillips's relationship is signified by a curved line that was first a curve of the link unemployment—variation of salaries, and later was a complete connection between unemployment—the variance of price-wage variation (fig. 12).

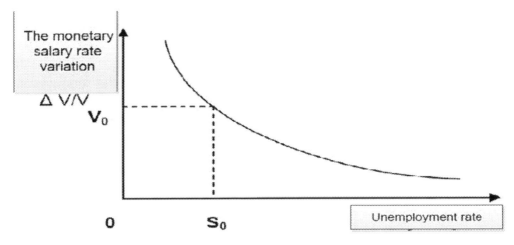

Figure no.12 – Phillips Curve –

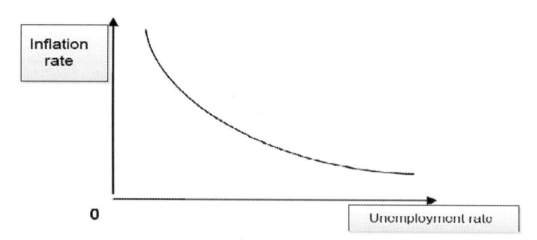

**Figure no.13 – Phillips Curve -The growing of the inflation rate
have the effect of reducing the unemployment rate**

The emergence of Phillips: higher prices and lower wages. In addition, when employees found that prices had increased apace with their wages, they revert to the original, reducing the supply situation, unemployment increase. Thus, the only result of action by the authorities is that causes an increase in prices to a sustainable level of employment the same.

If you want to reduce unemployment, they will have to enhance the creation of the currency in each period so as to maintain the idea that real wages increases, although inflation is accelerating. (See the Fig. 13).

The explanations above are valid under the terms of the labor market is in balance. Thus, unemployment is always voluntary: all those who want to work on the current salary can do it.

The natural rate of unemployment means that the rate does not increase with inflation. Traders expected inflation and adapts quickly to changes. At a time, agents can cheat on the re-launch, the unemployment rate is lower than inflation and progresses (fig. 14), but quickly adapts to the phenomenon of inflationary anticipation and the unemployment rate is at the level of balance. The conclusion is harsh: Friedman **if a Government persists in pursuit of budget deficit, would always be inflation and unemployment.**

In the Figure no.14 you see Phillips curve under non-inflationary

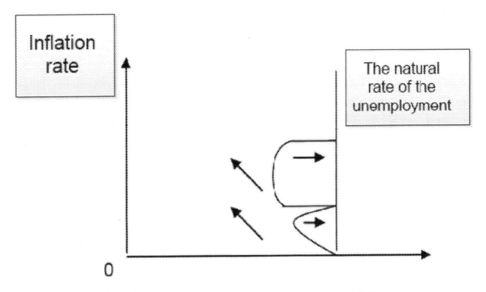

Figure no.14 – Phillips Curve -in the situation of the noninflationary

The complexity of the two phenomena, unemployment and inflation, but also the interdependence between them, requires a broader approach in the context of general economic policy, monetary policy, fiscal and budget.

The cycle of economic affairs

The cycle of economic affairs was the greatest controversy of our century. Some economic analysts have insisted on the regularity deduced from economic fluctuations, and which led to the introduction of the idea of cycle economy in movements. Incidentally, the fluctuations of wine to designate movements of increase and decrease of economic activity measured by several parameters, including the most used are GDP, prices, employment. Currently, there is a certain crush down in business cycle theory resulting mainly from the interpretation of the economy in the short term and long term. a) In general, the short-term business cycle refers to increases or decreases and the prosperity and recession, so the fluctuations in a time of 7-Eleven. Conventionally, such a cycle comprises several phases which follow each other in the following order:

- **Phase 1:** corresponds to expansion or the time of peak activity;
- **Phase 2:** depression is manifested through a brutal contradiction activity, characterized by the decrease in GDP, investment, etc. Where the reduction in activity is weak, the economy is in recession, and if there is a slight increase, something more than 0%, then the economy will be re-released.
- **Phase 3:** upgrade the supposed resumption of work on new bases, increasing tapping in general a higher level than the culmination of previous expansion. If the effects of the re-launch of the producer and the combined Accelerator, then increasing the investment produces a consumer request, which induce a raise investment that's refreshing in turn consumption. This incentive encourages mutual anticipation of optimistic and increase costs. The prices grow, grow, and stock ticker. Optimism reigns in the economy, which means that a boom. b) Long-term economic Cycle, known as the Kondratieff cycle, captures the behavior of the normal cycle of business throughout a period of 50-60 years. In the ascending phase of such a cycle, lasting 25 years, the normal cycles tend to have longer to kick and shorter contractions, and the downward phase, all twenty-five years, is shorter, boom and contradictions more protracted. In this regard, world trade index, which increases substantially during the period of "vitality" and tending to stagnate during the "decline" of it are, somehow, supposition long-term fluctuations and, even more, tends to give him a note.

Economists differ in interpretation of the crisis. In addition to Keynesian economics theory of imbalance of the markets and stimulation of investments, you know the Austrian neoclassical theory and theory monetarist theory.

1. Austrian Theory, the main rival of the theory of Keynesians, was made by I. von Misses and FR. von Hayek. It shows as a cause of economic crisis an expansionistic monetary policy. The theory assumes that the gap is the difference between the natural rate and the actual rate, difference generated by a policy favorable to increase investment. As long as the investments are based on voluntary savings of the population, everything is all right. When properly stimulated investment, they do not have sufficient voluntary savings to sustain and, therefore, the additional requirement of forced savings is covered, formed by inflation. Prices of consumer goods will grow, buyers will try to maintain their previous level of consumption, and money will stifle the economy. Any attempt to restrict credit will lead to the restriction of activity and unemployment. The theory says that the bigger will be the difference between natural and market rates of interest, the more difficult will be the recession.

2. The theory of monetarist is supported, in the case of m. Friedman.

If the State aims to achieve a certain combination inflation-unemployment, say 4-5%, the anticipation will cause inflation to rise up, and the Government will carry out the proposed unemployment at a rate much higher inflation and rising. If the phenomenon is enduring, stocks decline, the unemployment rate decreases, increases productivity, which means stagflation. There is a rate of unemployment which accelerates inflation. The explanation lies in the fact that the market cannot be found and remain so always in balance. Market must always be filled in order to meet the ongoing demands of the workforce. The same question, the market is always fraught with market gardening. Repeated mistakes of the State in economic policy (control of wages and prices) result in supra-investments not even justified in the new conditions. Thus, in a short period, unemployment and inflation coexist, and then, as entry into normal, subtract together.

3. Considers that the conditions of the neoclassical competition perfect return to balance are achieved automatically.

Fighting the crisis involves the reduction of State intervention alongside favoring competition.

4. Analysis of Keynesian economics, in contrast to the neoclassical, considers that the free market does not induce the game automatically return to equilibrium, leading more than another sustainable situation.

When global demand is expected to firm production below the level corresponding to full employment, they will decide to throw out part of the staff. Reduction of employment in the period ahead will lead to a further fall in demand and, on this basis, further reductions of production and employment. If the balance of the slop is set, it may be another instance and accompanied by a considerable unemployment. (See the Fig. 15).

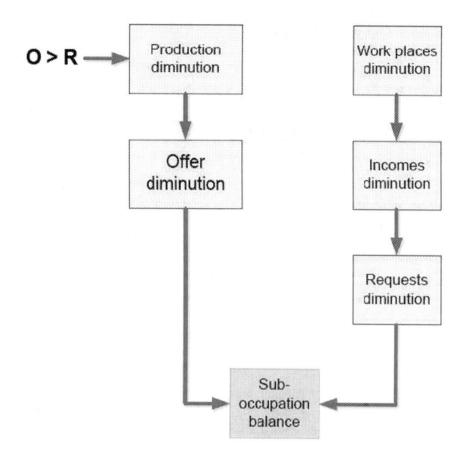

Figure no.15

In these circumstances, it is found justified the intervention of the State in order to achieve the objective of full employment. To this end, the State insist economic activity by increasing demand (supply-consumer and capital), using the levers of economic and financial.

Authorities in any economy is shifting to reduce unemployment and to full employment . . . using for this purpose by the theses and the views expressed by the experts, but that the experience of life highlights and demonstrates that the theses and the views designed by experts do not result in solving the problem of unemployment, most are enhance periodically. The Reason being that intellectual personalities from the field of economy, whether the big thinkers, working with "the effect of the case". The cause remains and for them a "conundrum".

Why force the dialectic of human intellectual and practical experience of life do not lead to the absolute truth "knowledge" by great experts on "the secret", "cause" of unemployment? Because human thinking in general is "polluted" with many psychological and various nuisances generated by the action of immunoglobulin of human forces and laws with which man/it dominates, action that works independently of the will and desire of man. This action combined, as I have demonstrated, "imagination", entails two processes which directs nature and human nature: a process of "psychological" invisible compasses and hardly perceptible, who directs the man being what it is, and the "psychological enchaining" of man in a "mesh" invisible and perceptible that it hardly restrain their locks, and even evolve dialectics from what is normal and should be rationally, since it is packed with thought.

Full consideration to the endeavor of many great thinkers in the field of economy to theorize economic notion of "unemployed", to characterize the way and chip, to conclude the effects of unemployment on those who become unemployed and highlight unemployment consequences on society, evil consequences. But that, at a time, you start to perceive that their work does not have the desired efficiency because theses and their points of view rests on knowing "the effects of the case", or "ignorance" of the case, they are unable to provide legal bodies which organize and conduct the Affairs of the country the necessary support for this social cancer "cure" so harmful in the life of the human species.

Absolute truth is that the work of the Organization and management at the level of State administration progressing dialectics, in line with the dialectic of human intellectual labor, even more, those of my invested do so, the political power, which holds people being psychological, are "compassing" as the nature and quantity of human immunoglobulin action between forces and laws with which man/it dominates, prompting him to do what they always do. Also, there are also "enchain psychologically" in a "mesh" invisible and perceptible action hard conjugate of human forces and laws with which man/it dominates, brake him, and even stranding them to practical work organization and leadership at the level of State administration, in line with the dialectic of human intellectual labor.

Scientifically, in the case of concrete economists should be organizations summoned Moldovan authorities that politics cannot be auto freedom from "trammeling" joint action between forces of man with man and the laws that/it dominates, taking place scientific, which is why, if the economy scientifically not know and does not charge connection stream of phenomena and processes based on knowledge and perception of "absolute truth", may not approach any of his knowledge he Spring, "and" engine that generates unemployment. Or, scientific, be able to assist in organizing and political management of the company, primarily involves him spiritually through theses influences and confusing points of view, some of which not only is not consistent with the ultimate truth, but more and pollutes the political thinking of such and such a size as aimed at "blocking" the type of business organization and management which would lead to progress. And so as not to remain at the level of abstract considerations, I have to give some examples:

1). "the condemnation of communism", i.e. We condemn a social-economic order, is such the historic mistake that can act with the condition of the dialectical development of the world in time and space for long periods of time. However, it is known from the evolution of human society that the world has gone through several socio-economic orders: common primitive, slavery, feudalism, capitalism and the emergence of socialism, which came at a time to be at the level of world-wide. Each of these socio-economic orders has had advantages and disadvantages. And you know that enslavement, as social and economic order, was in many ways superior to the primitive commune, and realizing it was in many ways superior to slavery, capitalism was superior feudalism. What deserves much attention is that the disposition of social-economic capitalism in its history, it was a movement and auto movement dialectic of primitive capitalism to capitalism developed environment, capitalism the environment developed in advanced capitalism, capitalism to capitalism developed and advanced capitalism developed in modern capitalism. The emergence of socio-economic and legal system of socialist-communist to be seen by his ideology, relations of production generated by forms of ownership of the means of production, designed many great thinkers of the time required for historical as can normalize the life of the human species in line with the laws of nature. Socialism-Communism did not have historical chance to modernize capitalism, did not have the historical chance to enter into a combat sport with capitalist socio-economic organization . . .

Communism as a social and economic order, must be perceived, as any other orders, perfectly framed in law of dialectic thinking, things and phenomena. The fact that the disposition of social-economic socialist-communist were identified through experimentation with the Marxist-Leninist theories to be a human society of abundance and general well-being is explained by the fact that she appeared on a concept thought of many great thinkers of the time who perceived historical State of the world in time and space "effect of the case", the cause remains a conundrum and thinkers who have thought of "scientific socialism". They, like many great thinkers of the time, were sensitive to the "General", "human society as a whole", "particular", "concrete man", and "life cell" of the "General", "human society as a whole" and that what characterizes the "particular", "General" normally and rationally is to characterize and "General-special", especially since the "particular-General" is also "the cell" figure. The existence of socialism-communism worldwide level revealed that human society is characterized by her, but through what characterizes his "living cell". Hence the conclusion is that it is a huge historical mistake to identify socialism with Stalinism, for example, or any other head of State from a formerly socialist-communist country.

I made this bracket to demonstrate that neither capitalism as a social and economic order, cause giving rise to depression: "unemployment-inflation" and so on and that 'unemployment and inflation "," sisters "who grafting with the life and work of the human species, is due to an unnamed, discovered as an" absolute truth "," source and engine "of the economic crisis," unemployment-inflation ", can be removed from the life and work of the human species.

This absolute truth is that "human psychological thinking is polluted". Human thinking, though evolving dialectic through the two streams: the dialectic of human intellectual labor and quantitative experience life collections in the human species, however, in terms of "quality", human thinking is "polluted" psychological action of conjugated with human forces and laws of human/it dominates and remains polluted long as does not know the absolute truth, "source" engine and giving the State the world form and content.

"Psychological Pollution of human thinking, which is generated by the action by the human forces and laws with which man/it dominates, makes the social consciousness a triad»: politics, religious and scientific, the work carried out is stopped, even more, to be locked in the dialectical to evolve in line with the dialectic of human intellectual labor, so that political democracy, though, through general elections, leaders of political parties shall be rotated periodically to the Organization and management of the company However, the "quality of work undertaken, due to" psychological pollution of thinking, remains unchanged. "Work organization and leadership at the level of politics do not benefit from the intellectual human labor dialectic, democracy and freedom of thinking, much needed progress of the human species, and prove to be insufficient, having no knowledge of the truth and absolute basis, "the source and engine" which gives the State the world form and content in time and content.

The religious is going the same phenomenon. Politics, religious and scientific have a common denominator that makes him "immune" to practice work to generate processes evolution dialectic in the life and work of the human species: thinking psychologically "polluted".

Politics and religious cannot be auto freedom from this psychological "emasculation" without the help of scientific, scientific, only that instead of "offer" of politics and religious theses and ways to assist them to practical work organization and management in line with the dialectic of human intellectual labor, they "offer" theses and ways that blocks the thinking in the practice of organizing work and driving always dialectic and in line with the dialectic of human intellectual labor.

I came to this effect the "condemnation of communism", another example would be to politely that socialism collapsed, that was based on "blue collars", and progresses that capitalism is based on the "white collars"; that socialism has collided with the future of knowledge: "computers," and so on (Alvin and Heidi Toffler, create A new civilization, p. 68).

Science, recipient of the largest potential of intellectual labor, does not make such assessment in bad faith, in our view, but because they are scientific and representatives of the people, and people being psychological, are "compassing", that kind of action yarn, and conjugate of human forces and laws with which man/I dominate remain psychologically in thought "pollute". Hence the conclusion that in order to help the political and religious work in the practice of organizing and driving always dialectic and in line with the dialectic of human intellectual labor, and they are auto freedom of "enchaining", as a kind of psychological and fire and act as informed on 'greening psychological thinking polluted "by the action of immunoglobulin of human forces and laws with which man/it dominates . . .

And in order not to create the impression that defend the political and religious and at the same time, not to charge some that defend an order socio-economic or other, make clear that no social economic Socialist Organization is that to ascribe merit for the launch of the Gagarin into space, not capitalism must assign the merit for the evolution of computers . . .

The intellectual dialectic forces of human is "cause" and "fount" of those great revolutions known at the end of the Millennium II, started the Millennium III. The examples may continue with much more . . . it is important to note that representatives of the scientific "at furrow" remained in the politics and religious theses and ways that the spiritual influence in organizing and leading the revolutionary processes which would lead to progress and general well-being, and the concern of many specialists in the field, to think of ways and means necessary for economic growth and sustainable economic development It is worth all the consideration, but that is not realizable until you know the "absolute truth", "source and engine" that generates unemployment-inflation and economic crises, social and political.

This is why scientific, through its representatives, through its peaks, pyramid shall levy the "valve" which opens in the chain, all "taps" general welfare, generating plenty of real economic benefit to the entire human species must be "greening psychological thinking" and "harmonization of the factors of production".

If the scientific will be able to "brainwash" of pollutants generated by the action of the conjugate base of the human forces and laws with which man/it dominates, then representatives will begin to make new bricks in the knowledge of truth absolutely endless column "by the theses and their points of view and their consequences will be of such size that the life and work of the human species will go into normality in line with the laws of nature.

Scientific, through its representatives, through its peaks, where the pyramid will have the wisdom to look human society through its particular, his "living cell", "practical man", then you will find the ways and means necessary to ensure that mankind to evolve dialectic without brakes and without barriers, without violent social revolution organized and run by a social class against other social classes, which becomes out of date at any given time and malevolent human life, creating national and world peaceful revolutions, social benefits to each class, each national State on Earth, rich or poor, revolutions whose platform-program to be: changing nature and human flesh, "greening the psychological pollution of thinking"!

Scientific, a form of social consciousness, through its representatives through the tips of his pyramid, knowing the cause that gave and which continue to give form and content of the world in time and space, through a "thinking ecologic cleaning of pollutants generated by the action of the conjugate base of the human forces and laws with which man/it dominates, will look at every socio-economic order through which he passed mankind, namely the mankind both in terms of advantages and the disadvantages.

This way of work of the scientific protects the theses and new points of view darkness, darkens the road to the knowledge of the absolute truth. This way of work of the representatives of scientific, scientific peak of pyramid opens the historical perspective, in providing theses and ways to influence the political and spiritual religious beneficial work. Will lead to qualitative leaps in regard to the work of the Organization and management of the company in contempt by those of my invested do so will result in a slight change to religious for the purposes of labor to participate actively in the generalization of "Heaven" for the entire human species in the world here, and will participate actively and tangibly reducing the "hell" in which survives a considerable potential of the human species in the world here.

If the scientific, a form of social consciousness through its representatives will be able to position themselves in a verticality as sports, knowing and perceiving what was good and evil in an order social economic socialist-communist falls at a time of world-wide level, will begin to know and to charge more and more is done to ensure that the fate of human life to be in line with the laws of nature.

The scientific, using the existence of the two orders socio-economic situation as a "huge fundamental scientific research laboratory", one of which with an ideology that promotes private property over the means of production, the other capitalist, which promotes an ideology on joint ownership of the means of production, the Socialist, will be able to conclude what alterations would be necessary to ensure that development of human society from one period to another are always capable of dialectic. The scientific, through its representatives, will be able to conclude what to do for the human species should not be so "rough" divided that a large part, a considerable potential of the active population, may not be able to valorize the "human capital" of the active population (according to the International Labor Office, is composed of those who have a job that paid employment and the unemployed, having no private ownership of means of production and don't find a job, are marginalized on the fringes of human society and, moreover, are "pushed" by the nature of ownership and relationships between people and between people and the environment to the mode of being of the animals from which they derived through work).

The scientific, on history how the ownership of the means of production, it will auto apprise that the ownership of the factor of production, land, human, preexisting element became privately owned in the disposition of social-political slavery, remained and was legislated in the feudalism and remains in the disposition of the capitalist. Why is maintaining private property over the means of production, land, and any pre-existing human element that, unfairly, became the private property of some families, while others are left without the resources necessary to be able to harness their strength, their "human capital" at their disposal? Because "nature and human nature", "compass psychologically conjugate of human action with forces and laws of human/it dominates", directs the way of being of the people, the relationship between them and also between them and work together, and the action of forces and laws of human/man, which it dominates, and "enchain psychologically" man, nature makes a "mesh" invisible and hardly perceptible for the conjugate actions of human forces with/and laws which it dominates from which one cannot auto freedom with on their own behalf.

The Science, through its representatives, through its peaks pyramid, knowing and perceive the laws of human society, as being generated by its "live" cell, knowing and perceive advantages and disadvantages of different forms of ownership of the means of production, can conclude what to do for life and work of the human species would enter into normality, in conformity with the laws of nature and with the dialectic intellectual forces of human generating the dialectic of the human live capital.

Scientific, recipient of the largest potential of human intellectual labor, may be apprise that "harmonization of the factors of production labor and capital accumulated, nature is an objective necessity as imposed by law and dialectic thinking things, phenomena, and the dialectic of human intellectual labor generated dialectic of live human capital requires the need for such forms of ownership of the means of production that those of my invested to organize and lead the human society can act without brakes and without obstacles, for the purpose of bringing out the rational, creative capital intensive and extensive live available to society at a time. ", a factor of production and passive, being on the one hand, and on the other hand, has been submitted and land degradation, in order to protect him, to maintain quality, it's a substantial amount of capital live", physical force and intellectual strength well above the one you have active population unemployed.

The scientific, a form of social consciousness, through its representatives, through its peaks stacked cars of a too high intellectual potential of the workforce to theorize on the various aspects of life and work of the human species and what deserves much attention is that it focuses too much on finding solutions to obtain profit for businesses and too little on what is done on the part of politics and religious the forms of social consciousness, for normalization of life and work of the human species in line with the laws of nature and the dialectic of force intellectual man, the main "source and engine" of dialectic "capital live" man.

Many great economists of the time going beyond what is necessary to give the economy a boost, companies in what is something better, so that, beyond the theoretical importance of the different mathematic of ties between the two types of economic units (households and firms) in the market of products and services and market factors, looks, looks, just what is the most important "organic connection between the factors of production labor and capital accumulated, nature".

Many great economists give their works a form such that any form of a work of mathematics, but may not be used for political organizing and directing universal "construction site", "human society as a whole", that site quality universal moves in time and space . . .

It cannot be said that a work of "MICROECONOMICS", for example, concerning the behavior of economic agents, theory and practice, would not affect the general influence of economy by using a number of exceptionally high, inordinately large mathematical formulas and all sorts of visions, but it can be said that if the great economists of the time would fail in the same proportion to theorize the connection between the factors of organic production work the nature and their accumulated capital contribution would be considerably, both in terms of development of the economy in general, but also in terms of changing social status in all respects-political, economic, social ".

Harmonization of the factors of production labor and capital accumulated is kind and "key" which will ensure economic growth and sustainable economic development.

I request at the scientific of looking at those written in this chapter as tips, not as a criticism to the address of scientific, but as an opinion regarding what should be scientifically to have political and practical religious to work for the Organization and management of nature dialectic and always in line with the dialectic of human intellectual labor. What have I written by those in this chapter is to raise awareness of the need to address the science of production factors in a correlation that could lead to the real possibility of recovery rational, creative, intensive and extensive "capital live" available to human society at a time my Creed. Is that it is much easier to harmonizes inputs than to find solutions for detachment strength and attraction of the Earth to the cosmos, conquest to chicken foot per month. If the scientific will focus on knowledge and perception of the factors of production labor and capital accumulated, nature will find ways and means necessary for the harmonization of the factors of production such as "living" human capital can be rationally exploit and creator and the unemployment rate to disappear from his life and work of the human species.

CHAPTER V

MAN POLITICAL LEADERSHIP, MAN REPRESENT ANT OF RELIGIOUS CULTS AND MAN REPRESENT ANT OF SCIENCE

Human society, throughout its history, from the primitive commune, then continuing with enslavement, feudalism, capitalism and socialism, has grown steadily from an order socio-economic groups, and the basis for the development of these socio-economic formations have state laws of dialectic in which the interaction occurs, loneliness and special universal. The common denominator of all socio-economic formations in the course of their history is "cell" of society, "practical man", "General particular", which, by its laws and forces acting shared throughout the life of a man; he has given and continues to give form and content of the world in time and space.

The man, from among animals, after Darwin, the biologist, the scientist is only a prerequisite for human appearance, **but** what he learned on the man from the animal world is work (Engels).

The work must be considered: 1 bidirectional) creative things necessary for human existence, that is to meet the needs (needs) and social-spiritual human in a dynamic always ascending; 2) creating many and diverse social wrongs, dividing people in the rich, middle and poor. The man, the leader of the political class, through the work of the Organization and management, was the one who raised the issue of social injustices, which, when raised, were maintained as a historic chain measured in thousands of years; the man's representative religious, priest, was the one who, along with politicians, contributed effectively to the creation of "Heaven" and "hell" in the world here, inventing that "Heaven" and "hell" would occur in the world by then. The man of science, intellectual work, he discovered many and various physical laws, chemical and biological, experienced and broad, led to the economic and social progress for the benefit of some to live in a sort of "Heaven" in this world here and the fate of the others have had to remain in a sort of "hell".

The scientific not ride high, thousands of years to discover the secret, the cause that gave form and content of the world in time and space. Human thinking, although it has always evolved, remained polluted dialectics of action between the forces of human immunoglobulin with/and law man that it dominates.

The man regarded historical, as a product of labor and regarded work perfectly for inclusion in the law of things, phenomena and dialectic thinking, it can be concluded that work through his dialectic process of dialectic human generated from 'primitive 'to a man of perfected man always, always, always civilized, modernized with a Word always developed, with peaks of pyramid, scholars and people in the process historical the man has two-way beneficial evolution: for the life and evil human species, beneficial by dialectic needs (primary needs and social and spiritual), evil by many and diverse social wrongs. The man and the human society are constituted in an organic, evolving in time and space dialectics. The dialectic unity of man, "organic particularly" and "cell" of the "General" and human society as a whole, the work carried out by the man sits in the production process, namely the physical work, intellectual work and the work of organization and leadership. However, work perfectly for inclusion in the law of dialectic thinking things, phenomena and should be seen and perceived this dialectic of labor efficiency in dialectic. Efficiency to be felt, complex and multilateral, of which the benefit is that labor productivity increases continually increase product quality, continuous, continuous decrease production costs, the conditions for continuously improve labor and remuneration for work done increases and so on.

In the production process people enter into two kinds of relationships:

1. Relations between themselves; and
2. Relations by that people enter into relationships with nature.

The experience of life reveals that within these relationships between people and between people and nature appears and malevolent side of the labor embodied in many and diverse social wrongs. Thus, some people cannot capitalize "capital live" available to them, either because the relations between the people themselves a certain part of the "capital live" consumed in the production process is appropriated by the one who organizes and manages the production process, and the owner of the means of production, either because many people active, don't have means of production and he found a job "capital live" is lost, it remains only as a prerequisite to produce different goods economic work. They live in poverty and misery of income support.

This phenomenon is the consequence of a work organization and leadership at the level of State administration, which develops dialectical, in direct proportion to the dialectic of human intellectual force and longer due to the fact that the factor of production, the production factor and primary passive, in time and space, became the private property of some families of large and very large and those who do not have the ground and not find a job are suffering misery and poverty and supports.

Social injustices were concerned about the large thinkers of the time of the historical and, depending on how the perceived cause of social injustice, formula theses and ways leading to the removal. Only history facts reveal that their efforts have resulted "only" to ease the social injustices of relative, the problem remains unchanged, so that social injustices continued to remain as a historical chain measured in thousands of years. This phenomenon characteristic of the life and work of the human species, has been and continues to be the "the things, phenomena and dialectical thinking evolves from the stage of" primitive man "to stage" man always modernized, always perfected, always civilized», with a word "always", with tips developed pyramid "mans of science ".

Making use of dialectic thinking, questions arise:

1. How is it possible that the "people" of time historical scholars have managed to make theses and ways to influence the spiritual organization and leadership of the revolutionary processes leading to the normalization of the life of the human species in line with the laws of nature?
2. That you have the secret of enigma, the cause, that the evolution of intellectual labor opposition of man, with the trend of development potential to infinity ($\rightarrow \infty$), did not manage to find ways and means of normalization of life of the human species, in conformity with the laws of nature?
3. That a man be secret that "scholar" he managed to find, to discover the law required that, as applied in the practice of the human species, to lead to the normalization of the life of the human species in line with the laws of nature? that you have the secret, enigma, recitals, cause that intellectual force of humans, with the trend of evolution towards infinity ($\rightarrow \infty$), n-generated "scientist" able man to demonstrate the ways and means necessary to ensure that the people time to get into the historical relationships of equality between them and between them and the wild?
4. As the physical and intellectual force of human force, formed in "live" human capital, not to be used rationally, intensive and extensive creator the benefit of the entire human species in general?

The explanation may not be other than the fact that the dialectic of human and intellectual force of life quantitative collections and activity of the human species, springs and motors of dialectic thinking, have generated a process of evolution, a dialectical thinking leading to the knowledge of the absolute truth ", the source and engine which gives the State of the world in time and space, the form and content". So the great thinkers of the time of history, as a confirmed history facts, imagine "cause social injustice" by "means" that it generates, "the effect of the case", the cause remains an unknown. Conclusions and views expressed in the books: democracy and social justice—the future of humanity, the dialectic of human society, man, let's change the world and Nature and human nature, "compass" targeting human society development, theses and ways that we infuse and we declare co-authors to them, they put a big "brick" historical knowledge of the truth "endless column", demonstrating absolute science that human society, like social economic order, are characterized by itself but by what characterizes "living cell", "concert man", "particular of General".

To support this thesis, the author of the books making a characterization of human offering sufficient elements that allows you to get to know nature and human nature. Thus, the term "imagination", the author of the books mentioned makes several theses which define the nature and human nature. The theses and the views formulated historical perspective open to influence the spirit of a triad» psyche: politics, religious and science in practice work only rational, but creative, beneficial to both the runs and human society as a whole. The theses and views aimed at knowing the absolute truth and perception, "source" engine and that gives motion and auto moving status of the world in time and space, with everything good and bad characterized; seeks ways and means leading to the normalization of life and work of the human species in line with the laws of nature. In this regard, to formulate the law of nature and human flesh from the "conjugate of human action with forces and laws of human/ it dominates" and it is shown that the "law of nature scientific and human flesh", the man being "particular of General" and "living cell" of the "General", "human society as a whole", becomes, by induction from private to general, "the law of human society development in time and space" to characterize everything good and bad.

The discovery of the "law of nature and human flesh" seems to be the most important law ever discovered by human thinking, she targeted and psychological thinking "greening" of pollution nuisances generated by the action of immunoglobulin of human forces and laws with which man/it dominates. "The key" ecologization psychological" of the nature of I and human flesh" by pollutants generated by the conjugate actions between the human forces with/and laws which it dominates human society, ecologization of many and diverse social wrongs and, finally, "greening the environment of physical and chemical pollution generated by human activities and natural" is "human dialectic as nature and temperament".

The discovery of the law of nature and human flesh is intended both to present and future of human society, in order to eliminate the social injustices occurring historical in slavery and maintained historically in feudalism and capitalism as a historical chain measured in thousands of years. As the future concerns for the security of each Member of the human species, each small or large national State, becoming the "protective shield" of the entire planet alive.

Greening psychological thinking of human pollutants generated by the action of the conjugate base of the human forces and laws with which man/it dominate would cause the human dialectic as kind and nature, of what it is:

When "man versus man";

When "man Fox devious manipulation and likely to man";

When "man versus man" crook;

When "man versus man killer "the normal and rational should be, to be always only:

"Man to man". In this process, the relations between people and between people themselves and the environment is a new mutually beneficial content and what is particularly important is the fact that social revolutions, the violence of certain social classes against other social classes, become dialectical, national and global peaceful revolutions, social benefits to each class, whose platform-program human dialectic as kind and fire, from what is normal and should be used judiciously, since it is packed with thought.

The man, the leader of the political class representative of religious man, and man of science enters a process of radicalization of work done. Work organization and leadership of the political class always begin to evolve in line with the dialectic and the dialectic of human intellectual labor; the work carried out by representatives of religious worship begins to adapt the general progress of human society, religion became a dogma a long tussle with science, I would say, she was one of the most important methods and ways of changing human nature and the temperament; work scientifically, representatives of the science pyramid, their tips, parallel with the work carried out in different areas of science, practice and scientific research work on knowledge and perception of man, the nature and temperament, concerned to formulate sentences and ways to ensure a dialectical evolution of nature and human flesh, human religious, man in general.

Triad psyche—politics, religious and scientific—getting as in a "purgatory", will start to produce a creative work always, always, always reasonable, beneficial to both the human dialectic concretely and human society as a whole. So the role of a triad» psyche fall in normal and should be used judiciously. As part of a triad» psyche, the lead role with science, the owner of the largest potential of intellectual labor and knowing evolution of riding the society in time and space, the evolution of human thinking know man about the State of the world in time and space. The science is a form of social consciousness that must draw up theses and ways to govern the work of the Organization and management of politics and religious. The fate of mankind no longer depends on the mode of thinking of a politician in any way, be it genius, nor of a group which is tasked to lead his country's Affairs, with the task and responsibility to organize and lead the country, "universal yard", based on fundamental scientific researchers developed in research institutions profiled on knowledge "of nature and human flesh "where large specialists will remove the tactics and strategies in order to make work politics, politics only having to apply advanced scientific projects very closely.

The role of the Organization and management of human society, namely the construction site of the "universal" in continuous motion, self-knowledge and modernization of a triad» "psyche".

Triad psyche will conceive a forum, which undertakes concrete to organize scientific research institute profiled on human knowledge, that such laws and fire, where they will be assigned higher intellectual personalities: philosophers, psychologists, historians, economists, biologists, writers of all genres, which are great connoisseurs of the law of dialectic, per man and perfect human society which is in the law of dialectic things phenomena, and thinking. They will design the tactics and strategies that govern the work of the Organization and management of "universal" is located in the continuous modernization. Forum of a triad» psyche will determine the order of application of tactics and strategies which will ensure their implementation and in practice.

The Triad of social conscience will know the "absolute truth", "source and engine" which gave and which continue to give the State the world form and content. Will know and "psychological" invisible compass and hardly perceptible as being generated by the action of the conjugate base of the human forces and laws with which man/it dominates, and the fact that the action by the human forces and laws with which man/it dominates generates and psychological process "enchaining" of man in a "mesh" invisible and perceptible which stifles hard, and even block the dialectic "compass" to develop psychological dialectic, in direct proportion to the dialectic of human intellectual labor. It will also charge that the "law of nature and human flesh" is from "particular", "practical man", the "General", "human society as a whole" were, without a magnetic induction, where the phenomenon taking place through the work of the Organization and management at the level of State administration. Conclusion that emerges is that practicing the work of the Organization and management of the human society on the basis of scientific research studies on knowledge and perception of nature and human flesh the "universal", located in the continuous modernization, project-based tactics and strategies developed in research institutes and design, profiled on knowledge and perception of man, the kind and nature, work organization and leadership will be continually upgraded, always in line with the dialectic and the dialectic of human intellectual labor. In this way to work to create the environment, by inference from the general to the particular question of the Organization and management of modern society, to be issued at that yard work "universal" enchain "by the invisible and perceptible mesh," strapped by the conjugate action between human forces with/ and laws of human which it dominates and that block the dialectic of "psychological compass" which directs the human nature and temperament to evolve dialectics, in direct proportion to the dialectic of human intellectual labor.

Changing the State of the world from what is normal and should be rationally is dependent on knowing the truth function absolutely, source and engine that gives the world socio-economic orders, form and content in time and space.

The historical experience of the life and work of the human species that highlights the relationship among people and between people and nature cannot evolve dialectics for the benefit of their unique and peculiar to the General, or for the benefit of protecting the environment, without the "greening the psychological pollution of human thinking".

Philosophy in historical times, some of whom are big thinkers, idealists, or materialistic, they have focused on "interpreting the world in chip and kind" (Marx), "but the important thing is to change" (Marx), and the historical experience of the existence of two socio-economic orders with different ideologies and different properties on the means of production—the capitalist private, the Socialist municipality—leads to the perception that human society cannot be changed as long as the absolute truth Spring, "and" engine which gives the State the world form and content in time and space, is not known.

In Marx's thinking further about how thinking of many great thinkers of the time, as a result of the existence of both social and economic orders and the result of historical events since the end of the Millennium II, Millennium III detachment of a large number of countries in socio-economic and legal system of socialist-communist and choosing the road to capitalism, which had been, offers the necessary elements to conclude that great thinkers historical times have managed to provide theses and ways leading to in preparing the world spiritual revolution with the aim of changing the State of the world because of her refusal by "effect" of the case, the cause remains an Enigma, an unknown thousands of years.

Those offered by the existence of two orders socio-economic one capitalist, based on an ideology founded on private property over the means of production, and other socialist, based on an ideology based on public property, are a result of the "cause", the cause remains a conundrum.

The emergence, in socialism, "the cult of personality" political leaders which resulted in the process of braking and even blocking of democracy and the right to think freely, and the relations of production were also influenced by the cult of personality the mischievous and had the beneficial to highlight and demonstrate that the source engine "and" which gave the State of the world in time and space form and content is the "law of nature and human flesh". This law of nature and human nature appears to be the "ultimate truth" which gave and continues to give State of the world in time and space, the form and content. Hence the conclusion that the class struggle, historically, loses its contents in the sense that, at one point, it no longer is beneficial to human society, dialectic and the violent social revolutions of a social class against another social classes become outdated, historical, and that they, according to the facts and phenomena of dialectic thinking, denied and replaced with national peaceful revolution-world, beneficial to each social classes, whose main objective is to improve the "law of nature and human flesh". Perfecting the law of nature and human flesh will result, by induction, after changing the State of the world from what is normal and what's supposed to be rational and will enter into normality, in conformity with the laws of nature.

CHAPTER VI
POLLUTED PSYCHOLOGICAL THINKING, COMMON FOR ALL THE HUMAN SPECIES

The man has thought is the greatest gift that can and should benefit the entire human species. Or, if the work was that it had stripped the man from the animals (Engels), all his work, by dialectic, with efficiency, was the one that has generated the process of dialectic human from the stage of "primitive man" from the stage that is found today, beginning of the Millennium III, "man always modernized, always perfected, always civilized", "always developed synthetic said," "pyramid spikes with people" (author of the books 'scholars: Democracy and social justice—the future of humanity, the dialectic of human society and human).

Experience the historical facts of his life and work of the human species reveals that man endowed with natural law thinking discovers, chemical, biological, and others of which and the law of things, phenomena and dialectic thinking (Hegel). Hegel claimed cognoscibility the world; he was the first philosopher who presented worldwide natural, historical and spiritual as a process in continuous motion, change and development of this process by assigning a dialectal character. In logic, Hegel developed a unitary system of categories, which they looked into their dialectical relationship. Hegel explained, on the basis of the contradictions, the passage of some categories in others. Hegel has the great merit of being historical developed multilaterally dialectic: the passage of laws in quality, quantity and unit fight contraries, denying the opposing negate and that thesis: things, phenomena and dialectical thinking evolve and progressively thinking that leads to the dialectic of the knowledge of the absolute truth.

Using this thesis of Hegel and taking into account that in the books in question is demonstrated that the scientific thinking of dialectic underlies the human dialectic intellectual force, which, through speech and writing process, the accumulate part, sometimes total, from man to man, from generation to generation, with the trend of development potential to infinity, is born the question how to explains that human thinking Although always develops dialectical though it resulted in knowing the truth, indeed, why the man, the kind and nature, there is dialectal? Question why is born, in the process of dialectic thinking, not lead to her knowledge by man, thinking, that human thinking is as it is and why it is not as normal and rational should be? The answer can only be one: "human psychological thinking is polluted," with many and various "nuisance generated by the action of immunoglobulin of human forces and laws with which man/it dominates". "Psychological" Pollution which, at the level of social consciousness a triad»: politics, religious and scientific, makes their work efficiency, as it cannot evolve dialectics, in direct proportion to the dialectic of human intellectual labor.

The secret, the cause of these phenomena, it seems that locate in the report ("R") of the weighting of the forces of good **(G.F.)** and share of evil forces **(E.F)** and which is found in a continuous process of internal fighting, beating when one when the other, with minimal breaks tie, relation ("R") to be "imagined" of the form:

$$R= FG/EF = 1; >1; <1.$$

Conjugate action between forces of good and evil forces with/and the laws of man which it dominates the psychological thinking "pollute", thereby hindering it and even blocking it to evolve in the dialectical "auto ecologization" of pollutants generated by the action of the conjugate base of the human forces and laws with which man/it dominates.

At the level of politics, social consciousness form, political leaders, people being due to the psychological pollution of groupthink pollutants generated by the action of the conjugate base of the human forces and laws with which man/it dominates, fail to practical work organization and management of human society has always dialectical, which would lead to progress and general well-being. Fail to practical work organization and leadership, always dialectic and directly proportional to the dialectic of human intellectual labor. Dialectical thinking and rationing, the phenomenon is because human intellectual labor dialectic has recorded that level of development which would lead to the dialectic thinking in getting to know the absolute truth. Political man is not in possession of such a potential of intellectual labor, and do not benefit from sufficient examples of life and work of the human species in order to know and to perceive himself as working for what works and what fails to work as normal and rational should work and what is even more important, fails to perceive that his thinking is polluted "psychological" pollution generated by the "law of nature and human flesh", which no-one knows.

The man, the political leader of the social injustices of this occurring, the patron and the snake grows historical existence, adding new links, social history of the inequity chain, chain whose length is for thousands of years. "Psychological" Thinking, the polluted level politics, has consequences particularly malevolent on life, so that the human species through the work of the Organization and management at the level of State administration, practiced by leaders of the political class who hold power in the State, instead of creating the environment necessary to lead progressively to abundance and well-being is complicated, and it distorts the functioning factor markets work the nature and capital accumulated, and the perception of organic links between inputs. Work, the main factor in primary production and asset, is not known, nor perceived by its sources: the physical and intellectual strength force of man, and of these, the intellectual force is not known nor is perceived in a continuous process of moving and auto movement of nature dialectic of "living" human capital, the premise of the factor of production work, which in the production process joins the factor of production nature and capital accumulated. It is not known nor is it perceived process of internal contradictions of the factors of production, generated by "live" the dialectic of human capital, the premise of a more productive and always work to be United with the factor of production nature and capital accumulated, which, in addition to that, their nature is not in line with the factor of production work, and degrade over time (the factor of production nature) so that the inputs of organic work, nature and the accumulated capital is found in a process of continuous crisis.

Dialectic thinking should raise the awareness of the role of politics in the need for the type of business organization and management harmonizing continuously functioning factor markets. Or, "polluted" psychological thinking results in practical political leader man to work for the Organization and management of the human society at random, as it appears some ideas or staff of close advisers. This work is out of date and lead to irrational exploitation of the living "capital" of the human factor of production work cannot operate at the level of its premise of human capital "live".

And what is especially difficult is the fact that, shape the political psyche through its leaders, who hold power in the State, due to "psychological pollution" thinking, practical work organization and leadership that gets in conflict with the law of dialectic thinking, things and phenomena. The consequences are mischievous multi-directional: lost a large share of the capital of the company of live human at a time; It erodes the continuous nature of the production factor; the level of living of a considerable potential of the human species is affected in every respect: food, clothing, housing, health and so on by politics, form of social consciousness through its leaders, who hold power in the State, in order to improve the status of poverty and misery of able-bodied families, but does not find a job, nor does it possess a minimum means of production in order to be able to harness the "live" capital at their disposal, works by well-known formula of "social assistance". Times to provide social assistance to families able-bodied amplifies evil consequences on families who do not find a job in the sense that if work was that it had stripped the man from the animals, "it pushes the non work man" to the way of being of the animals, which is particularly serious, both for the one who receives income support and human society as a whole. And when you think about that many do and great parade that through social assistance ensures decent living families of active-and finds a job.

"The Psychological Pollution of human thinking" is to be seen as the latest pollution of all types of pollution known to man!

"the Psychological Pollution of thinking", at the level of human, political and other evil consequences is: democracy and freedom of thinking, the means necessary to the spiritual progress of the society to influence more social justice, are decreased and, at one point, free elections, democracy by a party or the other: left, right or center-right loses its effectiveness and meaning as "psychological thinking polluted" by the action of immunoglobulin of human forces and laws with which man/it dominates, makes, no matter what the political potential is found in power, State of the world does not change, no more than to be improved, when and where, insignificant, so that social status of the nation a country remains relatively unchanged.

Psychological thought pollution, at the level of politics, the shape of the psyche through the work of organizing and driving behavior, maintain a system of social environment, with many and diverse social wrongs, and things do not stop here, because the law of nature and human flesh works as a "psychological" compass that directs development of human society to events and serious: terrorist and unjust wars that endanger human life itself. Terrorism is a "brother of war" which, owing to the psychological pollution of man, might give rise to a true "Hell on Earth", and the fight against terrorism with armored cars, planes and missiles is like a mentally handicapped should look for a "needle in a Hay reek. And Moreover, this strategy to combat terrorism is to enhance and promote diversification of terrorism because there was a battle against terrorism with armored cars, aircraft and missiles, in addition to that you cannot catch a terrorist leader, kill innocent people, and those of their becoming terrorists in many cases, because they are so severely affected by the death of loved ones that cannot wield the spirits and seek ways of vengeance and means of revenge . . .

Unjust wars have always been a great harm to a considerable potential of the human species, and modernization of weapons of mass destruction, nuclear, chemical and biological properties and the modernization of means of transport of weapons of mass destruction, at haul preconceived, does not exclude the possibility of an "ecological disaster" which could endanger human life on Earth!

Here's why "psychological" pollution of human thought to be seen as the most noxious pollution known to man. "Psychological" pollution, the man becomes unwittingly the greatest enemy of man and the environment.

"Greening the psychological pollution of thinking" is the priority of priorities for the triad psyche: politics, religious and scientific, say for the triad psyche because politics, though the specifics of the Organization and management of the human society is one which promotes the unjust wars, however, it cannot be "ecologization" of pollutants generated by the action of the law of nature and human flesh "without the help of religious and scientific.

Religious, a form of social consciousness, through its representatives that people being practical work, always with the same content, i.e. do today what they did yesterday, I do tomorrow what they did today and always so, or if the work was that it had stripped the man from the animals, all work is one that has generated the evolution of man from the stage of "primitive man" from the "man always modernized always, always perfected, "civilized," always developed synthetic said ", with peaks of" pyramid "of well-known people. The man from religious, religious, priests and their tips pyramid, practicing the same always, work with the same content, becoming at one point, by the way they work, at odds with labor in General, the dialectic that always develops dialectical, as efficiency, with influence beneficial to humans and human society as a whole, so also for priests. Representatives of the religious work which dialectical uninvolved, loses its value always so that, at a time, the priests and the tips of their religion, practiced by pyramid, religion being a dogma, their work is not consistent with the dialectic of human intellectual labor, to which representatives of religious benefit in full, their work does not contribute to the knowledge of "absolute truth", "source and engine" which gives the State the world force and content. Priests, no matter which religious belong to the religion as a form of social consciousness in along the way of the human species had a big role in shaping the "law of nature and human flesh" and still have for that segment of the human species that has a spiritual preparation consisting by religion, or they are subjected to everyday pressures generated by the complex dialectic thinking. Not incidentally appeared saying: "do what the priest says, not what makes the priest", hence the conclusion that the priest says it is beneficial to humans and human society as a whole, and what makes the priest is a "natural thing", common to all people and aimed at "the well-being of the world and his family". And then what would be the priests, religious representatives, so that the religion to become a dogma a science with beneficial influence on the action "law of nature and human flesh" from another dimension, non-braking and unblock the knowledge of truth "absolutely", "source" engine and giving the State the world form and content in time and space?: "Modernization of religion in line with the dialectic of human intellectual force". However, this implies "greening" psychological pollution of thinking of pollutants generated by the action of immunoglobulin of human forces which it dominates, at the level of religion.

The vast majority of priests are large and great philosophers and psychologists and may, if their thinking would be "ecologization" of pollutants generated by the action of the conjugate base of the human forces and laws with which man/it dominates, practice a dialectical work always and in line with the dialectic of human intellectual force, which means the dialectic of religion from a dogma in science. This would entail some changes with regard to the religious of the assumption of man on Earth as a divine creation submitted by "the Lord God in the image and likeness", the hypothesis that has many unknown: "who has ever seen God?" **No-One.** Then why this assumption created by the man that "the man is the Lord God beyond the image and likeness of HIM? Because so and imagined those who have made this assumption, or dialectical thinking evolves and then normal and rational hypothesis is as religious human encroachment on Earth to be recast, such that to characterize the man as a life experience confirms.

If the religious, a form of social consciousness, by representatives of religious worship, will ponder characterization made man in the books: democracy and social justice—the future of humanity, the dialectic of human society, man, let's change the world and Nature and human nature, "compass" targeting walking human society ", you might as well say:" the Lord God formed man as a being "biologic-social, owner of four forces physical strength: strength, intellectual force of good and evil force and it has been dominated by a series of laws so that the work to take lives throughout its existence and a lot of work to know good and evil generated by the action of immunoglobulin, human forces in the dualism of good and evil with/and the laws of man which it dominates ". And in terms of "Heaven" and "Hell" in the world of then a figment very beneficial to the influence of the spiritual man to do only good fellows, religious can mean: "The existence of" Heaven "and" Hell "in the world of opera man here is generated by the action of immunoglobulin of human forces and laws with which man/it dominates and the psychological thinking» «pollute such that he created the single" Heaven "and" Hell "," Paradise "for some and" Hell "for others. "Greening the psychological pollution thinking» pollutants generated by the action of human immunoglobulin and human laws forces that dominate it: «Heaven» in the world of here will be generalized through a rational and creative work, both of which benefit the one running, and society as a whole, and" Hell "that survives a considerable potential of the human species will disappear once and for all. Existence «Heaven» in the world of here for the entire human species will be the subject of disappearance "Hell", both from the world of here, where there is effective and in the world then, where he imagines to be ". This way of thinking, religion and no WINS coming in conflict with the knowledge of "absolute truth", "source and engine" that gave the world and give form and content in time and space. And what is very important in such conception, religion, social consciousness form, increases the influence on human spirituality and aligns with political form of the psyche, influencing the political to the practical work always dialectic in line with the dialectic of human intellectual labor, aimed at eradicating social injustices in the life of the human species, which are nothing but "Hell" in which survives a considerable segment of the human species.

I argued that the political, social, form of consciousness cannot go to practice a dialectic in the work of organizing and evaluating always dialectic and the labor force in line with the dialectic of human intellectual because I do not know and did not perceive the "General" by his "particular" and do not know nor perceive "particularly", "practical man", as wild and fire, "the law of nature and human flesh". Do not know and does not charge the two processes generated by the law of nature and human nature: 1) the process of "psychological" compasses "invisible" and "hardly noticeable," which directs nature and human nature) and 2 enchain psychological process "of man," like kind and fire in a "mesh" invisible and perceptible you hard blocks to evolve continually as a dialectical and threads, in line with the dialectic of human intellectual labor without the help of science. However, through its representatives religious, as it can help to stimulate the political work of organizing and driving always dialectic and the labor in line with the dialectic of human intellectual and he has great need of aid science to be able to work at a practice under which to hang a science, not a dogma! Which means using scientific to turn religion from a dogma in science?

The science, a form of social consciousness through the specifics of his work, gives a human intellectual labor movement and auto movement always dialectic and the trend of evolution, and potential, to infinity ($\rightarrow \infty$), and the intellectual force of man is the dialectic of human thought and the main source of dialectic thinking, and the second source of quantitative build-up dialectic thinking of the life and work of the human species.

The scientific, a form of social consciousness, does not make an exception to the "law of nature and human flesh", and "thinking" is also "polluted" psychological action of conjugated with human forces and laws of human/it dominates, only science is the recipient of the largest potential of intellectual labor and knows well the evolution of dialectic human thinking along historical times and what is very important that scientific know and perceive the law of dialectic thinking, things and phenomena.

The science, a form of social consciousness, due to the potential his intellectual labor, may find that the "State of the world" could be changed from what was over the historical times, with many and diverse social wrongs, because great thinkers of the time perceived state of the world historical times lived by her "cause effect", the cause remains an unknown thousands of years.

So that the theses and the views of many historical thinkers of the time, concerned about the State of the world, devoted their time to change the world from what it was, with many and diverse social wrongs, in what was to be the case, they were made in "effect", the cause remains an unknown. Tests of the great thinkers of the time to influence the historical spiritual organization of social revolution leading to the normalization of the life of the human species in line with the laws of nature, having no knowledge of the basic "absolute truth", "source and engine" which gives the State the world form and content in time and space, have led to changing the world, social injustices continued in the form of a chain history measured in thousands of years.

The science, in addition to the fact that it has known for thousands of years "absolute truth", "source and engine" which gives the State of the world in time and space, the form and content, due to "psychological pollution of thinking"/with pollutants generated by the action of the conjugate base of the human forces and laws with which man/

it dominates, and theses and the opposing views which have influenced those of my invested to lead the company to work for the Organization and management always with the same content. The fact that the political and religious have been and continue to practice a work which has led to the normalization of life and work of the human species in line with the laws of nature are due and how to work the scientific.

Many great thinkers of this pollution, due to "psychological" thinking, not between the way of thinking of many great thinkers of the time on the historical causes which have induced the social injustices and incurrence are not used by their way of thinking to give a new impetus to human thinking dialectics in knowing the absolute truth "," Spring "and" which gave the engine and gives the status of the world form and content in time and space. Some representatives of the science not only fail to make use of the intellectual and the dialectic of force build-up quantitative experience life and work of the human species to discover the cause, the secret that has generated the process of social injustice, but also politics and religious and offers views in contradiction with the real nature of things and phenomena. Such a situation you encounter at many large intellectuals of this, instead to take account of the law of things, phenomena and dialectic thinking and try to put a new brick in the endless column of dialectic thinking, a "psychological" causes many times with new items.

Many great thinkers of this instead to avail themselves of the existence of two orders socio-economic situation of the world-wide to see what should be done to ensure that the human species lives in normalcy, in conformity with the laws of nature, it is made to all sorts of opinions which do not result in anything other than the road of the darkness of the human species and the removal of "absolute" knowledge of truth Spring, "and" engine which gave and continues to give form and content of the world in time and space. Some large merges these intellectuals willingly or unwillingly, a social-economic order with different mistakes made by those of my invested to lead the country at a time, while others are confusing dialectic cognition, spring of which is the dialectic thinking, with disposition of social-economic . . . Asked the author of the books mentioned how he emerged the idea that "absolute truth", "source and engine" which gives the State of the world shape and content would be hosted by "particularly", "General" that is "private" General cell, we said that he has chained in his thinking what they thought of many great intellectuals of the time concerned about the historical fate of the human species and has been used by the existence of the two existing socio-economic orders at a time at the world level as a laboratory fundamental scientific research on the knowledge and perception of human society by reason of which determines the shape and consciousness. Came to the conclusion that human society is characterized not by itself but by its "particularly", "concrete man", and "living cell" of human society and that what characterizes the "particular" of General", particular being and living cell of the "General" normally and rationally is to characterize and General. Arrived at this conclusion meditating on what characterizes positive or negative, including using his own experience for over 70 years of work, remembering how he thought and work life.

On this basis, has given man a characterization that has sufficient human perception as necessary, such as fire, characterization and confirmed by the experience of life.

Using the characterization of human made and remembering the famous Greek philosopher maximum sought by Socrates, the opposite of knowledge: "know thyself", began a process of meditations on him and on many acquaintances, seeing what they do and how I think and so came to the conclusion that the man, the nature and consequence logical threads, is a joint action between forces of man with man and the laws that/it dominates conjugate action, which operates independently of the will and desire of man.

At one point he imagined that the action of human immunoglobulin/forces and laws with human forms in the central nervous system in the human brain, in a "psychological" compass and hardly perceptible invisible which directs nature, man and nature, as in its relations with his fellows and in relation to the environment, and "practical man", "particular of General and General cell 'by nature's nature and becomes "the compass" targeting human society development in time and space, the process taking place through the work of the Organization and management at the level of State administration.

Still, he "pictured", says the author of the books mentioned, that the action by the human forces and laws with which man/it dominates it constitutes as a "net" invisible and perceptible that it hardly "enchain psychologically" on man as kind and threads, braking him and even stranding him to evolve as a dialectical and wires, from what is normal and should be rationally, since it is packed with thought. But the "concrete" man, being "particular", "General" and "cell" of general human society, as a whole, "enchaining", as his psychological nature and fire, in a "mesh" invisible and difficult perceptible becomes, through the work of the Organization and management at the level of State administration, "enchain" society to evolve dialectics, in direct proportion to the dialectic of human intellectual labor. In this way, or due to this phenomenon, social injustices, characteristic of the human species, continued historical as a chain history measured in thousands of years.

Dialectical thinking and dialectical rationing, says the author, it can be concluded that the human society, in order to evolve constantly in line with the dialectic and the dialectic of human intellectual labor, action must be taken to his cell "vii", as "wild and fire". If "the cell", "particular of General", dialectal and always evolving in line with the dialectic of human intellectual labor, then the "General", "human society as a whole" will always evolve in line with the dialectic and the dialectic of human intellectual labor.

This way of thinking and to reason involves the violent social and dialectic revolutions of a social class against other social classes, the engine of dialectic national and world peaceful revolutions, each beneficial social classes whose platform-program would be "human-flesh and revolutionize the nature of what it is:" when man to man ", when" man versus man Fox-like "When "man versus man" biter, when "man versus man killer" in being always only "man versus man" man.

Knowing the absolute truth "," Spring "and motor" which gives the State the world form and content in time and space, is a first step and a new step towards normalization of life and work of the human species in line with the laws of nature. The second step is to create the environment necessary for work organization and leadership at the level of State administration to evolve constantly in line with the dialectic and the dialectic of human intellectual labor. This presupposes that the one who is made to the organize and lead the human society, "universal" site, in a continuous modernization to be based on projects of tactics and strategies developed by the institute of scientific research on the knowledge and perception of the profiled "absolute truth", "source and engine" which gives the State the world form and content in time and space. The role of political parties is radically so that they, the political parties, through their leaders,

What are my invested to achieve "universal" site in a continuous process of modernization, in line with the dialectic of intellectual labor, become only performers of the projects of tactics and strategies developed by some specialists in knowledge and perception of "absolute truth", "source and engine" which gives the State the world form and content in time and space.

The role of the historian to organize management of the company at the base of scientific research and design of tactics and strategies to ensure the movement of human society and auto moving dialectic and always in line with the laws of nature is the responsibility of a triad» psyche.

Triad psyche, to this end, he formed the Forum which probably should be called: the Supreme Forum of the human species history, whose role is to evaluate and approve the research studies and design of tactics and strategies developed by the great intellectual figures, philosophers, psychologists, theologians, historians, economists, writers of all genres. They are great connoisseurs of the law of nature and human flesh and large partisan's knowledge and perception of the law of dialectic thinking, things and phenomena and applying it to know about in the modernization of "universal" site, human society as a whole.

This historic task of psyche has a triad» and the Grand historic role to become a "live shield" in protection to protect man against his own actions generated by the action of immunoglobulin of human forces and laws with which man/it dominates when they are evil.

Greening the psychological pollution of human thought has a historic importance which will mark the passage of the "border" human species, the life and work, from a historical past and present history from a "sick" economically, socially and politically in a healthy socio-economically and politically.

Psychological pollution of human thinking is hardly perceptible. If natural environmental pollution is visible and perceptible, and chemical pollution is perceptible through the analyses made in different laboratories, pollution of psychological thought is invisible and hardly perceptible.

Psychological consequences of thought pollution are extremely evil and are much more serious than the physical and chemical pollution of the environment that affect the life and work of the economic, social and political organization of the whole human species.

"Border crossing" on a sick world economically, socially and politically in a healthy world economic, social and political can be done by "reagent", "rational and creative work".

They will make contributions to both physical and intellectual work in concrete terms, how beneficial values both the running and the whole of human society and the environment, benefit and work organization and leadership at the level of State administration, to become "change the world, reagent" in a world of their economic, social and political world, in a healthy economic political, social, and must be practiced by connoisseurs of the great men, work organization and leadership and to be equipped with "art organization and management".

This requirement is of decisive importance for that process to move the border from a world of their economic, social and political, to a world of sound economic, social and political means that those who organize and conduct the human society, lead a "universal" site, where you build the most advanced building in the world, whose form and content is in a process of continuous motion and auto moving in order to modernize them depending on several factors. However, human society is a building in "living brick" whose quality varies radically and all live "bricks" are also beneficiaries of construction. And the society is "living brick" to be organized and conducted in order to auto improvement themselves in to exploit rationally and creator "capital live" available to them. Hence the conclusion that all "living brick", "concrete people" must be given the environment necessary for their physical and intellectual strength, constituted in a vivid, capital can be harnessed through rational and creative by work.

CHAPTER VII
LABOR UNION AND HIS HISTORICAL ROLE

Trade unions, professional organizations of masses, whose purpose is to defend the interests of the working class and labor of all people, should be treated historical and placed in the law of dialectic thinking, things and phenomena.

The unions have appeared on a particular stage of development of human society and capitalist era, order social-economic system based on private property over the means of production and employment of workers. The appearance of labor union was an objective necessity generated by relations that have emerged between the owner of private capitalist and worker employed reports that have been characterized by many great intellectuals of the time as "employment service" private ownership to its employees. Marx to characterize the owner of private capitalist as "parasitic" and that Wikipedia endorses the gratis and work of his employees.

This way of thinking of Marx was the consequence of the fact that during his private capitalist owner employees worked 10-12-14 hours a day and receiving a salary which does not ensure basic needs for a decent life for their families, and working conditions were particularly heavy . . .

Marx discusses the work of the scientific and the profound as:

1. The physical and intellectual labor work;
2. Simple and complex work;
3. The abstract and the concrete work and employment;
4. Required and supra-work;
5. Work productive and unproductive labor;
6. Employment and labor last week and so on.

Work required and supra-work is characterized as a the historical process in human existence and human society in the sense that the work required is that part of the work done by the employee in the manufacturing process that creates the product, used for the upkeep of his and his family. Supra-work, historical, appeared on a particular step of social production and to a certain level of labor productivity, when each producer can produce more things than are necessary maintenance of himself and his family, the rest is appropriated by others. . . and that in capitalism work required, creates the equivalent of the value, referred price of the worker's employment, on which it receives in the form of salary While the rest of the value created by the supra-work is the capitalist free silhouettes, in the form of profit. This way of looking at work by Marx is due to the level at which it was to be her perceived intellectual force of historical time and practical experience in which the worker was working 10-12-14 hours/day, until exhausted. And also because Marx was sensitive to perceive that the owner of private capitalist practice of organizing work and driving without which the manufacturing process cannot take place, hence the important Special Labor Organization and leadership. In the book "democracy and social justice—the future of humanity" is formulated the thesis according to which "the work of organizing and driving is the most important side of labor" and that this side of the work cannot be confused either with the physical work, any work with intellectual. She is the one that ensures the process, became the capital of live human from a dormant potential, prerequisite for the creation of economic goods, in an active status function, hence the conclusion that the capitalist who organizes and manages the production process, either directly or through its officers, that is all the work of organization and leadership, practice the most important side of work, so he does-endorses free and supra-work workers. As regards plus—product, created in the production process, if we look at how evolving economic goods on account of the different sides of the labor (fig. 1-8), it is very difficult and even impossible set how much of the work necessary to get over the plus-product of workers, which operates in the production, a production cycle belongs to the workers, or practiced lest workers working on the capitalist enterprise they espouse a part of the goods obtained in the form of salary over the level of work required. The secret lies in the evolution and qualitative characteristics of bounds intellectual work and transformed into technological processes automated and mechanized, robotic, or sometimes, this process is the consequence of capacity for work by capitalism, private owner, who, by work organization and leadership, continuous production process modernization, source safe and always enhanced to ensure the greatest possible profit.

The role of trade unions, in socio-economic conditions of capitalist system, which has as its basic private property over the means of production are intended to represent the interests of employees by socio-economic issues, such as: size of wages, improvement and reduction of working time, etc.

In socialism, as you know from the experience of socialist countries, which is based on public ownership over the means of production, the role of trade unions was (e.g. in Romania Socialist) labor to mobilize people to produce more goods in their interest and human society as a whole, the supra-work in socialism by generating funds accumulation, which will ensure the development of the technical-material basis of society supra-work, benefiting the entire society: the development of modern education, schools, free tuition at all levels (primary, middle and upper), free medical care in hospitals and clinics, the building of resorts and recovery of the labor force, houses of culture and modern cinemas and, of course, the modernization and development of industry, transport, clothing, agriculture, etc. etc. In conclusion, the role of trade unions is one in the case of private property over the means of production and with everything in the conditions of a society in which human needs is public property on the means of production.

And labor, given that human society will build on the "law of nature and human flesh," whose objective will be the Supreme rational use, extensive and intensive live "capital" of man, and violent revolutionary processes will evolve the revolutionary dialectic to peaceful and beneficial processes of each social classes, will have to participate actively in the peaceful conduct of the revolutionary process.

CHAPTER VIII

RATIONAL AND CREATIVE WORK, ORGANIC "BENEFICIAL UNITY, HUMAN SOCIETY MAN AND THE ENVIRONMENT"

The factor of production, primary production factor and active, be known with its effects being approached by multi-directional, many large historical economists of the time.

In the book "democracy and social justice—the future of mankind", the work is seen as practical it day by day, namely:

- A. physical work;
- B. intellectual work and
- C. work of the Organization and management,

And in the book "dude, let's change the world", the work is regarded as a scientific hypothesis of the emergence of man on Earth, perfectly framed in law of dialectic, as rational, useful work and creative work, but also as irrational and evil society.

The law of nature and human flesh has influenced factor of production work when beneficial, when the mischievous. Between humans, human society and the environment there is an organic unit, which, in time and space, thanks to the action of the law of nature and human flesh, "organic unity is ever-changing qualitatively."

The Man. I am a man, you are the man, he is the man we are people, ye are people, and they are people. But what is man? "Man is a being endowed with thought and articulated language", says a classical definition of man. Man, being fitted with thinking, thought, and asked how he appeared on the world in the world here in the world of Terra. So the first assumption has been made about the emergence of religious man, recorded in the Bible: "Man It is a divine creation, made of the good God in the image and likeness ". Later, it was made and a scientific hypothesis regarding the appearance of man on Earth, the event founded by English biologist Charles Darwin, which mentions the thesis that man comes from among animals through natural selection and sexual selection. This assumption of Darwin is taken over by the German philosopher Engels and featured as deterministic, stating the thesis that the work was that it had stripped the man from the animals.

Man, since it comes with thinking, thinks and, at one point, asks the question, that we, as people issued with thinking, we ask the question: what is the man in this world? What are the role and the rationale behind him in this world? I, being a man endowed with thought, we, as people issued with thinking, we ask the question: what does a fi, the explanation that the man appeared on Earth, in the course of its history, did what it did and make and currently making? Want to be secret, unknown cause that the man was and is: when "man to man", when "man versus man" biter, when "man Fox devious manipulation and likely to the man", when "man versus man killer" in relations with his fellows?

With these questions, the classical characterization of man: "man is a social being equipped with thought and articulated language" is not sufficiently comprehensive to allow giving an answer to the questions above. Again, I repeat and emphasize/ repeat and emphasize that I, being a man endowed with thought, (or) us being people issued with thinking, start to think, we begin to think and to be able to give an answer to these questions, we take man as a being biologic-social, in possession of four forces: 1 physical force), located in the muscular system; 2) intellectual force, located in the central nervous system of human brain; 3) force of good and evil force 4), located in the central nervous system in the human brain, and that man is dominated by a number of objective and subjective laws, laws that its forces are acting shared with. Human forces and laws of man, by their combined action and with the forces of the environment, have led man to be what it was and is and what it is today.

Man thinking starts with a process of knowledge, discovering various laws (physical, chemical, biological, etc.), and at one point thinking reaches such a level of development as a general discovering and universal law and valid: "law of dialectic thinking things, phenomena and" law discovered by the German philosopher Hegel, who give it an interpretation, arguing the thesis that the idealistic man endowed with dialectical thinking, playing in almost nearly, is coming to the knowledge of the absolute truth. This law is General and universally valid silhouettes by Marx and Engels and perceived in a materialistic concept, stating the thesis of human society's historic materialism, according to which human society, like anything and phenomenon, it was moved and auto moving dialectic and that of the stage reached in their times will evolve from dialectical social-capitalist economic disposition towards a social-economic Socialist order in the first instance, namely to communism in the last phase.

New order, Socialist, is called imagination by Marx and Engels as being bigger than the capitalist, describing it as a imagine her. Imagination of Marx and Engels on the American capitalist system towards one Socialist was silhouettes and Russian political philosopher Lenin man and experienced, and after World War II to extend world-wide, cohabits parallel to that capitalist.

At the end of the Millennium II, disposition of social-economic Socialist enters a process of teasing at world level, while remaining, here, over, in several countries of the globe. Former socialist countries in Europe are in a process of transition from Socialist to form order an order social economic capitalist, where they had been. In this situation, the question arises: how should the perceived socio-economic orders dialectic?

Like humans, being "fitted with thinking", like people, being "gifted with thinking", start a process of "imaginary" research and, after a period of meditation, we come to the conclusion that the dialectic of a company of men to be seen by her particularly the man is also his" living cell". She, the socio-economic order, is being the General of particular man.

Perceive the dialectic of General, socio-economic order, by particularly them, man, begins a process of meditations upon him and we calculate enclosing it organic in the dialectic of things and phenomena and the law, that he, the man once appeared on Earth, evolved from the stage when the dialectic was "primitive man" to something higher, becoming now continuously at the beginning of the Millennium III-in the vast majority of the countries of the globe, Earth, "man developed, improved, modernized and civilized man", with peaks of "pyramid" of well-known people.

The man is the living cell of society, through its dialectic, generated and the process of dialectic human society. Or, the man, the living cell of society, as peculiar to the law of dialectic thinking things, phenomena, and will continue its process of dialectic and his dialectic will generate and dialectical process of human society.

Dialectical thinking and rationing and concluding that the dialectic society has its origins in the human dialectic and the source, I looked for the source and the engine of dialectic human and, through an imaginary research, we concluded that if the work was that it had stripped the man from the animal, all its work, through the dialectic, as efficiency, it must be spring, and the engine of his dialectic. Question that I put it/we weren't paying was: who provides labor dialectic? After a long search, on the basis of the characterization made man as owner of the four forces: physical strength, intellectual force, the force of good and evil force, and perceived work, consuming physical and intellectual energy, I have reflected on these two forms of human energies and I concluded that physical energy, physical force in the labor process, is characterized in that it is relatively consistent from person to person and that cannot be transmitted from human to human, so there may be the source of any engine of dialectic and the labor (labor efficiency). Meditating on the intellectual strength of a man, I have concluded that by the process of speaking and writing, to be transmitted, either partially or even totally, from man to man, which means a movement and auto moving dialectic of intellectual labor, whose potential can grow from person to person and from generation to generation, what, imaginary thinking, leads to the conclusion that the intellectual force of man tends to infinity $\rightarrow \infty$. So the intellectual force of man is the source of the dialectic and the labor (labor efficiency). Or, if the intellectual force of man $\rightarrow \infty$, then the process of dialectic and the labor $\rightarrow \infty$ (for efficiency), hence the conclusion that human natural dialectic will continue and that by his dialectic, will take place and the dialectic of human society as a whole.

If we thinking the imaginary, intellectual human labor dialectic $\rightarrow \infty$ and labor efficiency $\rightarrow \infty$, and the man and through him, as "cell" of society, dialectic society as a whole will continue. Be born a natural question: what is the future of humanity? World, is go whither?

This question is put and the phenomena that occurred at the end of the Millennium II, when the disposition of social-economic development of socialism, which was conceived by Marx and Engels, bigger than the capitalist, virtually collapsed from the level reached at the world level, while remaining "here and over".

The answer to this question, which is closer to the ultimate truth, require a moment of reflection in which to try to respond to phenomena that took place in the last part of the Millennium II, after whom the world socialist system collapsed?

From my point of view, there is an explanation of nature dialectic: a) The intellectual force of man, from the time of Marx and Engels, has achieved that level of development which will enable man to charge the dialectic of human society through his "living cells "by dialectic the man; b) Man, "living human cell of society", was perceived in those times of Marx and Engels, by its laws and its forces; c) The social-economic Capitalist Order was not perceived away in a moving and auto moving dialectic; d) Socio-economic Socialist Order was not perceived by his "living cell ", the man, but by itself; e) dialectic society was perceived by the dialectic of social revolutions, which, to a certain level of intellectual development of the human force of violent social revolution, can make the leap into becoming their dialectics, in national and world of the peaceful revolution in which to win every social class, each unique and peculiar to the General, human society as a whole; f) Religion as a form of social consciousness, was charged in moving and auto movement dialectic, be it and very slow, and so on, that was perceived as a very effective means for building socialism.

Deeply convinced of the existence of the law and dialectic thinking things, phenomena, law discovered by Hegel and perceived by Marx and Engels in a materialistic concept and extended to human society, after I researched imaginary which is the fount of human society and the dialectic, in the books "democracy and social justice—the future of humanity" and "the dialectic of human society and human needs" was enunciated the thesis that the socio-economic orders existing at the beginning of the Millennium III both the Capitalist and Socialist, where there is dialectal, will evolve towards an order social economic democracy and social justice dialectical opposition, and the process will be national and revolutionary world peaceful and from his will win every social class. The Platform-program peaceful social revolution program beneficial to each social class will be: "revolutionize the nature and temperament of the man, from what is normal and should be good!"

The books "democracy and social justice—the future of humanity" and "the dialectic of human and human society" in which the man and the human society in the process of moving and auto movement include the following: the dialectic of scientific demonstration of man and society were progressing dialectics in direct proportion to intellectual human labor dialectic, that dialectic human and human society is on a road full of obstacles and with many brakes. They generate a process of moving and auto movement at a rate like "movement with snails" and, sometimes, the movement is of the form "crab movement ". For the improvement of the road of dialectic human and human society, without barriers and without brakes, based on human perception through his laws and his forces were brought over 25 theses concerning changes of nature and human flesh.

Among the conclusions formulated in the books "democracy and social justice—the future of humanity" and "the dialectic of human and human society", claims were made by the following: 1) "socio-economic orders Dialectic existing now, at the beginning of the Millennium III (capitalist and Socialist), in an order social economic democracy and social justice dialectical opposition "and 2)" violent revolutionary Dialectic processes of social classes from other social classes in the revolutionary processes of national and world peaceful for all social classes . . ."

Making these expressions to explain what we understand by "Let's change the world".

Those who have read the two books and those who will read below, may be sensitized that man, owner of the four forces (physical strength, intellectual force, the force of good and evil force) and dominated by a number of objective and subjective, laws is "shackled" and "imprisoned" of action by human laws with those of the man in the dualism of good and evil. That he is powerless to break enchaining and be released from prison in which survives by himself, on their own behalf, hence the conclusion that he, the man must be helped to be free of this emasculation. The author, we, we've imagined as a "living shield of protection" that I've named "Supreme Forum of the human species." The changing world? The radical way of leading a country, a national State, by those of my invested do so, they are people. Her people are being "enchain" of action by human laws with those of the man in the dualism of good and evil and organize and lead under the action by human laws with human dualism good and evil, which is why they need help and the "live" shield of protection.

Intellectual force of humans to a certain level of development level will help her, the core members are organizations summoned Moldovan authorities that the fate of a people, small or large, can no longer depend on how the driver's seat, no democrat would have it, no matter how advanced the democratization of his country would be. The present state in which the human species is found to depend on the decisions of a political personalities, and highly personal orientations and aided by many and various advisors, is out of date, is outdated.

It is unacceptable that the fate of a people to depend on the mode of being of various heads of States, which, although they have a political platform, a political-economic-social superior of their other opponents in the struggle for power, yet they cannot resist joint action between human laws and human forces in the dualism of good and evil. And then, in what would be, say synthetic, "world changing "?

In the Organization and management of the company, on the basis of studies developed by the institute of design and research on the knowledge link sections of organic inputs on the knowledge of the link between economic activity and the environment, the organic link between the perception of the dialectic of human intellect, force the dialectic of human society, dialectic and dialectic of production factors. These studies will be developed by the intellectual personalities specializing in philosophy, theology, psychology, biology, economics, history, etc. and will be approved by the Supreme Forum of the human species established nationally and with the recommendation to sue and global political class being awarded to apply in practice these studies and only! Why only? In order to shun the political leaders of the danger for the type of business organization and management generated under the influence of joint action with the forces of human laws human dualism of good and evil, which can keep long in the position to do what they have done throughout history, human society, preventing them to do what he should do.

Organization and management of the company at the base of scientific research studies should be mandatory because human society should be seen as: "a worksite universal" in the modernizing continues. This universal "construction site", "human society" as a whole cannot modernize without scientific research studies prepared by the large intellectual personalities, who are great professionals in knowing and perception of the world in time and space. They, on the basis of scientific research to design tactics and strategies designed to ensure the dialectic of the labor organization and management of the modernization construction of the "universal" in line with the dialectic of human intellectual labor.

CHAPTER IX
THE MAN AND THE WORK

Meditating on the common denominator of the two hypotheses of occurrence of man on Earth, assuming religious and scientific hypothesis, namely that all human life on Earth is subject to the employment factor and influenced by the thesis made by Engels, that work is that it has removed the man from the animals, and based on my own experience to practice various forms of work and those referred by the course of my life, on how to be people who practiced different work, and upon those who do not really worked, I formulated the thesis in the book "democracy and social justice—the future of humanity": "Non-work is approaching its man of the way of being of the animals".

After a period of time in which we practiced, over ten years, physical work in various fields of activity (agriculture, stock raising and in different industries), I was favored by historical circumstances to practical and intellectual work, during which time I got acquainted with different views of intellectual personalities of the factor LABOUR. In the process of searching for the way of perception and interpretation of the WORK I took the cognizance with different opinions about the WORK factor of philosopher, political economist and human k. Marx. He comes to work like this:

1. Concerning the work of physically and intellectually, k. Marx concludes that between physical work and intellectual work, that there is a contradiction in the process of work increases. The opposition of physical work and intellectual work dates back to the slave era and that in capitalism reaches climax due to advances in technical and technological training and continuous development;

2. Seen the work in terms of simple and complex labor, Marx shows that simple work is work of a person who does not have special training that would be a labor unskilled labor. Complex work, be it physical or intellectual work, is a worker with a special theoretical and practical training and that all kinds of complex production process is reduced to simple, social work serving as a unit for measurement;

3. Seen the work in terms of concrete and abstract, Marx mentions the thesis that the concrete work is generation of value of utilizing goods and that abstract work, expense of employment in general, regardless of its form, set the value of the goods;

4. the work required and supra-work is portrayed as a historical process in human existence and human society, in the sense that the work required is that part of the work done by the worker in the production process, which creates the necessary product, used for maintenance of his and his family, and supra-work, historical, appeared on a particular step of social production and to a certain level of labor productivity. Each manufacturer may produce more goods than it needs to maintain his and his family, the rest is appropriated by others . . . and that in capitalism work necessary to create the equivalent of the value and price of the worker's employment, on which it receives in the form of salary, while the rest of the value created by silhouettes capitalist supra-work is free the form of profit, said Marx;

5. Work productive and unproductive labor, understanding productive work through work that is reflected in the material world and non-productive work through labor workers who do not participate in the creation of material goods;

6. Work life is defined by k. Marx as spending for manpower in the manufacturing process, in the production of material goods, and the last work is defined as work filed under previous production processes and embodied in the means of production (the totality of the work and the work that people use them in the production of material goods). Within the means of production, the role you have the means for work (all material means by which people act on objects work, adjusting them according to the aim pursued).

This way of looking at work by k. Marx and taking into account that I have practiced a lot of physical and intellectual work, a lot of work simple and complex and a lot of work, and the fancier things, phenomena and dialectic thinking, I was determined to involve work which is in the organic law of dialectic thinking, things and phenomena. However, these laws generally and universally valid by its contents show that: "the things, phenomena and thinking are evolving from what are at some point to something higher", which is why I started to consider the work and perceive the dialectical. I used as a basis two points of support:

    1. How to look and work by Marx
    2. The way in which people practice work, namely:
        a. physical work
        b. intellectual work and
        c. work of the Organization and management

These two points of support, passed through the filter, I started thinking concerning them and to perceive through the law of dialectic thinking, things and phenomena.

By doing this way of thinking and research, both imaginary and meditative, I concluded that the dialectic of work materializes, approves a dialectic of labor efficiency, and effectiveness of the work to be seen, respectively, complex and multilateral both from the point of view of labor productivity, as well as from the point of view of the many and various influences on concrete worker No matter where performs work, finally and human society as a whole. Therefore, these aspects of the efficiency of the work is known and are highlighted in different statistics regularly practiced, which shows that labor productivity increases continuously, working conditions improve continuously the quality of products is increasing, decreasing costs and so on.

So the efficiency of labor develops dialectical from what is at one point to something higher. Next, I looked for the source engine and auto movement and economic efficiency of work and, of course, other beneficial aspects of human life.

I started the process of the search engine and the spring providing the labor movement and auto movement efficiency in the work rendered, i.e. physical, intellectual work and work organization and workplace and leadership increased, practicing and diverse physical work, then a lot of intellectual work and a lot of work for the Organization and management, I felt my own person that any form of work behavior requires expenditure of labor force and require less battery power.

By me from my own experience of practicing physical labor, intellectual work and work of the Organization and management, I remembered the physical efforts made as a farm-worker as a worker and micro-stock raising, forestry, mining, worker as master in mining, as Chief Engineer of the sector, and teaching-assistant professor, lecturer, Professor and so on.

I remembered the physical efforts, sometimes suffocate in forest work, practicing various different mining and other work-work that you practice with classical, but primitive tools: back saw, shovel, axe, hoe, Pecker, wheelbarrow, etc. and noticed how, on a regular basis, with the advent of other gear, goods are produced increasingly more and with less physical effort ever. I remembered the intellectual efforts and why I made in the process of education and higher, graduating high school class 12 in the city of Cluj-Napoca, with diploma of merit. Also, I remembered the effort made in connection with the admission examination given to the Timişoara Polytechnic Institute, where I became a student, and after the end of the year I, with good results and very good, I was sent to my ongoing studies in Dnepropetrovsk, the locality was U.R.S., where, after 5 years of study, I received the diploma of engineer of mining. After graduation, I worked in the Institute's leadership—as master in the mining sector, head, head of aid at the evidence for Baia Sprie mine County Maramureş, where I was sent from the production to work on the Committee's Economic Commission, Regional Party in the position of Deputy Premier with economic problems. After one year in this job I was sent to the Academy of economic studies and Political "Stefan Gheorghiu", where I worked at the Department of Economic Construction, and then as Assistant Professor, lecturer, teaching the course "Technology of the main industries" students for five years, during which I supported and received a

Ph.D. in economic sciences with the dissertation "economic efficiency of introduction of modern technologies and equipment in the process of exploitation of deposits of non-ferrous mining ores in Baia Mare".

After supporting her doctoral degree, I worked 20 years in the work of director general of Mining Trust Baia Mare, the unit passed through several organizational forms (Central non-ferrous metal ores, Minerals and non-ferrous Metallurgy), where I was transferred to the Ministry of Mines, serving as director of Technical Division, where, after a year, I was transferred to the Central Salt and non-metallic ores, Bucharest occupying the post of director-general, hence I retired.

While I worked at Baia Mare, I taught students the "Organizing, planning and management of economic activity", as an associate professor and Professor.

I have reviewed these few works provided to reminds me of what efforts we have made in my lifetime, as a worker in various activities, in order to search for the source and the dialectic of the work, the work is a phenomenon that requires expenditure of labor for the production of goods required to meet the economic and social necessities of the human spirit.

Practicing different work, I began to perceive the physical and intellectual efforts involving various physical work, intellectual, organizing and leadership.

In order to find "fount" dialectic and the labor, I did a research on the evolution of the share of imaginary economic obtained on behalf of various kinds of research work—located at imaginary social—economic orders that passed that humanity, in which humanity is found at a time.

Research of the imaginary I represented a graphic in the book "democracy and social justice—the future of humanity". Stating that this research imaginary I made it through the prism of dialectic thinking things, phenomena and, taking as a support module to look at and interpret the work by k. Marx and on WORK and as it is practiced every day as a physical work as an intellectual work and, above them, and as a work of the Organization and management.

Dialectic laws are very complex and they must be discovered and deciphered in what's happening in the labor process, where man spends the workforce for the production of goods required to meet his needs and his family.

What special importance for humanity, today, now, at the beginning of the Millennium III, understands the deeper and more complex "group work"? Philosophical category "employment" and category "economic work" dialectical and historical should be viewed, that physical work should be viewed, rendered, and provided the intellectual work of organization and management chores, both individually and as an organic unity inextricably linked to each other.

If the physical labor—reflecting the physical muscle effort that a producer makes in order to ensure the goods required to meet those needs and of his family, over time, from the primitive and our times, the beginning of the Millennium III and intellectual labor and organization and management, we find that the relationship changes continuously both in quantitative and qualitative, increasing the share of the latter. The graphical presentation of the goods produced by the "man" in the socio-economic orders (figures 1-8) we note that in the entire production of goods primitive products achieve only by consumption of physical labor—muscular exercise. (See the fig. No.1).

In slavery, goods produced by the "man" in the overwhelming majority were achieved by physical labor—muscular exercise. At the same time, and buds appear to participate in the production of goods and labor passed (work gained in production tools) and intellectual labor-intellectual effort. See fig. nr. 2.

In feudal society, the goods produced by the "man", also in the large majority are caused by physical work—physical muscular, but this order goods produced as a result of past labor participation are starting to grow. Also, and locally produced goods on account of intellectual labor recorded a slight increase. See fig. nr. 3.

In the disposition of social-economic development of capitalism, the goods produced by the "man" I try to introduce you to different stages of development of the capitalist economy. Thus, in the Figure nr. 4, is presented a situation of capitalism. From this figure we see also that goods produced by the "man", in their great majority, are linked to the consumption of physical labor—muscular physical exertion, but at the same time, it is apparent that goods produced on account of work past grow significantly.

The same phenomenon is going on and due to the consumption of intellectual work. May we find a phenomenon particularly important, namely that the work of organizing and driving becomes in the production of goods towards one side of the very important work, which contribute to joining forces at work-physical, labor gained (last week) and intellectual labor.

I make this clarification because, even though in previous socio-economic orders and labor that existed inside the organization and leadership, in capitalism, this side of the work acquires a special importance.

In the figure nr. 5 are presented the production of goods produced in a late stage in the capitalist economy. From this figure we see that, although the share of goods obtained on account of physical labor, though the majority is living, the last work (acquired) and intellectual labor participates more substantially in the production of goods and the work of the Organization and management is becoming increasingly important in the production process.

In fig. nr. 6 is a share of production of goods in a stage of development of capitalist economy relatively average. From this figure we see a dignified namely that consumption of locally produced goods on account of physical-physical work the muscle begin to be less than 50%, and locally produced goods on account of accumulated work (past) and joint intellectual labor with work organization and leadership are beginning to be more than 50%.

Fig. 7 is a share of goods produced by the "man" in a developed stage of capitalism (modern capitalism). In this figure you can draw conclusions of utmost importance and that the vast majority of goods produced are carried out on behalf of past labor (accumulation of physical, intellectual work and work organization and workplace management). Also, and the production of goods produced at the expense of jobs, the vii, intellectual, and organizational and leadership is more sensitive than that of goods produced by the physical work. What deserves to be noted is that physical work is carried out by a staff with a highly qualified and in a reduced working time or 6 h/sch. six working days per week or 8 h/sch. of the five working days per week.

This process changes the relationship and between the owners of the capitalist-owner who was "man of labor". He, the man, the owner of private capitalist, practical side of the work of the utmost importance and knows how to organize and lead plant, factory, etc. depend on the economic and financial results. And to be better understood, it is sufficient to point out the following three examples:

1.) a unit of production, some with some degree of technical equipment, raw materials and materials existing in either the own or other facilities, with the same energy source, with the same personnel, but with "a work of the Organization and management" of poor quality, has the financial and economic results of monthly and annual unsatisfactory, leading eventually to bankruptcy;

2.) a different drive, or even the same drive from point 1, with the same technical conditions, but with a driving practical work "Organization and management", say, as satisfactory or average, economic-financial results monthly and annual satisfactory or even good, your lives and the lives and continues production;

3). an economic unit with the same degree of technical equipment as that laid down in paragraph 1 and 2, with the same staff of workers, but with a very knowledgeable in leadership to organize and lead the process of production, that is "a work of the Organization and management", modern economic-financial results monthly and annual great, exceptional, big profits This enables both current needs at a higher level (payroll), and new possibilities in perfecting the art collections and technologies work.

Fig. 8 is played a capitalist economic unit in which the manufacturing process is completely automated and mechanized warfare, mostly robotized. In this situation, locally produced goods, in their great majority, are conducted on the basis of past work and labor on behalf of the Organization and management, which is done either directly by the owner of private capitalist or its officers, who are very well paid. The goods produced by the labor raw (physical and intellectual), in addition to the fact that it is much lower than the share of goods produced on account of past labor (accumulated) and work organization and leadership, the work is alive and very well paid and are running in a pleasant ambience and a reduced working time.

This complex process of mechanization, automation and robotizes determined from almost close to production as "always enlarged and increasingly few people", and the number of unemployed is a social problem all the time particularly intractable by political and administrative organs of the State. Solving the problem of unemployment depends ultimately all of the capacity of the Organization and management of those who are part of the Government of the country and those who are part of the administration of the various areas of the country (prefects, mayors, etc.).

When the Prime Minister of any capitalist countries, Government Ministers will have the political will and ability to organize and lead the country as a capitalist has a highly endowed in the practice of work of the Organization and management in accordance with point three, the problem of unemployment will remain as a sad remembrance, and in that time, the disposition of social-economic capitalism are evolving towards "social-economic organization of democracy and social justice".

Make it clear that the share of goods produced on account of past work is the consequence of the dynamics of intellectual work which is to accumulate from generation to generation and to transmit to the next generations as a major force for action, namely the new intellectual goes on a road wide open, which enable the force to his intellectual to rest on everything you have given the best previous generation of intellectuals It may help to turn him to improve existing technologies and technique, which entails developing and continued development of the forces of production, labor productivity growth and the reduction of production costs.

The disposition of social-economic socialist-communist, where it remained, and it can be to reach to turn to build a new society and economic and social, "democracy and social justice", and the ways in which you can reach such a human society will be relatively the same as for the former socialist countries, which find themselves in a deep reform process, to move from socialism to . . .

Practicing the three sides of Labor: 1 physical work), 2) intellectual work and 3) work organization and leadership, which represented an expenditure of labor force, which in turn implies the existence of an energy source, making use of dialectic thinking, I have concluded that the man, since his birth, his body is stored in the two forces organic buds related to one another:

1) Physical force and

2) Intellectual force.

These two forces differ radically between them and follow their separate ways over time. Thus, physical force go away measured in years equal to the life of each individual man; physical force is found in the muscles of the body and the body is continually developed, parallel to the growth and development of his body, reaching a peak at the age of CA. 20-25 years, period after which the physical force remain for a certain period of time, starting as a relatively steady after the CA. 45-50 years to decrease continuously, up to such a level that man can use physical force in getting up, lightweight clothing, movements, etc.

Physical force differs from man to man, but has a certain limit that cannot be overcome (e.g. a man can lift a weight of 25 kg, 50 kg, and 100 kg). Physical force is characterized by the fact that it cannot be transmitted from human to human. Being then relatively steady all the time, physical force is easily perceptible to everyone.

Intellectual force in the human brain and therefore is perceptible and hard. Intellectual force in the human brain, in the form of "shoots", appears with the birth of the child and develops continuously throughout the life of man, with some exceptions. Development of the intellectual forces of humans takes place according to the law, the phenomenon of dialectic character of continuous quantitative accumulation and periodically and character of qualitative leaps, changes are generally all the time from lower to higher levels.

Physical and intellectual strength force of man is presented graphically kind of like this:

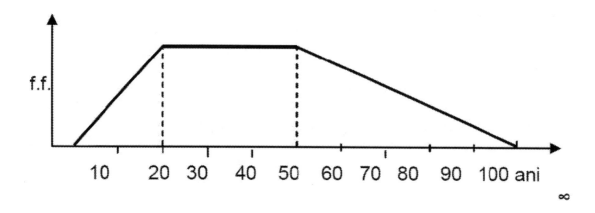

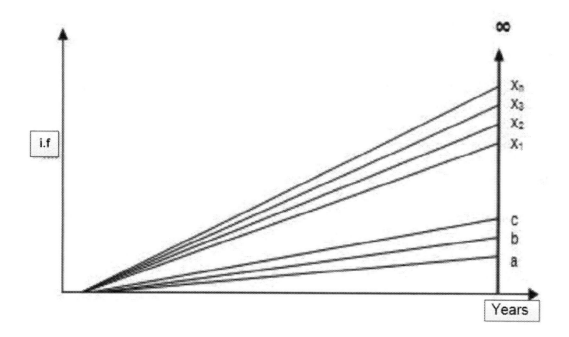

where:

    f.f.-is physical force of man;
    i.f—is intellectual forces of man
        a,b,c . . . x_1, x_2, x_3 . . . human generations
    i.f of man $x_n > x_{n-1} > \ldots > x_1 > \ldots > c > b > a$

Unlike physical force available to the body of a man, intellectual forces go a long way, equal to human life. The ways you browse is very long and are transmitted from human to human, and from generation to generation, what we can urge to believe and to imagine that the intellectual force of mankind tends to ∞. It should be made clear that intellectual force differs radically from human to human, what makes some people to be more successful and discovery of many laws that govern the world that surrounds us and the laws that govern nature and human nature, human society as a whole.

Intellectual force is a force without concrete, fixed size and very hard to imagine, and under no circumstances can be measured in physical units of measure, how to measure physical strength of human-muscle strength. Worldwide there are procedures for determining the precise degree of intelligence that is equipped with an individual.

Intellectual force of humans, with the hope that they make a mistake, highlight through increased labor efficiency always physical, that shall be also measured in natural units and value in highlighted man-hour productivity per unit of product. And synthetic, and highlight the intellectual force behind the forces of production, always the superior from stage to stage, means of transport (land, water and air), in the media, in the knowledge of the general laws governing the nature of the general laws that govern human society as a whole, close to the knowledge of the absolute truth.

Regardless of the content and form of manifestation of the two forces of man, of humanity, one thing is very clear, namely that these two forces find themselves in a dialectic, which influences each other and continuously up to ∞ (infinity).

To make myself understand how better and more clearly, I have to give some concrete examples which, I hope, that I will convince everyone of those said above regarding the unity of physical forces and dialectic of human intellectual forces, dimensions of these two forces:

1) a man picked at once detached from the animal Kingdom, begin to think and to discover that he, "the man" may use a stone which it helps to made those needed for his consumption and his family, which means a consumer intellectual force with beneficial consequences for physical labor;

2) Man imagines that by carving the stone he can produce more easily and in greater amounts of con-sum property required him and his family, which means that man can build tools from stone carved stone, or the process mean and the consumption of higher intellectual force, with beneficial effects on employment, on the use of physical force muscle;

3) Man discovers, through intellectual force that can use the bronze far better and more efficient as the stone carved stone and begins to produce the tools working in bronze, practicing and using physical work—physical muscle—giving life force intellectual—grey energy consumption—and then, later, the intellectual force behind

you helps the man to go forth and discover that iron is superior bronze to be used in the construction of machine tools;.

4) man in his dialectical manner, using grey matter, progress continuously building and practicing physical, workforce tools of increasingly enhanced, and in different time periods are held parallel to the collections, qualitative and quantitative advances leading to home's prowess to build ever-better machinery and equipment, which causes great progress in creating and developing productive forces, and so on;

5 Man, parallel with as shown above, on the process and progress of construction of production forces, discovers animal energy, water energy, power energy, electricity, hydro and Thermo and others, the energies used, put into motion the forces of production created, with the help of which one-man starts to produce consumer goods for the private and public in the most varied;

6) Man builds and diversifies the means of transport by land, water and air, and means of the documentation and information, with a Word, man progresses continuously from vintage to vintage.

7) Man invents writing. This great discovery enables replication of any medium, by conventional signs, or hand-drawn, painted, etched and thoughts of language spoken.

The oldest forms of writing have appeared in ancient Egypt, CA. 3,000 years BC, and after CA. 1500-year-old man discovers the alphabet. It is assumed that the first alphabet was composed by the Phoenicians by about 1300 years BC, the Phoenicians and has developed phonetic character writing. In the 2nd century AD, the Chinese invented paper. These great breakthroughs of grey matter and ordinary human in the form of intellectual energy, has enabled mankind to formula by writing on paper, the discoveries made at one time they were taken over by the next generations of people who, in turn, using everything you had discovered their predecessors, they could accumulate a rich material—a result of intellectual work and accumulated past—then stated in writing on paper could continue the process of development and improvement of the knowledge giving them then, such intellectual force behind the potent of this man and the *human future*.

As the human mind is enriches with new and new knowledge on how to produce the goods necessary for its existence and of his family, his dialectical works grey matter and in terms of how to understand the phenomena and processes occurring in nature. Man finds that periodically appears light and darkness, cold and heat, storm and silence, the seasons and so on.

The man starts, the dialectic, to explain these phenomena and natural processes, and the conclusions which we shall write to his followers. People think differently, the findings are different and they are taken over by the next generations, developed and improved. It goes with the intelligence up to ask questions like: what is nature? Who created it? Who made man on Earth? And others many questions. These questions arise about making the world religious assumptions by a divine force and scientific hypothesis that the world is material, that has always existed and that man is a product of biological kind of the animal Kingdom. These two assumptions, once raised, go parallel, and are continually by man, through various scientific arguments, some other dogmatic.

Important is the fact that man progresses continuously and that his way of life in general is improving from a historic step to another, that man starts to be organized in different social forms: races, tribes, States, which allow a life safer and more enjoyable.

The man, in the process of work, using the two forces, physical force and intellectual strength, make such breakthroughs that change and beautify by nature, a work of the Commission.

At one point, the man, accumulating a lot of knowledge in various fields of activity as: mathematics, physics, chemistry, biology, mechanics, etc. get to make such collections quantitative processing always jumps with pinhead, that quality, in the sixth decade of the 20th century, begins the launch rocket, artificial satellites and cosmic ships with tools for measurements on board and with television apparatus (flying dog Laika on Sputnik II "," after beginning in the early flight series: other cosmonauts Yuri a. Gagarin, etc.).

Flight of the cosmic opens a new historical stage in the way of thinking about the world of humans, Earth and celestial bodies. The human mind has new possibilities to auto exceed in the knowledge of truth.

Detach the conclusion that the source and the labor force is the dialectic of human intellectual, namely the dialectic process of dialectic intellectual force generates employment in general, as complex and multi-faceted training efficiency.

Labor dialectics of human intellectual and practical experience in quantitative collections of life and human activity, will present at one time the dialectic thinking, it is known as "the law of nature and human flesh" generated by the action of the conjugate base of the human forces and laws with which man/it dominates and the psychological human thinking "pollute" generating a process of relationships between people and between people and nature with many and various nuisances.

CHAPTER X
WORK DIALECTIC

Dialectic, science has the most general laws of development of nature, society and thought; theory and method of General knowledge of reality, infinite path through the dialectic of judgment, and dialectic of reason, it helps the man to come close to knowing the absolute truth.

Taking as a basis the two hypotheses of occurrence of man on Earth, assuming religious and scientific hypothesis, and the fact that these two hypotheses have a common denominator, work, and interpreting this phenomenon, in the light of the law of dialectic get to perceive that if work was that it had stripped the man from the animals, all of it, through its dialectic It is one that has caused, which resulted in the evolution of man from the stage of "primitive man" from the stage it is found at a time.

The work is that it has stripped the man from the animals (f. Engels). The work is a phenomenon without which one cannot conceive of human life on Earth, and this phenomenon, practiced by man, played by the law of dialectic, evolving continuously from lower to higher, from what is at a time, to something higher. Regarded the work as it is practiced every day as the physical, intellectual, work organization and leadership, we come to the knowledge that any work involves energy consumption, which is found in the human body's biological and physical energy is located in the muscular system of the human and intellectual energy to locate in the central nervous system.

The physical energy of humans is characterized in that it is relatively constant (50-75 kg strength rarely exceeds this limit) and is characterized by the fact that evolves over time, the evolution of human biological, i.e. her buds in biological body of each new-born and develops continuously up to a ceiling which remains constant until a certain age a man, after which it begins a process reverse out ongoing, tend towards zero. Intellectual energy of man, providing intellectual force, locates in central nervous system in the human brain. This intellectual energy is characterizes in that, through the process of speaking and writing, accumulates potential, from man to man, from generation to generation, what determines the evolution of his dialectic, hence the conclusion that this force intellectual human labor and that ∞ dialectics determines labor force intellectual dialectic (the dialectic of efficiency of work).

Physical and intellectual energy of human energy, through the process of labor are transformed into real economic and spiritual needs of man, in his lifetime, assuring them of the primary needs and social and spiritual in a dynamic growth. Stating that the potential physical and intellectual energy of man is found under a dormant and to become active in a functional State is practiced assiduously, expenditure of manpower in a process in which the economic and spiritual goods.

Practicing employment, physical and intellectual, on a particular step of the dialectic of labor and employment practice of organization and management to ensure consistency between the physical and intellectual labor and Union work their last work with the (attested)—work in production and processes embodied in the means of production and consumption evolve over time.

Energy conversion efficiency of physical and intellectual potential existing in the form is based on the latent ability of organization and leadership of those who engage in the work of the Organization and management-competence—not the least of art to organize and lead.

Work as you practice it every day—work intellectual and physical work, work organization and leadership—and using the way of looking at work by k. Marx, I formulated the thesis: "dialectic, Work is currently being carried out by labor dialectics dialectic of human intellectual labor; the opposition between intellectual and physical work shall be harmonized through the work of the Organization and management "and the sentence:" the most important side of the work is the work of the Organization and management; It ensures consistency between intellectual and physical work and work their vineyards with the last work of Union gained and embodied in capital goods and consumer goods, giving them their new dimensions of potential ".

Dialectical thinking dialectics, rationing, I worded the sentence: "If the work is hence who created man, detaching him from among animals (f. Engels), his work, by dialectic, determined and dialectical process of human generated from 'primitive 'man at the «man always developed, always perfected, always civilized and modernized, always from the mass and which have emerged and are always "new academics ".

K. Marx, by the way of work, as employment, labor and employment the abstract and the concrete, scientifically demonstrated that the work is one that creates economic value of goods and the value of their use. How to watch the work as it is practiced, in physical labor: 1); 2 and 3) intellectual work) work organization and management, which can result in the perception of labor side causes social injustices, which, when raised, remain as a historical chain measured in thousands of years. However, I have shown that the work of organizing and driving is the most important side of work, that it provides and the main physical and intellectual energy in a dormant state active creative, functional, economic and spiritual goods, that the efficiency of transformation of physical and intellectual energies of peoples in the economic and spiritual goods depends on the ability of the Organization and management of those people who engage in such work current capacity which depends on the force with which it is provided that organizes and leads. Work organization and leadership that generates the process of social injustice.

Meditating on work organization and leadership, we concluded that it should be considered at three levels:

1) Level of the family;
2) Level of company and
3) Level of local administration and the State police.

A. Regarded the work of the Organization and management at the level of family, it may be established, taking three related families, i.e. with the same number of people and with the same basic physical and technical, that:

a) one progresses continuously), and primary needs and social and spiritual ascending into a dynamic;
b) while the other stagnates and primary needs and social-spiritual, relatively, at the same level;
c) continuous, which weakens another beggaring from year to year, and may maintain primary needs and social and spiritual even at a constant level.

B. Regarded work organization and leadership at the level of companies, which have the same (or different profiles), have a technical-material base relatively comparable, the same number of employees and with comparable level of qualification, we note that:

a) the company develops) continuous production capacity increases continuously diversifying production, lower grades, increases continuously the quality of their cost price decreases from period to period, and activity-based balance sheet, a profit. This situation may occur and by keeping the number of employees or even reducing them;
b) a company which maintain a constant level of profit, constant production equipment with great effort, at a constant level, we note that the production activity on the basis of the annual balance sheet shall be concluded without loss, but also without benefits (profits), and the more we see that and validated from the staff of employees, as they can survive;
c) a company whose production in value expression, decreases continually, cost increases, product quality decreases, the number of employees is reduced,

and activity-based balance sheet, ending with the loss, sometimes leading to bankruptcy and closures.

In all three cases, the efficiency or inefficiency is the ability to organize and lead the company as Manager of the company.

Without highlight entirely internal consequences on workers, one a mention and a highlight: in all three variations can occur from staff layoffs, workers 'and in the case c) general availability may become unemployed workers becoming.

C. At the level of State administration, although there may be three States to be compared to similar cases in points A and B, however, the same State, got in early with different drivers, highlights the same issues. It is true that State level greatly complicates things, because you may experience phenomena generated by natural factors—weather: very favorable year for agriculture, favorable and unfavorable year, with the added potential evolution different from year to year, industrial activities, namely the economic-financial, which, although it does not belong to the Organization and leadership capacity of the national-State Manager However, in cases in favor of it and it assigns and vice versa.

It is Important to note that, at the level of the family, good or bad results generated by the work of organizing and driving affect directly and in the same direction on family members; good or bad results at the level of companies, although differentiated on the evolution of society evolves, however there are ways that workers should not bear the consequences of evolution, to underline that the Manager supports consequences in direct proportion to the results obtained. At the administrative level, things are changing radically, respectively, regardless of the evolution of the national economy, the State administration remains relatively the same, rarely changes on here or over one Minister, the political class in power makes the "tank" for the duration was chosen . . .

This situation generates a process of evolution of differentiated dialectic labor organizing and leadership. The leaders of the political class in power, and promote the

He could not be valued according to their own specific indicators, which characterize the quantity and quality of their work, do not make the necessary efforts to evolve dialectics dialectic evolution in direct proportion to intellectual human labor.

Dialectic differentiation of labor at the three levels has and that the particularity of the "labor" objects. If the first two, the family and company, the subject of labor is physical, in the political subject classes work is "the man". Hence, the conclusions formulated in the books social justice and Democracy-the future of humanity and the dialectic of human society, in the form of theses.

In order to ensure the political dialectic class leaders in direct proportion to the dialectic of human intellectual labor, it is necessary that the appreciation of the work they are extensive and make rational, intensive, live human capital, thereby ensuring and process of the abolition of existing social injustices as a chain history measured in thousands of years.

This indicator will highlight and direct contribution to political personalities of those who are in power over the economy himself on the evolution of the standard of living of the whole people.

The way of looking at the work from the point of view

1. physical labor;
2. intellectual, and
3. organization and leadership.

Give the Labor opposition sentiment and perception engine of dialectic and the labor of the spring. This way of looking at work does not exclude the way of looking at work by k. Marx, on the contrary, it builds on this, stating that the interpretation of the various sides express of work evolving towards approximation of absolute truth, and this development to be seen through the dialectical evolution of human intellectual labor. Thus, if the work was concerned, k. Marx in physically and intellectually in opposition to the socio-economic slave, feudal and capitalist orders, in the Socialist economic order, order that him see in a future history, the opposition would disappear. Historical reality shows that this opposition between the physical work and intellectual work existed and exists where there is socialism. For this unconfirmed should not be accused Marx, but it should be noted that the laws of dialectic thinking things, phenomena and human intellectual force helps to approach more and more of knowing absolute truth. Which is why I worded the sentence in the book democracy and social justice—the future of humanity, that: "the physical work and intellectual labor of man can be found in an organic and influence each other, generating process of dialectic at work whose source and engine is the dialectic of intellectual force".

Taking the analysis method of looking at work by Marx in the workplace also need to be supra-work, we will highlight several features. Such work required is a part of the work done by the employee in the manufacturing process that creates the product necessary for maintenance of his and his family, and historical supra-work appeared on a given step of social production and to a certain level of labor productivity, when each producer is able to produce more goods than it needs to maintain his and his family the rest is appropriated by others. . . That in capitalism work necessary to create the equivalent of the value and price of the worker's employment that you receive in the form of salary, while the rest of the value created by silhouettes, supra-work is on the free, capitalist form of profit. I repeat this way to interpret the work by Marx is due to the level where it has come to be perceived by human intellectual force. In the book democracy and social justice—the future of humanity, is formulated the thesis according to which "the work of organizing and driving is the most important side of labor" and that this side of the work cannot be confused either with the physical work, nor by intellectual work, it is that which provides the main live human capital in a latent state, potential, prerequisite for the creation of economic goods in an active status function, hence the conclusion that the capitalist who organizes and manages the production process, either directly or through its officers, that is all the work of organization and leadership, practice the most important side of work, so he does-endorses free and supra-work workers. As regards plus-product, created in the production process,

If we look at how evolving economic goods on account of the different sides of the work (figs. 1-8), it is very difficult and even impossible to find out how much of the work necessary to get over the plus-products of workers, in a cycle of production, belongs to them or not somehow workers working in an undertaking they espouse a capitalist part of goods obtained in the form of salary over the level of work required. The secret lies in the evolution and the quality of intellectual work jumps and transformed into technological processes automated and mechanized, robotic, or sometimes, this process is the consequence of capacity for work cap.

CHAPTER XI

ORGANIC UNITY BETWEEN THE DIALECTIC OF HUMAN LABOUR AND DIALECTIC

The man, once stripped from among animals, evolving dialectics from the stage of "primitive man" to stage "man always developed, always perfected, always civilized, modernized and from among the mass which have emerged and are always academics".

The work is hence who created man, detached him from among animals (f. Engels). The work is hence dialectic which generates the dialectics of man from the stage of "primitive man" from that in which it is located now at the beginning of the Millennium III (democracy and social justice—the future of humanity).

The man has a definition. According to the dictionary, "man is a social being which is characterized by the ability of forged tools and to transform with the help of their surrounding reality through thinking and articulated through language" (small Encyclopedic Dictionary, 2nd Edition, revised and reissued, Editura Ştiinţifică şi Enciclopedică, Bucharest, 1978). This characterization has man, to define the place of man in the world here, and the rationale behind his role in the world of Terra, in his book democracy and social justice—the future of humanity, man is characterized as "a biological being, in possession of four social forces, physical force located in the intellectual force behind the muscular system, located in the central nervous system, brain, muscle force of good and evil located in the central nervous system, brain, forces built up in the form of dualism of good and evil ".

Physical and intellectual strength force of man is like a "living" human capital, the generator of all forms of capital known. Force of good and evil force existing in the form of dualism of good and evil acts, throughout the life of a man, prompting him to do when good things, bad things, function ratio (R) of creation between the share of the good forces (G.F.) and share of evil forces (E.F.), report (R) that can be of the form:

$$R = FG/EF = 1; >1; <1.$$

The man is a being biologic-social dominated by a number of objective and subjective laws, laws acting human forces conjugated.

The man is "living cell" of human society. Forces and its laws are those that generate productive forces of socio-economic orders that retrieve the mankind at a time and orders the socio-economic laws that passed that humanity, in which humanity is found at a time.

The man, in his history, dialectics has evolved and will continue to evolve its dialectic, dialectic being generated by his intellectual dialectic of force, this force is characterized in that it builds continuously potential ∞, hence the conclusion that the man will continue to evolve dialectics. The dialectic of human is achieved through the work, whose source and engine is the dialectic of human intellectual force, the engine being put to work and remained in service for work organization and leadership.

The work of organizing and leading political personalities at the level of those artifact of which is man, their work has reached that level of development as the man to become the posture in which is found by doing what is in the position to do what they should do, in relation to his fellows, and with the surrounding world.

Delaying political man to become dialectical, from what is in what should be, was and is determined by the laws of man and human forces in the dualism of good and evil, and there is a danger, God forbid, that this situation be eternal, or at least very lengthy, maybe even thousands or millions of years.

These considerations are based on what happened in the last period of the Millennium II and the beginning of the Millennium III and constantly progress. The and more specifically, if we take the analysis as human intellectual force evolved during its history, starting with the jump of the primitive man's "dialectics" of hewn stone confectionary tools, and then of bronze, iron and so on, when man evolves dialectics dialectic process, generated by the work which rises and the engine movement and intellectual force "auto moving "gradually, gradually discovers the power of water, wind, heat, electricity, Atomic, build tools work increasingly more modern and more sophisticated. Using the energies found in historical times, get up there that detach from the force of attraction of the earth revolves around the Earth, put his foot on the Moon . . . and yet intellectual force of man has not achieved that level of development in order to assist the man may not be "prisoner", and its laws to be in position to do what they to do what they should do in relation to his fellows, and in relation to the environment.

Dialectic of man from "primitive man" to stage "man always developed, always perfected, always modernized, from among the mass which have emerged and are always people scholars" is found at the threshold of a new leap of becoming the dialectic what was and what it is, in what should be it, the man in this world on Terra.

His intellectual force has reached that level of development, however, in order to assist the humans to find the means necessary for the dialectical developments, the role and the point man in this world to become what it should be.

This means should be sought, in the dialectic of labor, labor in the dialectic of organization and leadership at the State level, at the level of those personalities whose labor is "man" and human society as a whole.

To make the work of the Organization and management of my invested by those to do so, the object of labor "man" and human society as a whole, to ensure the evolution of the dialectic of human posture to no longer be what it was, in the posture of not being what it is, as being what it should be perceived as a "revolutionary" and must be started with the auto-knowing "man", self-knowledge that starts with yourself, which answer the question "What are you? What is it? What are we? What are you? What are they?"

If the man will do this step to move closer to knowing the truth about the nature and its nature, will come to the conclusion that "man is a being biologic-social, in possession of four forces (physical strength, intellectual force, the force of good and evil force) and that is dominated by a number of objective and subjective laws acting shared with the forces of man".

Once the man auto-perceived, why is he in this world, the question arises: can he be issued from this "year prison sentence because" the "Cobweb" formed by the human forces and from the laws of good and evil, represented as a dualism of good and evil. From my point of view one cannot on their own power, he must build a "protective shield" to protect themselves to do what he has done in its history, to defend him to do what they do, to help him do the right thing to do in the world here in its relations with fellows and in its report with the environment, since it is packed with thought.

"The shield of protection" should be "alive and active," composed of national and international intellectual personalities of great prestige, knower and dominated by the law of dialectic thinking, things and phenomena.

Normal and rational would be that this protective shield to be called the "Supreme Forum of the human species 'and be composed of intellectual personalities, in possession of an intellectual force in the form of" intellectual force vector ", capable of magnetizes national and international intellectual force. The primary object and fundamental to the protection of the human face of the evil forces of the central nervous system, forces acting shared human laws and helping man to become the "only man, man to man", a process which requires that the ratio (R) of the share the forces of good (G.F.) and share of evil forces (E.F.) of the form:

$$R = FG/EF = >1$$

And from stage to stage $R_n > R_{n-1} > R_{n-2} > \ldots > R_1 > R > 1$, were $R_n \to \infty$, and E.F. $\to \emptyset$

(see the book democracy and social justice—the future of humanity)

This transformation process continues between G.F. and E.F. in favor of E.F. will result in almost nearly, the evolution of the human dialectic, so he will be in position to be:

When "man versus man killer";
When humans duffer to man ";
When "man Fox devious manipulation and likes to the man"

As being only "man to man", this will mark the abolition of social injustice and process-related history of human society and then kept as a historical chain measured in thousands of years.

The Supreme Forum of the human species must be very sensitive to the way of looking at work by k. Marx and to use this way of looking at and perceive the work as a stage reached by the intellectual force of man; to be very sensitive to look at the work as it is seen in the book democracy and social justice—the future of humanity, in:

- physical work
- intellectual work
- work organization and leadership.

To be very sensitive to the way of looking at work as an organic phenomenon, part of the dialectic of things, phenomena and the dialectic thinking, intellectual labor, "the source engine" dialectic and the labor. At the same time to be very sensitive to the role and importance of work organization and management, ensuring the process of improving the ratio of physical work and intellectual work, improve the ratio of production factor, a factor of production work and active and productive factor, a factor of production nature and passive, and any inputs, and to find the necessary strategy and tactics of dialectic work without barriers and without brakes, generator of dialectic human and human society.

The Supreme Forum of the human species must be sensitive to the organic link between dialectic and the labor and human dialectic, which is particularly important to perceive organic unity between labor and the man in a moving and auto moving dialectic.

CHAPTER XII
THE ORGANIC UNITY OF DIALECTICS THE DIALECTIC OF HUMAN SOCIETY AND HUMAN

The work he has created man. The Dialectic labor generated the process of dialectic human and through him to human society. Labor is the source of the dialectic in the dialectic of human intellectual labor.

Human dialectic progressing don't evolve generalized, which hampers the dialectic of human society as a whole. Also, the human dialectic is not appropriate to keep the pace of dialectic human intellectual labor.

Generalized human dialectic braking is determined by the laws and human forces. Thus, the political leadership vested in the man to lead the country's Affairs has managed to find tactics and strategies that concentrate the physical and intellectual strength force of man in a "vector force whose "potential" to be the sum (Σ) of the physical forces + intellectual forces of each man working on his own apt-i the country. People live, "cells" of human society, in addition to not-and can capitalize fully and rationally "capital live" available, more practical and work which are malevolent to humans and human society. Their range is, unfortunately, very diversified, which is why I regard the work and the

1. Productive
2. Unproductive
3. Destructive.

This way of looking at work has a particular importance that highlights, in addition, if more was needed, why is the man when not auto-knowing, or even if him auto-knowing is dominated by human laws of dualism of good and evil. In those moments when the ratio (R) of the weighting of the forces of good (**G.F**) and share of evil forces (**E.F.**) is of the form:

$$R= FG/EF = <1 \text{ respectively } R= FG/EF = >1$$

He can do much harm to its neighbor and human society as a whole.

A massive man dialectic is subject to the possibility of making conditions bringing out the "capital live" available to everyone, however, this work belongs to the environmental factor in the political personalities, entrusted with the power of decision and approved the mandate established by citizens of their country.

Experience living history—demonstrated—regarded that although parties follow each other at the head of the country, even in a democracy, however, the work of organizing and leading the political class, whose object is "man's work" and human society as a whole, not up to expectations, so that things perpetuates the injustices of the Sochi-flow as a "permanent drainage water "the form of a "historic" chain measured in thousands of years. This phenomenon is common to all countries of globe stating that he is differentiated from country to country, and to underline that this phenomenon in a country some further improves on behalf of other countries.

Generalized dialectic of man must be looked at through the prism of the factor labor. Therefore, if the work was that it had stripped the man from the animals, if the work has been viewed dialectics and is therefore gave rise to the dialectical process of man, then "non—work" it pushes the man to how to be animals; it approaches the environment from which it was spun off through work. However, this phenomenon exists and it perpetuates and can become, God forbid, an eternal phenomenon, putting in danger the dialectic of generalized all "living cells of human society."

At this phenomenon is particularly serious is added another phenomenon, and worst, the provision of work producing techniques and technologies dedicated to the destruction of accumulated work and materialized in the means of production and different economic and spiritual goods and even to the destruction of "living" cell of the society of human and physical mutilation of others.

Generalized dialectic of man requires a radical change in the way of being human political leader, whose object is "man's work" and human society as a whole.

To raise as much as the intellectual force of man, on these considerations, it is useful to ponder the phenomena that took place at the end of the Millennium II and the beginning of the Millennium III in the former Republic of Yugoslavia, the Middle East, in Afghanistan and in Iraq—destruction of dozens of economic goods, hundreds and maybe thousands of billions of dollars, the death or mutilation of thousands, tens of thousands of "living cells" of the human species and when you think that this phenomenon occurred after the second world war and after the dissolution of the Warsaw Pact military bloc . . .

Mankind fails to learn what has to be done to ensure that this way of being human to not repeat it. Moreover, some political figures speak of "Star Wars", others: "I and

I pride myself in my rocket and with it". The trend of mass destruction potential is constantly growing and when you think that this process takes place in circumstances when human intellectual force develops dialectical and trend to ∞.

I demonstrated scientifically in the book democracy and social justice—the future of humanity that the secret of this kind of human being is determined by the laws of political man and forces of the dualism of good and evil and that he, the man politically, cannot make up its main dialectal of posture of being what it is, as being what it should be compared with the objective of "the man" by his own forces, it has helped himself by his work, "the man".

"Help me that I can help" would sound the call to the object of man's political work, "the man".

My belief is that the laws of man, the human forces conjugated, should not be perceived as fatalities, but must be understood in the light of dialectic human intellectual labor, which, to a certain level of development, can generate process the rule of law and human forces and managing them in a direction that is beneficial to the human dialectic generalized.

Books on social justice and Democracy-the future of humanity and the dialectic of human society, through theses formulated by the author, is a platform-program change the man in what is supposed to be. Platform-program whose applicability is universally valid, at the level of municipality-City-County-region—country, regardless of the disposition of social-economic development in that country, and is found in the end, by expanding into more countries, generalizes worldwide—across the Earth. So, the platform-designed broad program of dialectic human is also a fundamental theme of scientific research on the applicability of all the steps of the administrative territorial unit of a country, the level of municipality at the country level and vice versa, generally in the singular, which is why those responsible for the subject at each level, should be the man political leader and representative of religious man, whose labor party is "the man".

Basic research, on ways and means of dialectic broad human starts from the scientific way of perceiving the work by k. Marx, from the scientific way of perceiving the work in the book democracy and social justice—the future of humanity, and as a phenomenon and process in a dialectical evolution, whose spring is the force of human intellectual, dialectical, who currently plays for the engine that provide movement and auto movement from lower to higher from what it is at one point to something higher is the work of organization and leadership.

Work organization and leadership at the level of State administration, in order to pass the threshold to something superior, must rest on the way of looking at work by k. Marx, in concrete work, and creative, abstract work. Making the call and the dialectic of reason to begin to decipher and what use is being wasted values generated by the physical and intellectual work carried out in research institutes and design profiled on finding techniques and technologies that will lead to the modernization of weapons of mass destruction and transported to certain preconceived distances; to decipher what usage value creates physical work and intellectual organization and leadership that is practiced in many factories and plants producing weapons of mass destruction, in technical and technological means, to ensure that weapons manufactured to reach its "target". The target value and utilizing weapons manufactured, whose content is to destroy the accumulated work and "live" cells of the human species, possessors of capital live. This pleasure of some is downright Satanic and is rooted in the way of being human, of those historical periods when the man was "man" killer to continue due to pollution and psychological thinking.

These people should be perceived through the prism of human laws and human forces in the dualism of good and evil, or they work conjugate and are common to all "living cells of the human species must be carried out, the fight against the evil forces of the central nervous system of the human brain, in order to help the man as the ratio (R) of the weighting of the forces of good (G.F.) and share of evil forces (E.F.) should only be of the form:

$$R= FG/EF = >1$$

And which will promote $R_n > R_{n-1} > R_{n-2} > \ldots > R_1 > R > 1$, were $R_n \rightarrow \infty$, and respectively E.F. $\rightarrow \varnothing$

However, this implies the struggle to change human nature and nature, a continuous process for that child, when born, possess the four forces in the form of shoots and buds, so has the force of good and evil forces buds. From here, and the need for informed, to help the man, still a child, to evolve and dialectic in terms of the ratio (R) between the forces of good weight (F.G) and share of evil forces (E.F.), so that the ratio (R) to be of the form

$$R= FG/EF = >1$$

Ways and means of defense was extensively featured in the book democracy and social justice—the future of humanity.

Being a man who lived and worked for over 30 years in a country where they were building socialism and pursue an ideology which regard and helping man "by critical and auto-critical", I found that this aid gradually becomes ineffective, the hierarchical scale, i.e. criticism and self-criticism are linked only from top to bottom, right and bottom-up. If kept, would have not arisen the cult of personality that has generated and dictatorship with all its negative consequences.

To make myself understood from "simple man" man, I have to scholar given several concrete examples:

1) Karl Marx and Friedrich Engels, philosophers, economists and politicians, were sensitive to the existence of some great social wrongs in their lifetimes and connoisseurs of the law of dialectic thinking things, phenomena, and have stated the thesis that the disposition of social-economic capitalist is limited in terms of history and that it will follow a different order straight, which they called a "Socialist" in the first phase Communist, in a higher phase. These two philosophers, economists and politicians have sought out and cause social injustices of the capitalist socio-economic order, perceived by them through capitalist private property and of the relationship between capitalist class and the broad masses of people the work, stating, on this basis, the fundamental contradiction of capitalism, the contradiction of social character of private capitalist production and the form of living results in production and so on.

2) V.I.Lenin, continuation of the work of Marx and Engels, organized and headed the socialist revolution in Russia and began the process of building socialism.

3) After the death of Lenin (on 21 January 1924), Stalin, as general Secretary of the C.C. al P.C.U.S., continued to lead the Soviet Union in the work of building socio-economic system of socialism.

4) After the Second World War, socialism was expanded, becoming a social-economic order worldwide have in parallel with that capitalist.

After Stalin's death was an imbalance in the Commandant general Secretary of P.C.U.S., and, somewhat, in normality with the Commandant general Secretary of P.C.U.S. 's N.S. Hrusciov, underlining that he was the one who made the great historical and legal system flaw in social-economic Socialist criticism of the cult of personality and highlighting tragedies caused by Stalin's cult of personality. This was a historic step to raise the intellectual force of mankind that the disposition of social-economic development of socialism, designed by k. Marx and f. Engels as something superior ideal and capitalism in all respects, the hypothesis of V.I.Lenin, handed over has not been confirmed in the process of building socialism and communism in the Soviet Union and for other countries which have become Socialist After the second world war.

After N.S. Hrusciov, Secretary General of the P.C.U.S. was taken over by Brezhnev, during which, in the global social phenomena took place (the events in Hungary and Czechoslovakia). Coming to the forefront P.C.U.S. Gorbachev gave many hopes for the improvement of relations with the Communists, in an order social economic socialist-communist. What followed is unknown: the collapse of the Socialist legal system, both at world level and in the USSR the purpose pursued by me is not to demonstrate in detail what was positive and the negative was in theory and practice of socialism, but to highlight that the dialectic of human society depend on the human dialectic as nature and temperament, and the dialectic of human intellectual force depends on the dialectics of man.

I have reviewed these historic personalities only to me that the dialectic of human auto—convince and human society is full of obstacles and various brakes and that improvement of the road of dialectic human and human society must be started with the man auto perception, the living human cell of society. The cell should be charged by its forces and laws, the cell should be seen as nature and temperament.

Make clear that I, being conquered by the law of dialectic thinking, things and phenomena and that my credo is not opposed to capitalism, socialism or capitalism socialism, but I wish to auto—convince the dialectic socio-economic orders, of the sources and movement engines and auto movement from what is the disposition of social-economic development at a time, to something higher. In doing so give a great esteem the ideas of Marx and Engels, in connection with the extension law and dialectic society, stating that the intellectual force behind the magnifying of the man of those historic times urged him to believe in some kind of laws orders the socio-economic, but sensitive to those of "the living cell" of society which generates the general laws of General (human society).

This account of mine is confirmed by the manner in which it functioned and the global social, organic tied to how to be "the living cell" entrusted to lead the Soviet Union and socialist countries.

The scale of socio-economic system of socialism in Romania, the same phenomenon is that it highlights, laws of socialism have been generated by the "laws" of the living cell and special concrete that was formed to lead the country during that period.

Historical phenomena occur at the end of the Millennium II and the beginning of the Millennium III, in which a number of former socialist countries are in a process of transition from socialism to capitalism, which never happened in the feudal era or in the capitalist, hence the natural question: "why?"

Why the events of 1989 in Romania are characterized by some as revolutionary process, the people's revolution, others . . . ?

I am concerned about the concrete conditions in Romania and those of the former republics of the USSR the dialectic movement and their auto movement? Lest human laws and human forces, the dualism of good and evil, and works such as dimensions, that it approves and ascending in a dialectic of society, be it and very slow, since through this process the historic level of life decreases continually, and the national economy collapsed? Their ignorance of the Revolutionary Committee "of Romania" and the program Committee and revolutionary platform that, suppose acted in 1989, I cannot allow me to do and I another point of view than to argue again that the laws of man and human forces in the dualism of good and evil are those that have acted such that the transition period of Romania of those 300 environment generated by billionaires, a capitalism which is false, after Petre Roman, a capitalism, christening party, after Ion Iliescu.

Comment lines can continue indefinitely and although may result in the approximation to the truth, however one thing to be considered, in terms of Romania, during the transition period, the economy has come a "moving from what was something less than", that the advent of billionaires and enriching the eighty leaders political class held in conditions of degrading radical in the level of the life of a substantial segment of the human species.

This phenomenon I explain it to me by the laws of man and human forces in the dualism of good and evil.

If you consider what role the world-wide history marked the Gorbachev's political personality towards the global disposition towards socialist and social-economic socialist-communist U.S.S.R., seeing and experiencing the consequences of historical and making a parallel to what happened in the world capitalist system, we can conclude, without fear of err, that the laws of man and human forces in the dualism of good and evil works differed from human to human and personal example that does not serve to improvement ratio (R) of the weighting of the forces of good (F.G) and share of evil forces (E.F.).

The ratio (R) of the weighting of the forces of good (F.G) and share of evil forces (E.F.) does not change through personal example of political personalities, regardless of the scale on which they are located. The reason being that the millions of logic, "living cells", "billions" of living cells-human work individually under the pressure of human laws, and these acts conjugated with the forces of good and evil in the dualism of good and evil in the central nervous system of the human brain, independent from those of one or other of the "live" cells of the human species. It is true that the staff can help mild improvement in (R)-between the share of the good forces (F.G) and share of evil forces (E.F.), but this phenomenon can be component and a concert of the adage "do not bring spring swallow."

Auto-knowing its forces and man by his laws, although it is particularly important, it does not mean that from that moment the man, "living cell" of society, they change the role and the sense that it has the world here. For that man to become of what is in what should be in the world of here, have made many and various efforts to generate the human process of change, so that his laws beneficial to work both for him and for the human society as a whole, and human forces to be used rationally, intensively and extensively for the good of each "living cells", which means a road reclaimed, without barriers and without the brakes of the dialectic of man and the man, the dialectic of human society as a whole.

These many and diverse efforts involve WORK. What kind of WORK? The first response would be "WORK in GENERAL." These multiple and diverse efforts involve "CONCRETE and ABSTRACT WORK USEFUL to SOCIETY", so it's not any kind of WORK.

EMPLOYMENT factor, viewed through the prism of the law of dialectic thinking things, phenomena and should constitute a major concern of the entire human species, and the leading role in the WORK as it is, in fact, it belongs to the intelligentsia. If the intellectual force of the human species will perceive the dialectical "phenomenon" and will take into account that the two hypotheses of occurrence in the world of man on Earth, in the world of here, have a common denominator—WORK, then, to a certain level of potential development of her WORK, not only will be charged as a main factor because the man in the row of animals WORK and will be charged in a dialectical process. It has to generate the dialectics of man from the stage of "primitive man" to stage "man always developed, always perfected, always civilized, modernized and from which have emerged and are always people and scholars". Will be charged at the "threshold" of a new DIALECTIC LEAP that will generate the dialectical nature of change and human flesh in what was, what it is, in what must be, against himself, against his fellows and in relation to its environment. It will charge and WORK through the prism of the human that is dialectal to auto-perception and to charge on his fellows, deciphering what is the role and the rationale behind the world of here. Will charge informed WORK, as a phenomenon generated good things for man and society as a whole, but also the bad things for the human species, dividing it into social segments, some of whom live in some kind of heaven, and others in a sort of hell, with the chance of a dialectical leap that will generate dialectical process of the abolition of social injustice. This process will be organized and conducted under the supervision of the intellectual force of human labor so that the dialectic to be channeled towards intellectual perception of dialectic human and human society as a whole.

The starting point in order to organize and lead the human dialectic and human society as a whole will be "human perception as living cell of society", which by his forces and laws give rise to the socio-economic orders laws that passed that humanity, in which humanity is found at any given time and, once this condition being met, starts work on a change of nature and human flesh from what is what needs to be.

The dialectic of human conscious acting is appropriate to the laws of man and using all the means necessary for rational recovery, intensive and extensive, live human capital and human forces in the dualism of good and evil must be mastered and acted on them so that the ratio (R) of (P.F.B.) and (P.F.R.) is always of the form

$$R= FG/EF = >1$$

And from stage to stage $R_n > R_{n-1} > R_{n-2} > \ldots > R_1 > R > 1$, were $R_n \to \infty$.

Transforming dialectical of the man in what is in what must be assumed that a jump in dialectical side of labor, known as work organization and leadership, practiced by those whose object of their work is "the MAN". It requires a process of meditation on the evolution of Division of labor at a different scale of perception. Thus, if the Division of labor in the production of economic goods generated a continuous progress in all respects, this improvement has been favored radical and intellectual human labor dialectic and Division of labor intellectual.

Now, at the beginning of the Millennium III, the natural Division of labor is in a highly developed stage, and that of intellectual work is even more developed, allowing you to resolve the "outer" at first glance. The bottom line is that potential human intellectual force has reached, in my view, that level of potential development which will enable man to use his physical and intellectual forces only worthwhile, useful only for the benefit of each and all members of the human species, which will enable a control and a strategy in which the ratio (R) between F.G and E.F. to be in the form.

$$R= FG/EF = >1$$

Thereby the functioning of the general law enforcement objectives and fundamental human law of accumulation of wealth (wealth), beneficial to the whole human species.

Intellectual potential of human force, in a moving and auto moving dialectic, is found near the threshold of a development that may act upon a change of nature and human flesh to become what it was, of what is, what needs to be.

Potential human intellectual force, dispersing through the Division of labor in all fields of intellectual activity, resulted in the overall progress of the human species, and currently it requires a change of action in the sense that each intellectual, regardless of their field of activity in which they work (mathematics, physics, chemistry, biology, philosophy, economics and so on) must contribute and in the direction of a change of nature and human flesh.

SENTENCE: "Potential human intellectual force, now at the beginning of the Millennium III, is the greatest wealth, riches, treasure of the human species, potentially in a continuous motion and auto movement from that which is at one point to something higher". This treasure-human potential, acquired during the history of human society, is found at such a level of development, from my point of view, that can act and on the change of nature and human flesh. Man, through his auto-knowing as being social-biologic holder of four inner forces (physical, intellectual force, force of good and evil force) and dominated by a number of objective and subjective law, making use of dialectic thinking and the dialectic reasoning, may collect what was throughout its history, why is he currently and what is particularly important, is that the intellectual potential of labor can help to perceive what he must be in the world of here; allows him to perceive what is the role and the POINT MAN in the world here.

To be able to change the nature and human nature, human intellectual labor potential, once perceived, is to be MASTERED, to be organized and led in the knowledge of the facts to change nature and its flesh.

Intellectual potential labor force is found in two areas:

1) Over passive latent gained in various stages and
2) In the active zone of existing latent brain billion people.

Potential intellectual force currently dynamic ascending and periodically leaping dialectical and the process takes place from private to general, so that intellectual force of special (the great chemist, mathematician, physician, biology, the philosopher, Economist, etc.) in an evolving dynamic-ascending, sometimes with jumps dialectical, generates general intellectual dialectic, force that imaginary thinking, ∞.

Experience proves that the lives of people who are currently particularly dynamic-ascending using the accumulated intellectual potential, strength, and in various writings which, when levied in their brains, may give rise to a potential new intellectual force, both quantitatively and qualitatively in a moving and auto moving from the stage reached at one point to something higher. The process occurs thanks to the work performed, and finally particularly ensuring a reward which he uses to meet its needs and primary social-spiritual and of his family.

This work was generalized and evolved in a direction of improvement continues, however, reaching, from my point of view, at a stage where the intellectual force of special you are not using any rational or intensive and extensive. The secret of the case found in dialectic thinking things, phenomena and that in the process and creates motion and auto movement internal contradictions, which periodically relieves partly through the work of the Organization and management at three levels (family, company and State Administration).

Demonstrating the scientific book democracy and social justice—the future of humanity, that man's intellectual force, through the process of writing, speech and accumulate continuously from man to man, from generation to generation, and the idea that we can develop the potential of intellectual labor currently dynamic-ascending and periodically leaping dialectical purporting to infinity (∞), and another conclusion, that the internal contradictions among different sides of labor will become increasingly more pronounced and even more complex.

Improvement of the road on the rational recovery, intensive and extensive live human capital implies that a change in the nature of logic and human flesh from what is in what must be, because this implies and psychological pollution "greening" of thinking. Who can perform this function? In order to fulfill this function, the intellectual force of man must act bidirectional. How I imagine myself this intellectual bidirectional labor?

Every peculiarity, intellectual man carrying an intellectual work, be it philosopher, psychologist, economist, mathematician, physicist, chemist, biologist, etc., wherever they operate—education, research, design, production, etc.—are obliged to charge the man "as a social being equipped with thought and articulated language", the classical definition, but also as a social being, licensed biologic-of the four forces—physical strength, intellectual force, the force of good and evil force. Of these, physical and intellectual strength force of man is to be perceived as a "capital live" latent human, the premise of creating all the phenomena known and necessary capital to meet the needs of the primary spiritual and social-and the force of good and evil force must be perceived as a "dualism of good and evil" in the central nervous system in the human brain. This dualism results in a man to do when good things, when bad things during his life, good or evil being size depending on the ratio (R)

What is between F.G and E.F., report (R) that can be of the form

$$R = FG/EF = 1; >1; <1.$$

Also, that man, being social, biologic-is ruled and dominated by a series of laws, one objective and fundamental-' law of accumulation of wealth (wealth) by any means and at any price ", law no limit, which is doubled, tripled . . . by a series of other laws (law of selfishness, individualism, law appetite, and so on). See the book dialectic of man and the human society.

Each intellectual, regardless of the scope of his activity, knowing the law is the most universally valid, the general law of dialectic thinking, things and phenomena, Hegel formulated and interpreted on the materialist position of Marx, Engels and Lenin, but also collected by himself physically and intellectually evolves, from birth until death, and by his fellows, and especially on man by social forces biologic-and by its laws can act on it and on its fellows to change nature and human nature. Will influence and the forces of good and evil forces in the dualism of good and evil exist in the central nervous system in the human brain, watching as the ratio (R) between the forces of good weight (F.G) and share of evil forces (E.F.) should only be of the form:

$$R= FG/EF = >1$$

This concern of human intellectual must be continuous because the human body's biology is such that from birth is in possession of the stems are physical, intellectual, forces of good and evil, dark forces that move and auto move throughout life. And because maxima and noble adage: "healthy mind in a healthy body" to retrieve the body of a man biologically, have worked with yourself and with your fellows, so sane to retrieve and change the nature and the human flesh.

I stated that all intellectuals need to use their intellectual force "bidirectional", two-dimensional—understanding through this bidirectional start small corrections of the social division of labor. Thus, any specialized intellectual within the social division of labor in a given activity (mathematics, physics, chemistry, biology, philosophy, psychology, history, geography, etc.), you need to practice and a minimum work required a change of nature and human flesh, perceived the man by his forces and laws and then watching it "organic" within the law, things and phenomena of dialectic thinking, Picturing and what to do for that man to be as close to what needs to be.

Mini-vectors intellectual forces of millions of intellectuals, tens of millions, hundreds of millions, used for changing the nature and the human flesh will generate INTELLECTUAL FORCE VECTOR which will ensure the change of nature and human flesh from what was in the way of humanity, of which what is, what needs to be.

Voicing my written these considerations with beating long historical way, because of a change of nature and human flesh to be as smooth and to benefit from the process of change the nature of human flesh and even human generation of "third age", the vector of intellectual labor of the human species must be directed and to help those people whose object of their work is MAN they are the leaders of the political class and religious representatives.

The leaders of the political class should be sensitized for their role in the process and rationale behind the object of their work, the dialectic of man in general, in the process of dialectic human society. They have sensitized that their way of work is out of date and that it requires a radical change, because as they generate many and various brakes, obstacles in the dialectic of human and human society. If you don't believe me, unless you can convince these considerations my, please reflect on how to work the political class in Romania after the popular uprising in 1989 and until now, when I write these lines. I for one, I meet with different people, different levels of training, different domain in the active, different as different as ethnicity, sex, different as religious practiced in their great majority say: "not that we wanted our new by the rebellion in 1989, what happens today in Romania". Please remember what happened in 1989 when in all the cities of the country demonstration shouting slogans, including "Ole, ole, ole, Ceauşescu not anymore!"; What happened in 1996, the Market revolution, where the crowd shouting: "Emile, Emile, we've saved! '; What was come up in 2000, when groups of people celebrated the victory of Iliescu's and P.D.S.R. 's; What happened in 2004, the month of December, when President Traian Basescu won the election with 51,23% and Adrian Năstase it has lost, being voted 48,77% of voters, and the world scan: "Victory in the election of President Traian Basescu has brought Romania into the street!", "Ole, ole, ole, P.S.D.-not anymore!" Let us remind the election slogans of Emil Constantinescu: "faith in God, the monk Basil, how can live on a minimum wage on economy a four-person family" etc. Social life situation worsened during the period 1996-2000.

In Truth, of 17 March 2004, page. 3, shows the graph showing the level of living in Romania in the period 1996-2000.

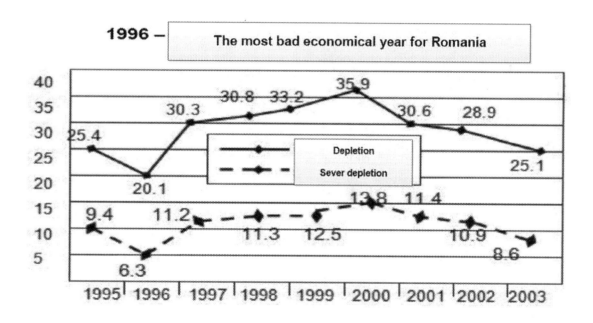

1996 best and 2000 the worst year of Romania Slogans "the 2000 election with people and with them"—it has followed a statistical recovery of the economy and the reality of life, top 300 billionaires and maintaining poverty at the level of many millions of people, and as a result of winning the elections by Traian Basescu's Adrian Năstase is assigned a black ball by Evenimentul Zilei, December 14, 2004, page. 2: "for four years, the leader of the PSD was charged that he had lied to the public opinion, favored corruption, it was mixed and influenced the decision of the courts, has curtailed press freedom," gyrate "open auctions which have proved good for its customers business policies, held in the arms of local barons are, tried to bribe people with large or rolls. For however, Adrian Năstase deserves a black ball ".

Traian Basescu in a new formula repeated what made Emil Constantinescu: "If you know Mr. Ion Iliescu, how can live on a minimum wage on economy a family made up of four people". Traian Basescu says, among other things, that "are retirees who have a pension of less than the monthly invoice to heat . . .", accusing this way how to be the politicians in power from 2000-2004 period, during which political leaders have used the electoral slogan: "close to the people and together with them . . ."

Traian Basescu, on his first crowd after winning the elections, the press, and has presented and the priority of priorities: "I will introduce in strategy the defense of the country the problem of corruption . . ."

Reviewing, very synthetic, names of political leaders and their sloganeer, and how things have evolved after winning the election, so the power, I did not for anything other than for what they have in common: human laws acting shared with those of the man in the dualism of good and evil, existing in each of the central nervous system of the living cell "of society human-man. It also may be perceived that the political leader is making it not only by himself, but also by those who are helping to do what it does—the Government, MPs, councilors and others, and they are "living cells" dominated by human laws acting shared with dualism forces of good and evil forces. Moreover, groups, whether they are closer or more distant from the political leaders, also manifests in the Dominion of the same elements, human forces in the dualism of good and evil and human laws.

Hence the conclusion, without fear of err, that human society course change from what is she at some point, to something higher, boosted by a certain alternation to the leadership of certain political leaders, however, the problem of background does not change in the interest of eighty citizens than improving on here and the evolution of life color course, a process stimulated, and the ability of leaders and art that you have to organize and lead.

Any critical position does not help us at nothing, sometimes destructive, by point of view morally, of some against others who succeed to power.

Let us remember the euphoria of those who gathered in the square of the revolution, in 1996, when Emil Constantinescu won the election, where the crowd shouts of whom and why, "Emile, Emile, you saved us! . . ." It is known that followed; menses came in 2000, when Emil Constantinescu he candidate, because he was convinced of what will happen, and the party that propelled him to Presidency of the country has lost the support of the masses (P.N. Ț. C.D.). Of note is the fact that Mr. Emil Constantinescu made "tank" and many of his other close relatives.

The year 2000 appeared to be turning year, Mr. Iliescu, who won the election for the post of President of Romania, stated: "the alternation is a means to encourage the Romanian society to hope that better days will come to the level of life . . ." "Close to the people and together with them . . .", it was the electoral slogan. What followed is unknown . . . An increase, at least in economic terms, especially in 2004, but the level of life remained to a large segment of the citizens under decency required. Retired men's mortal starvation, from city, maintenance bills, higher heat and light as a pension to a large number of them. Instead, top billionaires grew the political class and increased wealth, etc.

The surprise policy appears in 2004, the presidency country is won by Traian Basescu. Repeat the euphoria of 1996, the crowd gathered in the streets of towns exiles call his name Basescu. At the first sitting of the CSAT, Basescu concluded the meeting with a flurry of drawings to the "old Europe": "Romania no longer supports labeling corrupted country" . . ."Rejecting the crusty idea that Romania is a country corrupt, just two months after the election campaign in which the candidate Basescu attacking former power exactly the same argument: under the Iliescu-Nastase, Romania became the absolute champion in the field, in Europe. Then, all international organizations reports that general corruption in Romania present were high. Now, they no longer matter. Who speaks of corruption extended invents. Unwittingly, Basescu has done a service to the PSD. What will people say? Well, if the Impaler-Basescu argues that Europe has no reason to believe a corrupt country, means that Nastase and Iliescu were accused unjustly that have powered conservation and multiplication of that scourge in Romania. However, no further from the day before yesterday ", U.S. Department of State the report of 2004, established the former cohabitation of power and corruption." (The comment on Europe in the newspaper Evenimentul Zilei, March 2, 2005, page 1).

Conclusion: democracy and human rights, through the process of presidential and parliamentary elections are a big step towards always better, but the leap of the human society dialectics is conditioned jump of human nature as a dialectic and yarn, and man remains a too long period of time the prisoner from the forces of good and evil dualism of good and evil acting shared human laws. There is a danger that this situation be eternal, while maintaining social injustices in the world of hell on Earth, maintaining that survives a considerable segment of the human species.

There are, however, the prospect that, with the human perception through his laws and his forces as kind and wires and acting on them informed as to begin the process of changing the nature and the human flesh. One step would be to the human species to practice a democracy which edged and even exclude the possibility of repeating phenomena in different countries, on the occasion of the presidential elections and parliamentary votes of "stealing" or to influence the voters whom to vote. For example, would be positive if the Constitution should provide for a new conception of electing the President of the country, and that instead of choosing a President to select a group of Vice-Presidents, three, five, seven, based on the mandate established by the territorial dimension of the country and of course the number of parties and of the population. And the President to be elected either Vice Presidents or by order of the percentage of votes cast or for the Office of President of the country to be determined annually for each Vice President, in order of votes received on the occasion of the election. This procedure would preclude any suspicion of fraud to the elections and would end up with those actions, as occurred in Romania during the elections in November 2004, not to mention what happened in Ukraine and other countries.

This principle of Vice-Presidents to insist at Chairwoman would create the premise that man President to be more: "man, man to man" and as infrequently or not at all, "man Fox devious manipulation and likes to the man," etc.

CHAPTER XIII

DIALECTIC DIFFERENTIATED STRENUOUS WORK.

RULING

Regarded the work as it is practiced it day by day, and the perceived phenomenon, generally as a peculiarity of the dialectic, but law and taken in isolation, each side of the labor (labor, intellectual and physical work, work organization and leadership) we find that they are evolving dialectal differences. Thus, potential physical labor of man should be seen as a summary of the physical forces of man in his lifetime. As I demonstrated in the book democracy and social justice—the future of humanity, has a moving from ø (zero) to the maximum (50-75 kg, rarely 100 kg force), and then, after a period of time (20-25 years) begins the process of lowering levels of physical labor of man, reaching ø when man passes in the world here in the world by then. Imaginary thinking, human physical strength remains the same all the time, and potential physical force is the sum of the human species physical forces of members of the society to which you want (the national State, continent, planet Earth). Intellectual force of humans, though, as I demonstrated scientifically in the book democracy and social justice—the future of humanity, is characterized by the fact that differs radically from man to man and that evolves dynamic-ascending, throughout the life of a man, sometimes with jumps and dialectical, and through the process of speaking and writing accumulate, potentially, from human to human from generation to generation, what imaginary thinking intellectual force of human potential, as tends to infinity (∞).

The dialectic of human intellectual force is constituted as a spring, with permanent drainage, the dialectic of work in general. So that through the dialectic of human intellectual labor, takes place and the dialectic of labor (for efficiency).

In the labor movement and auto movement are many and various contradictions between the laws of the physical, intellectual, organizational and managerial, contradictions which relieves according to labor organizing and dialectic at three levels—family, company and State administration.

Work organization and management, regardless of the level at which it occurs, is not likely to be confused with any physical work, nor by intellectual work. Work organization and management is that part of labor, which is designed and intended to harness the potential of physical and intellectual labor force set up as a live human capital ", existing as a prerequisite for the creation of the necessary economic and social needs of the primary human-spiritual, generating the capital became" live "from dormant in active and functional. The efficiency of transformation of live human capital (physical and intellectual energy) of the dormant, prerequisite for the creation of economic goods, able active and functional, depends on the dialectic of Labor Organization and leadership of those who practice at three levels: the family company and the State administration, the dialectic which in turn depends on organization and direction of the Manager.

In the work of the Organization and management at three levels, some special features on the performance of live processing of capital available to the grouped in the premise of the creation of economic goods, existing latent form, whether actively functioning. Thus, at the family level, a good manager continuously diversifies activity, seeking to tap the capital live members of the family, through the Division of labor: agriculture, animal husbandry, poultry, often through area-and qualification of members of the family to be able to execute various other works outside of its own activities. The company, the manager shall primarily and fundamentally "obtaining of profit", which is why he, according to the art that you have to organize and lead the recovery follows the live of employees of the company capital commercial. However, as I pointed out several times, due to the intellectual force of dialectic, which accumulates and turns on the techniques and technologies constantly upgraded, generating reliable solutions for increasing production, and quality, reduce production costs and ultimately, increase profits, which may take place even by reducing capital live, so the layoffs capital live the ready availability of a number of staff.

At the level of State administration, things from was complicating several points of view. Living capital available to that country is in a continuous internal contradiction, which is generated on the one hand the consequences of the release of live at the capital the first two forms of organization and management, on the other hand due to the economic and social indicators of efficiency to be achieved. At the level of State administration, the indicators must be perceived by a shape object of labor and radical content particularly towards those which characterize indicators track the level of company, meaning that the subject of work is man and human society as a whole. Or, work organization and dialectic at the level of State Administration has other values and is practiced by the leaders of the political class who hold power in the State, power gained through periodic general elections. Therefore, the evolution of society depends on the political leaders of my invested to lead the country's Affairs which are not elected or appointed on the principles of "the art of organizing and leadership", but to the sloganeer election the radical masses, influencing voters.

In this way of looking at and perceive the work organization and leadership, she plays dialectic, but provides the PARTIAL recovery of physical labor and intellectual labor at all three levels of organization and management: family, company and State administration.

Historical human experience and highlights that particularity that those people who engage in management the work organization evolve dialectical with some gap in relation with dialectical intellectual force of man. Those people who are engage in organization and management works having the subject of work the "man" are decelerate, his dialectic is broken by human laws and human forces in the dualism of good and evil. These people are political leaders and representatives of religious worship. The secret lies in the possibility of a delay in the political and religious personalities to ensure the operation of the law and fundamental human targets, "the law of accumulation of wealth (wealth) at any cost and by any means, without making efforts to auto-exceed.

The consequences of this mod to work also has an impact of a substantial segment of the human species, over thousands of years to survive in an environment of social injustice, in a sort of hell in the world here, spurred by religious representatives to wait "their happiness in the Eden".

These considerations my are confirmed by what is happening now in the vast majority of the countries of the world and in the State of the world at the end of the Millennium II and III Millennium.

A few concrete examples of Romania today are edifying in the sense that the leaders of the political class compete among themselves in the slogan to convince voters that a political leader is superior to the other.

Without making a political and electoral history of Romania, in general, it is worth reflecting on that period's Ion Luca Caragiale, Romanian classical writer, playwright and journalist, who, in the comedy a letter lost, corrupted, unmasks political immorality and human uncultured, unmasks hand and glove political parties interested in looting and deceive the masses of ordinary people. This characterization made by I. I. Caragiale "refers to the Romanian political class 120 years ago.

Characterizing the political leaders of the 1989 and until now, when I write these lines? In Romania, all political parties, almost without exception, were and are driven by politicians with its preparation, the vast majority of the leaders of which are envied in terms of their level of general culture and in terms of human intellectual

These people, political leaders, however, does not differ from those of i. I. Caragiale in terms of tactics and strategy applied to influence the broad masses of the population, to elect, to empower with the power of decision in The State.

It was changed to political leaders, who are, as I pointed out above, intellectual personalities, people of culture? Slogans underestimate the electoral use religion as a means to influence the masses as to elect. As, for example, Emil Constantinescu, Professor, and in 1996, in order to influence the masses to choose him and not on the Ion Iliescu, and using a "chord" very sensitive to the Romanian honest and religious, asking questions, time peak, contra part, Ion Iliescu, if you believe in God and give him the monk Basil. Or otherwise of questions: If you know how lives a family of four people (husband, wife and two children) of a minimum wage on economy and so on.

What ensued after winning the elections by Emil Constantinescu? Living standards have worsened even more, due to reforms, but political class continued to be carried out under the basic law and of human: "the law of accumulation of wealth at any cost and by any means".

But let us remind electoral slogans and underwritten by Ion Iliescu and others who have gained power in 2000: "alongside the people and with them". As with people and how together they were in 2000-2004 is well known, and now, at the end of their mandate, to make new efforts to make the electoral slogan that will help to maintain power, and other practical opposition to win the election.

Here's how to characterize the publicist Cristian Tudor Popescu election campaign of 2004:

Until yesterday, I was thinking more in the elections of 1990 as the political-electoral pre-history of Romania. Barks since then, the nerve exits the blare demenței, frustrations as a doctrine, propped by the street seemed to me forever dusty magnetic tape memory and yellowed newspapers on the shelf. He was hallucinating to hear and to see their gloomy echoes today in Romania in 2004, country in NATO and the EU threshold. Large newspapers and claimed serious and have first page covered with propagandistic Photomontages with explosions and words as Turks. I had to read the repeated electoral post editorial, răcnete despair sublimate in Mystic, and apocalyptic swing taking place exhortations of political analysis. No more talk of «brink to lite» uncultured people like Roman Martin distinguished or abject sub-humane in Romania. At the same time, however, evidence that the press in Romania is freer than that in Burkina Faso, Congo and Namibia, despite report Reportes sans Frontières. The election came but hysteria in these last days of the campaign until Romania with Ukraine post-election threshold in civil war: that there is freedom of the press and expression, political freedom is troglodyte, irresponsibility, laughing stock to their countries 'electoral, with at least a decade ahead of Ukraine's political civilization on the ladder.

Forced to face the pressure hired mans of all sorts, the newspaper Truth strove to maintain sobriety, line balance, critical description, but impartial, of reality these days, with the regular readers of the row. Not incidentally, the only newspaper in this country where presidential candidates have agreed to meet in a debate at the Newsroom was, as in 1992, 1996 and 2000, the newspaper the truth. I dedicated these debate three pages of newspaper: not the same thing I did with big quantity of «secret» verbatim records of the meetings of the SOCIAL DEMOCRATIC PARTY received from editorial. After I published some extracts something more interesting, I considered that the texts of these otherwise untrusted audio tape, have nothing sensational, on the contrary, shall submit to the PSD politicians in a downright idyllic versus hardness analyses and to their shock debunks published in Truth in recent years. That Democrat Party members are cynical, they want to control everything, including the judiciary, that are obsessed with the press, in the case of the newspaper the truth, as evidenced even so-called verbatim records, that I knew very well, and I constantly informed audience. The question is: do you think some transcripts and the like, obtained from the other party, in power, it would be far more different?

I have not published the Armaghedonul anti Basescu, on the internet or the poster in PSD forged that Basescu was joined by a pair of gay kissing, because I considered multiply also abjectness on the circulation of truth, and be accompanied by a critical text.

In this campaign, the ruling party has adopted the tactic of fundamental electoral alms. PSD has rolled on electoral a gush of aid increases, bonuses, grants from the State budget or palpable only promises, hoping to cover such body ground of corruption, theft and assuredness.

On the other hand, the Alliance, primarily through the voice of Traian Băsescu, accused of corruption in the PSD all positions, hoping to cover such serious shortcomings with regard to program governance and skilled people; political error crimes of Basescu and his own dubious characters. Definition: the Dole campaign against corruption.

The logical conclusion of the above should not prevent the hysteria and dirt is to be placed in the urn with the ballot. We do not have a choice between good and evil, between monsters and pick up the queue on white horses, the archangels we have chosen, as a curse that we follow for so many years, between bad and worse. "(Cristian Tudor Popescu, hysteria and the URN băgăm dirt in the truth of 28 November 2004, pag. 1.)

Here's what says a political leader whose party has participated since 1989 until 2004 on governance: "Romanians, but I want and I can eradicate the mafia!

Dear countrymen, as a writer, sociologist and historian, I think you know better than you are aware of all other politicians. I have written thousands of pages about Romanian people, which I consider totally and utterly wonderful, with exceptional talent in all fields. Us, Romanians, we can be proud of with epochal creations, through which I lit and I made progress Humanity: the famous Christian hymn Te Deum is written by an ancestor of ours. The pen is invented by a Romanian, as all we win jet plane, insulin, Cybernetics, sonority etc. Unfortunately, such a brilliant people came to Earth, and have lost its compass. Barely longer lead existence on one day to another. The 15 were reached years of plunder of anarchy to give us back with at least 150 years. During these 15 years deep national shame, Romania has lost about 300 billion dollars due to Mafia, pilferage national heritage, destroy industry, agriculture, tourism, trade. The standard of living has collapsed at unimaginable odds, producing humility, psychosis and suicides. Reignite those miseries, which had been stamped out within a few decades ago. The country is depopulating from year to year, because Romanians die on heads and those who remain on the head take the world for a piece of bread. Who did that in this country was no longer bound by any law and should no longer go aright, than anything the Mafia? Who has turned his life into a nightmare, making sure to think about, with fear, tomorrow and in the jungle where they will be forced to live, soon, your children and grandchildren?

The answer is one and you know and you, better than me: guilty for the disaster of the country are all those who for 15 years have been in the Government, and now you appeal again votes, and with how you are going to the poorest, are rich Princes PSD + PUR and PNL-PD, as the Commission and the last of the top billionaires in dollars. More than 15 years of nightmare you want? Then vote for him all those who were. If you want to end this cycle of 15 years, Satanist, join me and my team of hardworking and incorruptibility of Great Romania Party!

Brothers help me that I can help! It's a crucial moment in the modern history of Romania. Only the PRM was not in the Government until now, because they formed a coalition against his evil forces. But I want and I can eradicate the mafia witch suffocate Romania. But I do not have any bank account anywhere and are not involved in dubious business. Only I can set up a new Moral Order in our beloved country, based on honor, national solidarity, social justice, hot love God. Do not vote for me to vote for you! Romanians, vote United, real change! To get the shot if not will pan out!

Dr. Corneliu Vadim Tudor, a Senator for Bucharest Great Romania Party President"

Whether for reflecting on how to be the leaders of the political class, we can find a great truth: human laws and human forces in the dualism of good and evil are not allowed to be what it should be. They need help to become what they are into what should be.

CHAPTER XIV
WORK WISE, USEFUL AND CREATIVE

Work is the one who created man; detach him from among animals (FR. Engels). That phenomenon, the work is perfectly and easily discernible in the laws of dialectic thinking, things and events, General and universal law valid, collected by Hegel in a process of continuous motion and auto moving, from lower to higher, whose source and engine would be internal contradictions, the absolute spirit "imagined".

According to Hegel, "absolute spirit" is auto-develop by going through the three stages of a triad»: thesis, antithesis and synthesis (understanding by thesis, antithesis engaged Hegelian dialectic idea by idea "alteration", i.e. objectification and alienation of her as a kind and understanding the spirit as the synthesis of the unit and the nature of the idea, as the basis of their absolute).

Hegel was perceived and presented worldwide natural, historical and spiritual as a process in continuous motion, change and development, attributing this process a dialectal character. On this basis, the objective idealism of footing, the dialectic of Hegel, applying the theory of knowledge, presented knowledge as a process of progressive approximation of groupthink absolute truth. The dialectic of Hegel, perceived as a general and universal law applies, the laws developed multilaterally: quantitative and switch quantity collections in a new quality, unity and struggle of contraries, denying negation. As regards the factor labor, Hegel has noticed the role human labor in the process of transformation, but only in the form of abstract work, spiritual, i.e. in the form of action, the "absolute spirit would produce" facts.

Dialectic engaged Hegelian dialectic is silhouettes k. Marx and Engels and FR. interpreted on the materialist dialectic positions, expanding on human society.

K. Marx characterized the 'class' complex and multilateral work. He comes to work like this:

1) Work, work done in concrete terms in a special form, directed towards a specific purpose. For example: work bricklayer, carpenter, taylor, etc. This form of labor creates value by use of the goods;

2) Abstract work, understanding thereby spending of the workforce in general, regardless of its form and the concrete manifestation. It creates the value of the goods;

3) Required, that part of the work done by the worker in the production process, which creates the product necessary for maintenance of his and his family;

4) Supra-work historical is appearing on a stage of development of social production and to a certain level of labor productivity, the manufacturer can produce more than is necessary for the maintenance of his and his family;

5) Simple work, that part of the work that you submit a worker who does not have special training to work unskilled labor;

6) Complex work-is physical or intellectual work by a worker with a special theoretical and practical training, the same as the simple times work;

7). Productive labor, work which translates into material goods;

8). Non-productive labor, work to workers who do not participate in the creation of material goods;

9). Norm of the work, work on the measurement of the amount they make using rules.

10). Not norm work is done on a full time job-board;

11). Physical work;

12) Intellectual work;

13) Work, spending by labor in the production of material goods;

14) Last (attested) work, work in production processes and embodied in previous means of production and consumer goods.

The work involves and actually represents a spending of labor force in order to produce the goods required to meet the needs of the primary social and spiritual man, without which human society and man cannot exist and is therefore a necessity eternal for man and society.

The process of economic labor category knowledge is dialectic and is directly proportional to the dialectic thinking, which depends on the dialectic of human intellectual labor. However, I have demonstrated scientifically in the book democracy and social justice—the future of humanity, that man's intellectual force currently dialectics, which urges labor process knowledge, believed to approach the "ultimate truth".

Having knowledge of the law of dialectic thinking, things and phenomena and perceived category philosophical and economic work as part of the dialectic, we formulated the following sentence: If the work was that it had stripped the man from the animals, all "work is his dialectic has generated through the process of dialectic human from stage to stage of primitive man always developed from among and by mass which have emerged and are always academics".

To me that auto convince has generated the process work the dialectic of history of dialectic human, I based on the laws discovered by Hegel, I pondered on how to look at the work by Marx using i mode of interpretation of the work, and to find the source and the dialectic of work, as I have pointed out, I reflected on labor as practice it day by day in physical labor, employment and intellectual work organization and leadership. After a period of meditations on these sides of labor, based on my own experience in practicing, I concluded that the intellectual work is that which accumulates in quantity, the process of gathering being generated through speaking and writing and, periodically, the quantitative accumulation of intellectual labor of man turns in a new quality and intellectual labor potential increases. I also noticed that between the different sides of the labor (physical, intellectual, work organization and leadership) there is always an internal contradiction, maintained by the intellectual evolution of labor which, through the process of accumulation potential, generate and process logic of denial negation.

Performing this process by imaginary research, confirmed by the practice of life, I approached by knowing the absolute truth ", that" the work evolves, that labor dialectics dialectic is the dialectic of human intellectual labor, which accumulates from man to man, from generation to generation, generating a new potential, as well as the denial process being continuously negation—due to the fact that the intellectual force of man is dialectal.

The work is specifically human activity, it being that it has created man, detaching him from among animals, it is that which, by its dialectic process of dialectic human generated, and as a result is one which take the form of a live human capital, the generator of all forms of capital and the necessary needs (needs) and social-spiritual man.

Work and the man shall be set up as an organic unit and dialectic with mutual influence in that work, in addition to that they are the eternal human condition of life in the world here, she, by dialectic, and ensure the human dialectic of dialectic human labor ensures dialectic. Imaginary thinking, the process tends to infinity.

The organic unity of the work and, between man and man, seen through the prism of dialectic, laws of dialectic, is reflected in that process of dialectical unity between "organic" and man, between man and not place in direct proportion to the dialectic of human intellectual labor, often, the road is full of obstacles that hinder the dialectic of human labor the end, hampers and organic unity between dialectic and man between man and, respectively.

Practicing an imaginary research, we can see that the laws of dialectic in the organic unity between man and the work of the Labor and radical man "work differently than any other thing or phenomenon. The cause lies in the fact that man is a being biologic-social form of "cell" of human society as a whole, "cell" in possession of four forces (physical, intellectual, the force of good and evil) and is dominated by a series of specific objective and subjective law of nature and human flesh, laws which, as I have pointed out, you are the man to be what it is and not let it be what it should be. Human forces and laws of human acts, in his lifetime, conjugate, prompting him to do what he did, making it and preventing it to do what he should do.

Intellectual force of humans, although evolved dynamic-ascendant and sometimes with jumps dialectical, however has not reached that level of potential development that would help the man to auto knowing and to define the role and purpose in his world here.

This account of mine is confirmed and how it is used "live" human capital. Or it is known that the dialectic of human intellectual force generated dialectic of the work which, in turn, changed continuously and share economic goods produced on account of the different sides of the work.

The share of economic goods produced on various sides of the account (physical, intellectual, organizational and managerial work, and acquired last) is presented graphically in the book democracy and social justice—the future of humanity, beginning from the primitive commune until the modern era of capitalism.

Graphical presentation of the weighting of the various products on the economic side of labor, matched by what takes place in all countries of the globe, the intellectual force of coated man linked to the problem of recovery "live" human capital, which raises major problems.

Harmonization of the work of organizing and leading to the three levels of the relationship between the different sides of the work has not been managed so that each unique and peculiar to the General (human society as a whole)-the man, "cell" of society to harness the capital live available at true value.

Use "live" human capital, the generator of all forms of capital, must be seen and felt, complex and multidirectional so that, in addition to the fact that it is a prerequisite for the creation of potentially economic goods and necessities of the human spiritual and human society as a whole, however, not all human accomplishment is useful and human society as a whole. What is more important, it is perceived that the work he has created man, detaching him from among animals, and the dialectic of dialectical evolution of human-generated from stage to stage of primitive man always developed, always modernized, always perfected and always civilized people, always defending the scholars. Non-valorization "live" human capital rationally, intensively and extensively generalized to restrain their dialectic, as a consequence of humans and the dialectic of human society is slowing down. And what more must we take and which has a major importance is the fact that if the work he has created man, detaching him from among the animals, if labor dialectic has generated human dialectic from primitive man from what is now at the beginning of the Millennium III, non-work it coming man of the way of being of the animals or/in the best case, to how to be human primitive.

These theoretical considerations are found in the translation of social and economic life of the human species in almost all countries of the globe, with an indication that the scale of a differentiation between the members of the human species is variable from country to country.

Intellectual force of man is to meditate on the causes leading to rational non-valorization, intensive and extensive live human capital and search tactics and strategy required allowing recovery of dialectical rational leap, intensive and extensive live human capital.

To raise awareness on the core intellectual force of the man that "State of the human species on the whole earth, so the world of here, from certain points of view, it is more unjust than the animals from which comes through the process of work", I'm looking for the secret, the cause.

The secret, unknown cause of this phenomenon is refined in nature and human nature. The man, as is characterized by historical personalities of all times, as "a being social integrated with thought and articulated language "is not enough to perceive and decipher the" nature and human nature." There is not enough to charge the man in terms of joint roles and that he should have in the world of here, which is why in his book, democracy and social justice—the future of humanity, we have formulated and a characterization that would help to perceive man why do what they do and what not to do what they should do.

Thus, man is characterized as "a being biologic social, in possession of four forces":

1. Physical Force, located in the muscular system, relatively constant from man to man, which is not sent.

2. Intellectual Force, located in the central nervous system in the human brain, characterized by that it is radically different from man to man and that are transmitted from human to human through the process of speaking and writing, what makes this force the human to accumulate and to move towards infinity ∞.

3. The force of good and

4. The force of evil, established as a dualism of good and evil, located in the central nervous system in the human brain.

The first two human forces shall be formed as a "living" human capital, as a prerequisite for the creation of savings necessary to meet the needs of primary mice and human social-spiritual. This live human capital, through the process of work, place of spending (consumption) of the physical and intellectual energy, energy is becoming as the prerequisite creation capital living economic goods, whether functional active, generating all forms of capital known to man.

Force of good and evil force in the human brain is constituted as a dualism of good and evil, which results in a man's life in all the time to do when good things, when bad things, good or evil that makes him being according to the report (R) which takes place between the forces of good weight (F.G) and share of evil forces (E.F.) report (R), which may be of the form:

$$R= FG/EF = 1; >1; <1.$$

Also, it can be demonstrated scientifically that man is dominated by a series of laws between objective and subjective, one fundamental objective: "the law of accumulation of wealth (wealth) by any means and at any price," law without limits. This fundamental objective law and of human is doubled, tripled . . . by a series of other laws, such as:

- -law of selfishness;
- -law of individualism;
- -law of rational, and irrational dualism;
- -law dullness and diligence dualism;
- -depth of dualism and law superficiality;
- -law of optimism and pessimism dualism;
- -the law of forgiveness and Cossette's dualism;
- -patient and non-patient law dualism;
- -the law of relative happiness (to be nicer, richer etc.);
- -the law differentiated facilities (to paint, sculpt, create literary, to organize and lead, etc.);
- -the law differentiated the pleasures (the pleasure of being the head, to be appreciated, to be heard, to decide to do some sport and so on).

Human forces acting shared human laws, generating both the progress and development, economic and spiritual and on the other hand, divides the human species in social segments of which lives in a segment, "a galore of heaven", and another segment is living in poverty and misery, "a kind of hell". Between these two extremes of the human species there is an intermediate step that moves toward an insignificant when the pole when towards the other.

Laws and human forces, through their combined action, it is what it is:

-When "man to man, man"

-When "man Fox devious manipulation and likes to the man"

-When "man versus man" crook,

-When "man versus man killer".

Man, through laws and his forces due to the intellectual work of dialectic, consequence of the intellectual force of dialectic, he progressed steadily, from "primitive" man up to what it is today. This improvement has generated and human as main phase to be more "killer man against man", characteristic of the slave era, when the man, dominated by his laws, began the process of "rip" the human species in rich and poor. Then the objective law of man and fundamental Law, "the accumulation of wealth (the city) at any cost and by any means" was based on exploiting the "capital live" man existing only in the form of physical force, prompting the wealthy to transform the poor in slaves, in speaking of the rich tools of the slave owners.

The dualism of good and evil forces, which in that era was set up in the form of historical

$$R= FG/EF <1. \text{ respectively } R= FG/EF >1;$$

It was the slave owners to be more "killer man to man". Slaves owned, owners tools-speaking slaves were kept bound in chains, beaten and burned with red hot iron when opposed to perform the commandments of their owners and kill when the ratio (R) of P.F.R. was much too large to P.F.B. intellectual human labor Dialectic has generated continuous growth process of living human capital potential and as a result, the source of law and fundamental human targets, "the law of accumulation of wealth (wealth) by any means and at any price", dialectical evolved allowing law enforcement objectives and functioning of the human and fundamental under continuous improvement of the report (R) of F.G. and E.F. It is always being found in the form of

$$R= FG/EF = 1; >1; <1.$$

What has determinant as the man to become as close to permanent "man versus man killer" as

-"man Fox devious manipulation and likes to the man"

-"humans duffer to man" and, in a growing dynamic, "man, man to man" and, in a dynamic decrease, "man versus man killer".

The dynamics of human intellectual force generated dialectical process towards law enforcement objectives and fundamental human so that "the law of accumulation of wealth (wealth) by any means and at any price" to be able to achieve thanks to tittuped for quality jobs, the accumulated intellectual and transformed into technological processes mechanized and sometimes partially robotic. This represents an inexhaustible source and always enhanced to ensure the accumulation of wealth in increasingly large, generating and process of reducing capital consumption continue to live in the form of physical force.

The dialectic of human intellectual labor does not limit and is characterized in that it builds up potential from man to man, from generation to generation, and imaginary thinking, intellectual force of man tends to infinity ∞. which means that live on human capital and tends to infinity ∞, because if we do physical labor performance-the sum of human, which is relatively constant (A), of human intellectual labor that ∞, then SJ $A + B = A + \infty = \infty$.

This trend of evolution dynamic-up capital of live human picks up in front of mankind, the human species, a complex issue that cannot be resolved, meaning to harness this capital live man, tending to infinity (∞), and assumed that intellectual labor dialectics leap to generate forms of organization and management to enable and ensure the recovery of the gigantic live human capital both in extensively and intensive, but mostly "GOOD".

The intellectuals at the national and international scale, irrespective of the objects of the intellectual work practice falls to a higher level of Division of labor has the historical task of intellectual, devote part of its force in order to harness the intellectual capital of live humans as rational, so intensively and extensively.

Intellectual force of man has reached, in our view, the level of development as to perceive what is here "; "what is the man in this world away"; "why do what they do and what not to do what they should do". And, what is of particular importance, is that the intelligentsia, by his intellectual labor potential and its coefficient of intelligence that characterize, should define what is the man in this world here, which should be the role of and rationale behind in the world of here and be informed because "MAN" to become what it is what it should be.

The man is found at the threshold of auto-knowledge and its perception. Intellectual force of man can and must act to ensure that this threshold to be crossed.

When the man begins its process auto-knowledge, process its perception starts and begins the process of perception, what is the man in this world here, what are the role and the rationale behind him in this world here?

This step of the dialectical approach to human knowledge of the absolute truth and helps man to about is the posture in which he lived thousands of years, making what he has done and to get in position to do what they should do so using its forces and laws of his knowledgeable, surrounding them with forces and laws of nature for the good life in the world here. This function is not only capitalizing on extensive and intensive live human capital, but is based on and exploitation of creative and rational of this capital live.

CHAPTER XIV
WORK WISE, USEFUL AND CREATIVE

Work is the one who created man; detach him from among animals (FR. Engels). That phenomenon, the work is perfectly and easily discernible in the laws of dialectic thinking, things and events, General and universal law valid, collected by Hegel in a process of continuous motion and auto moving, from lower to higher, whose source and engine would be internal contradictions, the absolute spirit "imagined".

According to Hegel, "absolute spirit" is auto-develop by going through the three stages of a triad»: thesis, antithesis and synthesis (understanding by thesis, antithesis engaged Hegelian dialectic idea by idea "alteration", i.e. objectification and alienation of her as a kind and understanding the spirit as the synthesis of the unit and the nature of the idea, as the basis of their absolute).

Hegel was perceived and presented worldwide natural, historical and spiritual as a process in continuous motion, change and development, attributing this process a dialectal character. On this basis, the objective idealism of footing, the dialectic of Hegel, applying the theory of knowledge, presented knowledge as a process of progressive approximation of groupthink absolute truth. The dialectic of Hegel, perceived as a general and universal law applies, the laws developed multilaterally: quantitative and switch quantity collections in a new quality, unity and struggle of contraries, denying negation. As regards the factor labor, Hegel has noticed the role human labor in the process of transformation, but only in the form of abstract work, spiritual, i.e. in the form of action, the "absolute spirit would produce" facts.

Dialectic engaged Hegelian dialectic is silhouettes k. Marx and Engels and FR. interpreted on the materialist dialectic positions, expanding on human society.

K. Marx characterized the 'class' complex and multilateral work. He comes to work like this:

1) Work, work done in concrete terms in a special form, directed towards a specific purpose. For example: work bricklayer, carpenter, taylor, etc. This form of labor creates value by use of the goods;

2) Abstract work, understanding thereby spending of the workforce in general, regardless of its form and the concrete manifestation. It creates the value of the goods;

3) Required, that part of the work done by the worker in the production process, which creates the product necessary for maintenance of his and his family;

4) Supra-work historical is appearing on a stage of development of social production and to a certain level of labor productivity, the manufacturer can produce more than is necessary for the maintenance of his and his family;

5) Simple work, that part of the work that you submit a worker who does not have special training to work unskilled labor;

6) Complex work-is physical or intellectual work by a worker with a special theoretical and practical training, the same as the simple times work;

7). Productive labor, work which translates into material goods;

8). Non-productive labor, work to workers who do not participate in the creation of material goods;

9). Norm of the work, work on the measurement of the amount they make using rules.

10). Not norm work is done on a full time job-board;

11). Physical work;

12) Intellectual work;

13) Work, spending by labor in the production of material goods;

14) Last (attested) work, work in production processes and embodied in previous means of production and consumer goods.

The work involves and actually represents a spending of labor force in order to produce the goods required to meet the needs of the primary social and spiritual man, without which human society and man cannot exist and is therefore a necessity eternal for man and society.

The process of economic labor category knowledge is dialectic and is directly proportional to the dialectic thinking, which depends on the dialectic of human intellectual labor. However, I have demonstrated scientifically in the book democracy and social justice—the future of humanity, that man's intellectual force currently dialectics, which urges labor process knowledge, believed to approach the "ultimate truth".

Having knowledge of the law of dialectic thinking, things and phenomena and perceived category philosophical and economic work as part of the dialectic, we formulated the following sentence: If the work was that it had stripped the man from the animals, all 'work is his dialectic has generated through the process of dialectic human from stage to stage of primitive man always developed from among and by mass which have emerged and are always academics".

To me that auto convince has generated the process work the dialectic of history of dialectic human, I based on the laws discovered by Hegel, I pondered on how to look at the work by Marx using i mode of interpretation of the work, and to find the source and the dialectic of work, as I have pointed out, I reflected on labor as practice it day by day in physical labor, employment and intellectual work organization and leadership. After a period of meditations on these sides of labor, based on my own experience in practicing, I concluded that the intellectual work is that which accumulates in quantity, the process of gathering being generated through speaking and writing and, periodically, the quantitative accumulation of intellectual labor of man turns in a new quality and intellectual labor potential increases. I also noticed that between the different sides of the labor (physical, intellectual, work organization and leadership) there is always an internal contradiction, maintained by the intellectual evolution of labor which, through the process of accumulation potential, generate and process logic of denial negation.

Performing this process by imaginary research, confirmed by the practice of life, I approached by knowing the absolute truth ", that" the work evolves, that labor dialectics dialectic is the dialectic of human intellectual labor, which accumulates from man to man, from generation to generation, generating a new potential, as well as the denial process being continuously negation—due to the fact that the intellectual force of man is dialectal.

The work is specifically human activity, it being that it has created man, detaching him from among animals, it is that which, by its dialectic process of dialectic human generated, and as a result is one which take the form of a live human capital, the generator of all forms of capital and the necessary needs (needs) and social-spiritual man.

Work and the man shall be set up as an organic unit and dialectic with mutual influence in that work, in addition to that they are the eternal human condition of life in the world here, she, by dialectic, and ensure the human dialectic of dialectic human labor ensures dialectic. Imaginary thinking, the process tends to infinity.

The organic unity of the work and, between man and man, seen through the prism of dialectic, laws of dialectic, is reflected in that process of dialectical unity between "organic" and man, between man and not place in direct proportion to the dialectic of human intellectual labor, often, the road is full of obstacles that hinder the dialectic of human labor the end, hampers and organic unity between dialectic and man between man and, respectively.

Practicing an imaginary research, we can see that the laws of dialectic in the organic unity between man and the work of the Labor and radical man "work differently than any other thing or phenomenon. The cause lies in the fact that man is a being biologic-social form of "cell" of human society as a whole, "cell" in possession of four forces (physical, intellectual, the force of good and evil) and is dominated by a series of specific objective and subjective law of nature and human flesh, laws which, as I have pointed out, you are the man to be what it is and not let it be what it should be. Human forces and laws of human acts, in his lifetime, conjugate, prompting him to do what he did, making it and preventing it to do what he should do.

Intellectual force of humans, although evolved dynamic-ascendant and sometimes with jumps dialectical, however has not reached that level of potential development that would help the man to auto knowing and to define the role and purpose in his world here.

This account of mine is confirmed and how it is used "live" human capital. Or it is known that the dialectic of human intellectual force generated dialectic of the work which, in turn, changed continuously and share economic goods produced on account of the different sides of the work.

The share of economic goods produced on various sides of the account (physical, intellectual, organizational and managerial work, and acquired last) is presented graphically in the book democracy and social justice—the future of humanity, beginning from the primitive commune until the modern era of capitalism.

Graphical presentation of the weighting of the various products on the economic side of labor, matched by what takes place in all countries of the globe, the intellectual force of coated man linked to the problem of recovery "live" human capital, which raises major problems.

Harmonization of the work of organizing and leading to the three levels of the relationship between the different sides of the work has not been managed so that each unique and peculiar to the General (human society as a whole)-the man, "cell" of society to harness the capital live available at true value.

Use "live" human capital, the generator of all forms of capital, must be seen and felt, complex and multidirectional so that, in addition to the fact that it is a prerequisite for the creation of potentially economic goods and necessities of the human spiritual and human society as a whole, however, not all human accomplishment is useful and human society as a whole. What is more important, it is perceived that the work he has created man, detaching him from among animals, and the dialectic of dialectical evolution of human-generated from stage to stage of primitive man always developed, always modernized, always perfected and always civilized people, always defending the scholars. Non-valorization "live" human capital rationally, intensively and extensively generalized to restrain their dialectic, as a consequence of humans and the dialectic of human society is slowing down. And what more must we take and which has a major importance is the fact that if the work he has created man, detaching him from among the animals, if labor dialectic has generated human dialectic from primitive man from what is now at the beginning of the Millennium III, non-work it coming man of the way of being of the animals or/in the best case, to how to be human primitive.

These theoretical considerations are found in the translation of social and economic life of the human species in almost all countries of the globe, with an indication that the scale of a differentiation between the members of the human species is variable from country to country.

Intellectual force of man is to meditate on the causes leading to rational non-valorization, intensive and extensive live human capital and search tactics and strategy required allowing recovery of dialectical rational leap, intensive and extensive live human capital.

To raise awareness on the core intellectual force of the man that "State of the human species on the whole earth, so the world of here, from certain points of view, it is more unjust than the animals from which comes through the process of work", I'm looking for the secret, the cause.

The secret, unknown cause of this phenomenon is refined in nature and human nature. The man, as is characterized by historical personalities of all times, as "a being social integrated with thought and articulated language "is not enough to perceive and decipher the" nature and human nature." There is not enough to charge the man in terms of joint roles and that he should have in the world of here, which is why in his book, democracy and social justice—the future of humanity, we have formulated and a characterization that would help to perceive man why do what they do and what not to do what they should do.

Thus, man is characterized as "a being biologic-social, in possession of four forces":

1. Physical Force, located in the muscular system, relatively constant from man to man, which is not sent.

2. Intellectual Force, located in the central nervous system in the human brain, characterized by that it is radically different from man to man and that are transmitted from human to human through the process of speaking and writing, what makes this force the human to accumulate and to move towards to infinity ∞.

3. The force of good and

4. The force of evil, established as a dualism of good and evil, located in the central nervous system in the human brain.

The first two human forces shall be formed as a "living" human capital, as a prerequisite for the creation of savings necessary to meet the needs of primary mice and human social-spiritual. This live human capital, through the process of work, place of spending (consumption) of the physical and intellectual energy, energy is becoming as the prerequisite creation capital living economic goods, whether functional active, generating all forms of capital known to man.

Force of good and evil force in the human brain is constituted as a dualism of good and evil, which results in a man's life in all the time to do when good things, when bad things, good or evil that makes him being according to the report (R) which takes place between the forces of good weight (F.G) and share of evil forces (E.F.) report (R), which may be of the form:

$$R = FG/EF = 1; >1; <1.$$

Also, it can be demonstrated scientifically that man is dominated by a series of laws between objective and subjective, one fundamental objective: "the law of accumulation of wealth (wealth) by any means and at any price," law without limits. This fundamental objective law and of human is doubled, tripled . . . by a series of other laws, such as:

- -law of selfishness;
- -law of individualism;
- -law of rational, and irrational dualism;
- -law dullness and diligence dualism;
- -depth of dualism and law superficiality;
- -law of optimism and pessimism dualism;
- -the law of forgiveness and Cossette's dualism;
- -patient and non-patient law dualism;
- -the law of relative happiness (to be nicer, richer etc.);
- -the law differentiated facilities (to paint, sculpt, create literary, to organize and lead, etc.);
- -the law differentiated the pleasures (the pleasure of being the head, to be appreciated, to be heard, to decide to do some sport and so on).

Human forces acting shared human laws, generating both the progress and development, economic and spiritual and on the other hand, divides the human species in social segments of which lives in a segment, "a galore of heaven", and another segment is living in poverty and misery, "a kind of hell". Between these two extremes of the human species there is an intermediate step that moves toward an insignificant when the pole when towards the other.

Laws and human forces, through their combined action, it is what it is:

-When "man to man, man"

-When "man Fox devious manipulation and likes to the man"

-When "man versus man" crook,

-When "man versus man killer".

Man, through laws and his forces due to the intellectual work of dialectic, consequence of the intellectual force of dialectic, he progressed steadily, from "primitive" man up to what it is today. This improvement has generated and human as main phase to be more "killer man against man", characteristic of the slave era, when the man, dominated by his laws, began the process of "rip" the human species in rich and poor. Then the objective law of man and fundamental Law, "the accumulation of wealth (the city) at any cost and by any means" was based on exploiting the "capital live" man existing only in the form of physical force, prompting the wealthy to transform the poor in slaves, in speaking of the rich tools of the slave owners.

The dualism of good and evil forces, which in that era was set up in the form of historical

$$R = FG/EF < 1 \text{ respectively } R = FG/EF > 1$$

It was the slave owners to be more "killer man to man". Slaves owned, owners tools-speaking slaves were kept bound in chains, beaten and burned with red hot iron when opposed to perform the commandments of their owners and kill when the ratio (R) of P.F.R. was much too large to P.F.B. intellectual human labor Dialectic has generated continuous growth process of living human capital potential and as a result, the source of law and fundamental human targets, "the law of accumulation of wealth (wealth) by any means and at any price", dialectical evolved allowing law enforcement objectives and functioning of the human and fundamental under continuous improvement of the report (R) of F.G. and E.F. It is always being found in the form of

$$R = FG/EF = 1; >1; <1.$$

What has determinant as the man to become as close to permanent "man versus man killer" as

-"man Fox devious manipulation and likes to the man"

-"humans duffer to man" and, in a growing dynamic, "man, man to man" and, in a dynamic decrease, "man versus man killer".

The dynamics of human intellectual force generated dialectical process towards law enforcement objectives and fundamental human so that "the law of accumulation of wealth (wealth) by any means and at any price" to be able to achieve thanks to tittuped for quality jobs, the accumulated intellectual and transformed into technological processes mechanized and sometimes partially robotic. This represents an inexhaustible source and always enhanced to ensure the accumulation of wealth in increasingly large, generating and process of reducing capital consumption continue to live in the form of physical force.

The dialectic of human intellectual labor does not limit and is characterized in that it builds up potential from man to man, from generation to generation, and imaginary thinking, intellectual force of man tends to infinity ∞. which means that live on human capital and tends to infinity ∞, because if we do physical labor performance-the sum of human, which is relatively constant (A), of human intellectual labor that ∞, then SJ $A + B = A + \infty = \infty$.

This trend of evolution dynamic-up capital of live human picks up in front of mankind, the human species, a complex issue that cannot be resolved, meaning to harness this capital live man, tending to infinity (∞), and assumed that intellectual labor dialectics leap to generate forms of organization and management to enable and ensure the recovery of the gigantic live human capital both in extensively and intensive, but mostly "GOOD".

The intellectuals at the national and international scale, irrespective of the objects of the intellectual work practice falls to a higher level of Division of labor has the historical task of intellectual, devote part of its force in order to harness the intellectual capital of live humans as rational, so intensively and extensively.

Intellectual force of man has reached, in our view, the level of development as to perceive what is here "; "what is the man in this world away"; "why do what they do and what not to do what they should do". And, what is of particular importance, is that the intelligentsia, by his intellectual labor potential and its coefficient of intelligence that characterize, should define what is the man in this world here, which should be the role of and rationale behind in the world of here and be informed because "MAN" to become what it is what it should be.

The man is found at the threshold of auto-knowledge and its perception. Intellectual force of man can and must act to ensure that this threshold to be crossed.

When the man begins its process auto-knowledge, process its perception starts and begins the process of perception, what is the man in this world here, what are the role and the rationale behind him in this world here?

This step of the dialectical approach to human knowledge of the absolute truth and helps man to about is the posture in which he lived thousands of years, making what he has done and to get in position to do what they should do so using its forces and laws of his knowledgeable, surrounding them with forces and laws of nature for the good life in the world here. This function is not only capitalizing on extensive and intensive live human capital, but is based on and exploitation of creative and rational of this capital live.

CHAPTER XV

THE DIALECTIC UNITY OF ORGANIC BETWEEN MAN AND MAN, BETWEEN WORK AND

Of those, about work and man, it appears that the WORK he has created man, detaching him from among the animals, that dialectic historical process generated the WORK of the HUMAN dialectic, hence the conclusion that between the work and there is an organic unit MAN currently dialectics.

Reflecting on the organic unity between man and man, between the work and, in a process of continuous motion and auto moving, dynamic-ascending and periodically with qualitative leaps, can perceive the live human capital. It has been shown that the man, the owner of a premise of the capital, the creation of goods required to meet the needs of the primary economic and social-spiritual, physical and occupational work transforms the intellectual capital live dormant, active and functional. Also, it has been shown scientifically that this capital live actively existing in the form of latent premise of the creation of economic and social-spiritual becomes functional only in part. A large part of the live human capital is lost, the efficiency of its existing transformation—in the form of physical and intellectual energy—energy is based on "the art of organization and management" of those who engage in this work at three levels—the family company and national State (State Board).

The dialectic of human intellectual labor, slave labor, and the dialectic and the source of the dialectic of live human capital, the ratio of the potential failure of much live human capital, latent, existing as a prerequisite for the creation of economic and social-spiritual, and live active and functional capital. Thus the efficiency of transformation of latent capital live in capital assets and the efficiency decreases, the functional transformation of latent capital live in capital live active and functional in time t2 is smaller than the time t1. The reason is that behind the quality of work organization and leadership to the movement and intellectual force of human auto moving, that dialectic of intellectual labor force > dialectic of organization and management or dialectic of live human capital than labor dialectic > organization and management.

This process should be understood as a general trend, and this should be seen at all three levels of organization and management, a phenomenon that requires a long and deep meditation. Thus, the first two levels of organization and management-family and company—the capital of the live human potential is better exploited, return on transforming the latent state of premise in living an active capital tends to keep the pace of dialectic human intellectual labor. As regards work organization and leadership at the level of State administration, the efficiency of transformation of latent capital live as prerequisite for the creation of economic and social-spiritual capital actively and functional, in addition to not keep up, in percentage (%) with the dialectic of labor, generated by intellectual human labor dialectic, and decreases. We present an imaginary example.

Suppose a company that: a) the intellectual force behind during : t_1 b) intellectual and physical work (capital live) in : t_1 c) work organization and leadership in : t_1

$\sum$. (amount) of the transformation of the dormant capital live in the capital living active level company let's say is:

$\sum_1 \approx$ 80-90% during t_2, when capital live active under the form allowable is $> t_1$ and the efficiently of work transformation remains relatively constant, namely all 80-90%, $\sum_{\cdot 2} \approx$ 80-90%.

At the level of State administration, under the same conditions capital live latent form of pre-requisite for the creation of economic assets is higher for t_2 to t_1. Suppose that in t_1 the efficiency of work is $\sum_1 \approx$ 70-80% (t_1); in t_2 the percentage decrease $\sum_{\cdot 2} \approx$ 65-75%.

This situation is consequence of two major factors:

1) Dialectic of organizing and managing labor, political personalities entrusted to conduct Affairs of State, does not keep pace with the dialectic of capital to existing live latent potential as a prerequisite for the creation of economic goods, and sometimes more beat up on the spot and more and give back.

2) forms of ownership of factors of production, mayors and derivatives, have no necessary mobility which will allow the harmonious Union of primary factor (factor of production) with the primary nature of the production factor (air, water and Earth) and with any inputs.

If you consider the first factor, the "dialectic of labor organizing and driving behavior of political personalities who hold power in the State and we will search for unknown," the secret ", because that causes the offset of the motion and auto moving dialectic between work in general and the work of organizing and leading political personalities who hold power in the State, with a small intellect we find that this phenomenon is due to the environment created with thousands of years ago. Objective law and fundamental human, "the law of accumulation of wealth (wealth) at any cost and by any means," law without limit, it works without making the effort required to maintain a constant gap between dialectic at work in general and the work of organizing and leading political personalities entrusted with power of decision in the State, within a consistent and rational. In addition, we may find that the struggle between political leaders to power is not based on rational exploitation of intensive and extensive subject-matter of their work—man.

Electoral slogans are always the same ruling, the only form of expression changes and sophistry always such that to determine the voter to vote on the same form of expression that finds the most accessible to the masses of voters.

It is very important to note that after winning the election, political leaders who hold power in the State objective and realize the fundamental law of man, "the law of wealth at any cost and by any means, "law without limit, regardless of the evolution of life of citizens. If economic indicators (GDP) grow, begin the process auto-computation the learn to power, and if remain constant, and sometimes more and less, begin the process of justification of the impact of external factors attributing their work organization and leadership, as for example on account of the transitional period (the case).

Reflecting on the ownership, the second major factor that determines the gap between the work in general and the work of organizing and leading political personalities entrusted with power of decision in the State, we find that, historical, the most important factor of production after work, primary factor, land, gradually-gradually became private property of increasingly higher or it is a factor of production is already existing human, is a good natural created by man and man wrongfully appropriated as private property, especially the sizes that exceed workforce potential. If our historical on the primary factor of production, land, we can conclude that when production tools were very poorly developed, then weak and so on, the consumption of agricultural work necessary work was really great at first, and gradually, parallel with the development and improvement of the tools of production, consumption has declined, peaking at a time when large landowners to work the land with a very small number of employees sometimes even just with the family. And what is totally unacceptable, great owners use the Earth as her will, irrespective whether it is a good natural nourish mankind through its products. Many areas of land are not worked, and a large portion of them degrade from year to year, from period to period, under the influence of natural factors, thus reducing continuous areas of arable land and grass and productivity per hectare, which is why, in his book democracy and social justice—the future of humanity, and sentence is formulated on the need for a conspicuous forms of ownership in a motion and auto moving allowing rational exploitation the intensive and extensive live human capital. Private property on the primary factor of production nature (air, water and Earth) can no longer constitute grounds for private properties, with minor exceptions, the production factor of the Earth where there may be private properties up to 2 to 5 hectares, more than 10 hectares where justified economic-social. The main production factor of land privately owned must be carried out in a form and a strategic concept to incentive on great landowners to sell or concede the State. This process is extensively presented in the book democracy and social justice—the future of humanity.

Improvement of the road for the work of organizing and leading political personalities to keep pace with the dialectic of capital live, human potential, ultimately is braked by human laws and human forces, political leaders, and her people, acts during their investiture under the action of human laws, which dominates and make are always what they are and aren't allowed to be what it should be.

And those people, political leaders, who hold power in the State and the sincere desire to change the course of affairs in their country, to the benefit of the entire nation, fail do so because of the laws of man and of the report which is between P.F.B and P.F.R. (R) report, which, as I pointed out, can be of the form:

$$R= FG/EF = 1; >1; <1.$$

Also, the political leader who win power through the election process operates with a large variety of live cells "which", under the action of laws and human forces, in addition to that I do what I do and he influences and from the tip of the pyramid to do what he did and what he does.

The dialectic unity between organic and between man and man, work, labor is subject to the dialectic of organization and management at the level of State administration, however, historical experience. highlights the great gap between the intellectual and labor force dialectic of organization and leadership and to decrease this delay time, you must set the economic and social indicators for the leaders of the political class parameters, based on the rate and the moral and material incentives. These indicators are set out in the book democracy and social justice—the future of humanity.

CHAPTER XVI
IRRATIONAL AND EVIL SOCIETY WORK

The work is a primary factor of production and active, the most important factor of production. The work is one which, by its action on the primary nature of the production factor (air, water and Earth) and the factors of production, resulting from any work performed previously and acquired, it has generated all the goods of the economic and social and spiritual human needs of the person and society as a whole.

The analysis of labor as a factor of production was a major concern of many intellectual personalities of the time. K. Marx, as I have pointed out, the viewer work in terms of Labor:

- physical and intellectual;
- simple and complex;
- concrete and abstract;
- necessary and unproductive;
- vivid and attested;
- with norm and without norm etc.

In the book democracy and social justice—the future of humanity, the author, using this way of looking at work by k. Marx and being captured by the law of dialectic thinking, things and phenomena, he imagined work organically incorporated into that law applies universally—dialectic—stating the thesis work of dialectic. Scientific work demonstrating that if it was that which he has created man, detach him from among animals-scientific hypothesis after the emergence of man on Earth—all work shall be that which, by its dialectic, generated the dialectics of man from the stage of "primitive man" to stage "man always developed, always perfected, modernized and always civilized, from among the mass which have emerged and are always academics ".

153

The dialectic of the work is demonstrated by the author in his book, using it to look as it performs work in reality, day after day, in the workplace:

* physics;
* intellectual and
* work organization and leadership

Demonstrating the scientific, through concrete and abstract arguments, that the dialectic of intellectual labor is work the dialectic, as a result of the continuous growth of the potential energy required the provision of intellectual work, which the intellectual energy quantitative collections lead to qualitative leaps, beneficial in every respect for upward growth efficiency of work in general.

Work in a dialectical concept and as the main factor of production and organic perceived a related factor of production nature (air, water and Earth) and any inputs, resulting from the action of the first two primary factors—labor and nature, whose potential plays dynamic-ascending, as a result of the accumulation process-generated quantitative accumulation of work last sentence "organic Unity between inputs: 1 production factor); 2) factor of production nature (air, water and Earth) and 3) inputs derivatives, resulting from the production processes. They are found in an organic, in a moving and auto movement dynamic-jumps up and periodically with dialectical whose source and engine "intern" is "work".

Organic unity between these three groups of factors of production is in the process of motion and its auto moving in a continuous contradiction; contradiction between the factor of production work and the nature of the production factor (air, water and Earth) and periodically with possible contradictions between the first two inputs and inputs derivatives.

The contradiction between the organic unities of the internal factors of production is generated and maintained by movement upward and auto moving dynamic-element production work, its motor and spring is the force of human intellectual dialectic.

The internal contradictions of the organic unity of the factors of production is continuously improved by that side of the work known as the work of the Organization and management, practiced at three levels: the family company and the State administration of work organization and leadership at the three levels is almost always one step behind to the dialectic of intellectual labor what is normal, only that if you meditate on those three groups of factors of production, we can conclude that one of them, natural production factors (air, water and Earth) not only progressing dynamic-ascending, but there is also a process of continuous degradation because of the strenuous work of man, which in some cases generate a process of air pollution, water and Earth. More is added and the action of natural factors, which also generates processes to reduce the surface temperature of the Earth, natural production and its surface remains as a factor of production is more functional and degrades quality due to the way how it is practiced in production work factor.

The nature of the production factor (air, water and Earth) is a pre-existing human element and cannot be influenced by humans, to liaise with the dialectic of production work, and what is even more serious, the advent of private property on land, especially large or very large prevents the possibility of major actions to restore areas of land lost; It hampers the work of organizing and action at the level of State administration, even if the political leaders who are my invested to lead the country's Affairs holds art organization and leadership at high level.

Dialectic thinking things, phenomena and universal law, valid through the dialectic thinking, consequence of the movement and intellectual force of human auto moving, always dynamic-ascending, may, at any given time, to help the man to charge which is the rationale behind and its role in this world on earth can help the man, the political leader with power of decision in the State, to charge that is "the role and the rationale behind his" as a work of the Organization and management of quality can be improved or even remove the internal contradictions of the factors of production. If the leaders of the political class are dominate by human laws, and acting shared with the man in the dualism of good and evil, which does not allow evolving dialectic, then the fate of the human species is still unable to live auto-valorization its capital at its disposal. More seriously, is that part of the live human capital will continue to be used in techniques and polluting technologies which degrade continuously factor of production nature, becoming an evil standing—determined by human laws. If we add to this phenomenon as "super evil", which means consumption work to decipher the vines to produce no real economic and social-spiritual human life but also the necessary technical means and technology for the destruction of a great potential for the inputs, then the picture is grim. This, unfortunately, accumulates in quantity and quality of jumps with regularly, generating a technical and technological potential of the mass destruction of such size that it is possible that by using the existing potential to end life on earth or humiliate such dimensions as woe to the one that will stay alive! Man intellectually, through his intellectual force, if you will auto perceived of his role as the owner of an intellectual forces concentrated in the form of "intellectual force vector" may by dialectic thinking to charge that the time has come to initiate the jump's dialectical mode of being, "a human intellectual" in his way to work and do not let the human species is the consequence of decisions on the use of nuclear and chemical potential of mass destruction. The core intellectual force of the human species must be organized horizontally and vertically, so the personalities, able to act on urgent, very urgent, to "stop" action man laws and human forces in the dualism of good and evil, which generates "pollution harness human capital live".

In this sense, the intelligentsia should be organized horizontally and vertically in a "Supreme Forum of the human species", owner of a "vector inner force" able to magnetizes all the intellectual force of the entire human species, capable of conveying human action laws and human forces knowledgeable for the good of each unique and peculiar to the human species, to harnessing human capital live sensibly extensively and intensively right up to rational. In this context, human power, political leader with power of decision in the State, it should be resized in the sense of not being able to take decisions which may cause much harm to large groups of people, or, possibly, the entire human species.

Dialectic thinking can help man to charge and "organic unity between democracy, human rights and duties of man". A dialectical step in this regard would be the election of a Governing Board, composed of Vice-Presidents, three, five or seven people, after they are elected, one of them to occupy the post of Chairman for a period of time, say one year, after which follows the Commandant Vice President another.

The order of the Employment Office of the President to be based on the number of votes received from the voters or, where appropriate, depending on the decision of the Vice Presidents to be expressed by the vote. This democratic system would preclude the possibility of electoral fraud, cases much commented, justified or unjustified.

The Supreme Forum of the human species to meet and function of supervision of the work of the President and Vice Presidents, and according to work to make regular assessments and the organization able to act on them.

The Supreme Forum of the human species, organized horizontally and vertically, to be endowed with the power to organize the process halted production of means of mass destruction and on the basis of a program to begin gradually the total disarmament of all countries and General globe and for safety to be organized an army under central control, with subsidiaries all over the world who can act in the knowledge that when a certain State, through its political leaders, violating the principles of equality, liberty and fraternity among the human species, which is dispersed on the Earth.

The second step, as a priority to be to make the production activity of the company's such that between the profile of production and environment (ecology) to be a positive report.

The third step is the imposition of conditions for the Government to ensure the rational exploitation of the whole live capital available to the country, and in the conduct of democratic and social justice, to devise tactics and strategies that would lead to the improvement of the forms of ownership of factors of production, so that the unit of organic inputs to be able to provide a moving and auto movement dynamic-ascending and with the leaps dialectical. And the relationship between man and man, between man and nature to be so dimensioned that every unique feature of the human species and to harness its capital live. Through a creative and useful work, and society to ensure objective and fundamental law of man, the law of accumulation of wealth (wealth) by rational recovery, intensive and extensive "live" its capital to ensure that at first "primary" happiness of each unique and special—man L'appel (the human) and continue to provide "diversified" happiness, depending on the amount and quality of work performed.

These relations of production will lead to human species to a new form of existence, which at first will have a basis in which all social segments of the human species will have ensured the primary needs (food, clothing, and housing), which builds and then happiness diversified, with a complexity of factors.

The human species will cease to be divided into social classes and will be discontinued chain social injustices as a river course with permanent drainage, measured in thousands of years, and the relationship between economics and ecology into normality.

Unreasonable work to be seen as a true "cancer" that sick human species. "This must be urgently cured cancer", because if it put down to develop intensive and extensive potential-, can attain such dimensions as to endanger human life in the world here in the world of Terra.

CHAPTER XVII
ORGANIC UNITY BETWEEN FACTORS ORGANIC PRODUCTION AND THE DIALECTIC OF UNITY FACTOR MARKETS

Economists, watch as a subsidiary of the intelligentsia, because human intellectual dialectic of force which, as I demonstrated in the book democracy and social justice—the future of humanity, it accumulates from man to man, from generation to generation, which potentially increases the imaginary thinking, ∞, are they of this phenomenon, helping them to formulate views and theses that lead from almost close to knowing the truth absolutely in their field of activity.

Some examples which, in the evolution of economic trends led from almost close to the appearance of an economics that has State and forms the basis of decisions of leaders are important economic activities such as: the mercantilists of economists) the 16th-17TH century and first half of the 18th century in Italy, Spain, Germany and England, who claimed that the money in the form of ingots of gold and treasures of all kinds, represents the essence of wealth; b) fizio-crats, economists in the mid-18th century, who felt that agriculture is the only branch of execution of product net; c current classical economists) English school, which were enunciated by Adam Smith (1723-1790), thesis that there is wealth of goods on which all members of society they consume, and the Economist David Ricardo (1772-1823) analyzed, in its work, the theory of labor value, the theory of market and its role, the theory of differential rent and, especially, theory of comparative costs. In the works of classical English school were grounded principles of economic liberalism, demonstrating that the market is engine of economic activity, impulsion it on the manufacturer to produce and to increase the offer; that supply and demand have essential role in the formation of prices and economic orientation, and so on.

In the classical English thinking detached two streams; two directions of movement of economic thinking. The first is that of k. Marx, which continues to develop labor value theory, dividing (on) the work in various forms: concrete, abstract, necessary and supra-work, simple and complex, the physical and intellectual, productive and unproductive and so on.

Using this way of looking at work, k. Marx concludes that the economic is the fount of all riches. The second way of economic thinking was that neoclassical theory is that our opponents, claiming labor value theory of utility value. In the early twentieth century appeared the current economic know under the name of kinesis, whose founder was John Keynes, who argued the theory of the use of manpower. After Keynes, the use of labor has a central role. At the end of the Millennium II, Millennium III, economists make great efforts to find solutions to intellectual property required for economic growth and sustainable economic development. Branch intellectuals, economists were focused and meditate on the State of the world in terms of economic imbalances. Economists, on the perception of the economic cycle and its phases (expansion, crisis, depression and refreshing) seeks sustainable solutions and not in any circumstances but only in the version to ensure this beneficial influence on the future, both in terms of sustained economic growth, as well as the relation between economics and ecology.

The influence of major economic imbalances phenomena is viewed and analyzed in the concept, handles of the causes of unemployment, inflation and the implications thereof for the human person and of society as a whole. All are concerns to theorize that the definitions of causes, forms and level.

Many economists are worrying and complex to find the necessary solutions to those dealing with organization and management of various companies with production profile, so that their work should be as effective. But the man's intellectual force builds up, potentially, from man to man, from generation to generation, with a tendency to evolve to infinity, as economists normally would have to do and they leap to thinking dialectics, theories to formulate sentences which should govern the strategies in the work of the Organization and management to which I have referred several times, and particularly for the companies and especially for the level of State administration, which aims to improve the relationship between factors of production. Why this view? Because if we look at the factors of production in an organic and in a moving and auto moving dialectic unity organic factor markets, whose source and engine found in the organic unity of production factors, demonstrate scientific production work that factor, the primary factor, dialectical and active currently. His dialectic being generated and maintained in a continuous motion and auto movement of human intellectual force, which, potentially, are evolving towards infinity, which implies, in particular, technical and technological processes, automation and mechanized robots station even in a dialectical movement and auto movement all to obtain production additionally. Therefore, on account of increased labor productivity, achieved at the level of their management companies, has one major goal—getting profit. Managers of companies are not too much concerned about social issues; the attribute belongs to those dealing with organization and leadership of the State administration. "what is of particular importance is the perception that his intellectual dialectic of force pushes the antennas in all areas of economic and social activity, hence the conclusion that the organic unity of the inputs is and will be in a continuous process of internal struggle between inputs. This report calls for the necessity of the opposition of labor to organize and manage the level of State administration, close to the dialectic of force sensitive intellectual man, allowing continued improvement in factors of production.

Based on different theses formulated by some personalities profiled on issues related to economic activity, which I managed to know during his studies, grandaunts and during my work, chores and rendered, based on my own experience in practicing various forms of physical, intellectual, work organization and leadership, in his book democracy and social justice—the future of humanity, I highlighted the sentence "the organic unity between the various sides of labor". Work in a circle in chains in a moving and spiral-shaped auto moving, whose horizontal projection is continually increase, resulted in the conclusion of dialectic in terms of its efficiency.

Meditating on the way of looking at work by various historical personalities, intellectual history as the source of all riches, and on some theses on "wealth", and perceived work and wealth as part of the dialectic, we concluded the necessity of looking at work and in terms of usefulness to man and humanity as a whole society and sometimes even evil of such a size that endanger life on Earth.

Making use of dialectic thinking and reason, formulize thesis: "the wealth evolves, it is the result of the dialectic unity of organic inputs in moving and auto movement dialectic, active and decisive role of live work, useful to both humans and human society as a whole". Dynamics of some wealth of a country is based on the degree of realization of capital live humans, exploiting useful and beneficial to both humans and human society as a whole. The use of live human capital for research, design and production of technical military: atomic bombs, chemical, bacteriological and technique for transportation of their preconceived distances: airplanes, missiles, tanks, cars, stifle dialectic riches required dialectic primary needs and social and spiritual man. Demonstrates that man, though it is equipped by articulated language and thinking and being and a social being, however, thinking of his dialectic generated by intellectual human labor dialectic, imaginary thinking, which tends to infinity, he managed to get it done on humans to perceive what is this world here on Earth, the world has managed to collect what is the role and the rationale behind him in this world rather, they should be the role and the rationale behind him in this world. There is only one explanation, which makes man to be what it is and not let it be what it should be: "force intellectual man still failed to help the man to auto-knowing; He managed to discover the secret of unknown cause, nature and human flesh ".

My attempt to know the man, the man why do what they do and what not to do what they should do, as it forces man by characterize they possess and what laws are their own, I do believe that if intellectual force of man will be channeled, directed to deep process knowledge of nature and human flesh then the human dialectic and through him, dialectic of human society will be placed on a road asana, unimpeded and without many brakes. What will make the great leap in human thinking dialectics is the possible beneficial influence on the relationship between the proportion of the forces of good and evil forces share, so that this report (R) should only be of the form:

R= FG/EF >1 and from step to step

$R_n > R_{n-1} > R_{n-2} > \ldots > R_1 > R\,1>$, where R_n go to ∞, which means that the share of the good forces tends to maximize the share of evil forces, and tends to minimize ø.

This phenomenon and the process is possible with only one condition, to charge the man, that by itself, cannot-and "select of the laws that it dominates only on those that are beneficial to both his human and society as a whole and the environment", that he himself cannot improve the ratio between the weight of evil forces (P.F.R), so this report (R) should only be of the form:

R= FG/EF >1

For this reason, the intelligentsia, which benefit from a concentrated intellectual force in the form of "intellectual force vector, perceived the man by his forces and laws, as kind and fire should be organizations summoned Moldovan authorities that she is to be incorporated into a" human shield of protection "that will help him to become the man from what is in what should be.

"The shield of protection" shall be located around and help those people who occupy positions of leadership and organization in the State administration, which by decision and their power can generate both good things and bad things among the human species. "The shield of protection" should be composed of living cells licensed intellectual force concentrated form of a "vector intellectual force" able to magnetizes the entire intellectual force of the human species or at least so far as is necessary to change the nature and the human flesh. Makes me think that this "protective shield" should have a name that the form of concentrated and its contents to generate and dialectical process of organization and management of human society both nationally and statewide—globally—the whole human species. This "protective shield" called: "the Supreme Forum of the human species", have, in turn, subsidiaries in all countries of the globe, what might be called the "Supreme Forum of the citizens of country X".

Priority and fundamental task of the Forum of the human species, aided by its subsidiaries, are changing the nature and the human flesh. This will lead to the interruption of the chain of social injustice, the chain measured in thousands of years, will generate the broadening of Heaven in the world of here, for the entire human species and the exclusion of hell in which survives a considerable segment of the human species.

If not it will proceed in this way, the dialectic of human intellectual labor will vary and the dialectic of means of mass destruction, and the laws of man and human forces can cause the man political leader with power of decision in the State to act in the direction of using the potential of mass destruction, which is so large that may lead to the death of life on Earth.

If the human mind will help man to auto-know and informed to contend with himself to become what is in what should be, then the organic unity between the inputs and the dialectic of the organic unity of production factors may provide for the entire human species happiness "primary" and "diversified happiness" in a dynamic growth. The human species will fall under the era of historical wisdom and reasoning, age where terrorism will become historical as a remembrance of what man is able to do because of a psychological and steps of polluted wars between peoples will sink once and for all.

Chapters IX-XVIII, chapters of this book to work, were presented in the book man, let's change the world, and in this book were again presented with small changes, considering that can influence social consciousness a triad» spiritual representatives to initiate, organize and lead a peaceful world revolutionary process, beneficial to each class, each small or large national State rich or poor, regardless of the disposition of social-economic development is located.

We could say that these chapters, with slight modifications, constitutes a "recycling" useful and beneficial to humans in order to raise awareness in addition to what has to be done to ensure that the work they provide is only rational and creative, for the benefit of organic unity "man, human society and the environment".

CHAPTER XVIII

THESES CONCERNING CHANGES OF NATURE AND HUMAN FLESH FROM WHAT IS NORMAL AND SHOULD BE RATIONALLY

Theses concerning changes of nature and human flesh at the level of social division of labor: politics, religious and science whose historical dialectics of role playing what is at the level of a triad» psyche as normal and should be used judiciously. This role of a triad» psyche: politics, religious and scientific will be to organize and lead the human society, seen as a "universal" construction site, in a process of continuous modernization, so that "man step", "particular of General" and "living cell" of General to enter into a process of peaceful revolutionary nature, which was beneficial to each class, the social revolutionary process, once started, is always directly proportional to the dialectic and the dialectic of human intellectual labor.

To the characterization of theses submitted formulation is: "Man to man is a being biologic-social thinking and language provided with articulated, owner of four forces: physical strength, intellectual force, the force of good and evil force and dominated by a number of objective and subjective law."

This characterization of human knowledge and perception opens the perspective of human society by his "particular", which is his "living cell ".

1. **Sentence on physical and intellectual force of human labor**. Physical and intellectual strength force of man is in a "live" human capital. Demo made on the existence of these two forces: the physical force that is relatively consistent from person to person and does not exceed a certain limit, and intellectual force, which is characterized by the fact that through the process of speaking and writing sometimes accumulate part of the total, from man to man, from generation to generation, with the trend of development potential to infinity ($\rightarrow \infty$) leads to the conclusion that, however, "living" human capital, currently always dialectics. Or, "living" human capital is the premise of all forms of capital known to man.

"Live" Human Capital is found in a latent form and he can become dormant in active, functional status, through work. The transformation of "live" from capital to capital form latent live in action, functional, process is very complicated and unwieldy because he always evolving because of intellectual labor dialectics dialectic and the LABOR by which "capital live" becoming dormant in Active status, functional, is based on dependent "art to organize and lead to the three levels: the family company and the State administration in the first two levels: organizational and management—family and the company—«capital living» art function is used to organize and lead the family company, respectively. Harnessing capital live available to human society at a time is dependent on the function of art to organize and lead the human society by those of my invested it do so.

Life experience that highlights the dialectic between "live human" capital and labor "dialectic of organization and management at the level of State administration" appears an increasing "gap" with the evil consequences of recovery capital live, only that at one point, the contradiction between capital and work the dialectic of organization and management at the level of State administration makes the gap to take the proportions. Such economic crises arise, political, social and unemployment, inflation occurs with evil consequences on the entire human society. But many appear great intellectuals that characterize the unemployment and its consequences, comment on the economic crises, a veritable "Army" of great intellectuals who use thinking and intelligence to comment from infinite crisis economic-social and political. Nothing did wrong in it but that does not solve the problem . . . crises continue unabated, the consequences are diversifying, leading to despair of a great potential the human species. What to do? The harmonized capital ratio of dialectic and the labor of man live organizing and leadership at the level of State administration, namely the harmonized work of said organization and management at the level of State administration with the dialectic of live human capital. How? The answer will be given in a different sentence . . .

2. The sentence of the labor force of good and evil force set up as a dualism of good and evil. The demo made the existence of the force of good and evil force in the human brain leads us to the idea that these two forces of humans, find themselves in a process of internal struggle continues, beating when one, when another with minimum breaks a tie which generates a report ("R") between the forces of good weight (F.G) and share of evil forces (E.F.) form:

R= FG/EF = 1; >1; <1 the knowing of this report are very important

According with this report ("R"), when people do good things, when bad things in the relationship between them and in relation to the environment. The existence of the forces of good and evil forces in the form of dualism of good and evil generate both things beneficial and evil things to the three forms of organization and management: the family company and directors of State if the household both good things and bad things are generally resolved within the family, at the level of company things start to get more complicated when F.G.> E.F. good benefits, the company personnel differed; all differential treatment acts on the staff of the company and the F.G. <E.F., respectively F.G > E.F. With regard to the existence of the dualism of good and evil at the level of State administration, those who organize and lead the company at a time where F.G. > E.F. situation of the society members even if not granted equally to all members of society, however, at the level of life is improve. When F.G <. E.F., respectively F.G. > E.F., the consequences will incur only a certain category of people. In this way, in human history, appear on a particular stage of humanity, social injustices, which, once raised, remain as a historical chain measured in thousands of years. What to do because of social injustices to disappear from his life and work of the human species? Influenced by "R" between F.G and E.F. to be always "> 1". How? The answer will be given to another sentence.

3. **The Sentence to the laws of man.** The history of the human species reveals that man is dominated by a series of laws:

a. the Law of accumulation of wealth) (wealth) at any cost and by any means, without limitation, regulations;
b. the law of thirst appetite, power, law no limit;
c. the law of selfishness;
d. the dualism law of rational and irrational;
e. the dualism law of activeness and laziness;
f. the dualism law of depth and superficial;
g. the dualism law of optimism and pessimism;
h. the dualism law of forgiveness and revenge;
i. the dualism law of patient and inpatient;
j. the law differentiated facilities (equipment to paint, sculpt, create literary, the Endowment is to organize and lead an economic and social activity or policy);
k. the law differentiated the pleasures (the pleasure of being the head, to be appreciated, to be heard) and so on.

Human laws Act conjugated human forces throughout his life, independent of human will and desire.

The action of immunoglobulin of human forces and laws with which man/it dominates defines the nature and human nature. At one point, nature and human nature are highlights to be in relations between people:

- ♮ When: "man to man";
- ♮ When "man Fox devious manipulation and likes to man";

↳ When "man versus man" crook

↳ When "man versus man killer".

In the slave era, relations between people were prevalent in the form: "killer man vs. man" so that the slaves were treated their masters with a ferocious cruelty held slaves bound in chains, he struggled, he turned red with iron, sold like any other tool, actually slaves were considered "tool speaking ", and when it opposed the judgments of the owner of slaves and kills.

Historical, man, like nature and temperament evolve benefic, so it plays in the era of feudal land owners never held on serfs bound in chains, were no longer burned with red hot iron, no more were killed and were no longer sold in fairs; but they were kept in serfdom.

In capitalism, man, nature and threads, as making up the dialectic to be more "man to man", "devious manipulation and Fox man likes towards human's duffer", "man versus man" and, rarely, "man versus man killer", dividing unjust wars.

In socialism begin to dominate mode of being that kind of man, and fire, so it is more: "man to man".

History facts reveal, however, that although the man, the kind and nature, however, is beneficial and nature's nature does not change radically in relations between people, so that at one time, reaching a tipping point, which cannot be exceeded, the critical point is generated by the nature of ownership of the means of production, any pre-existing human element-Earth, created by man and unfairly become the private property of some families of large and very large. Existence of socio-economic system of socialism, falls at a time of world-wide level may reveal that nature and human nature is a legality hardly perceptible, generated by the action of the conjugate base of the human forces and laws with which man/it dominates the relationship between people and that can change radically as long as it is known as "the law of nature and human flesh".

4) **Sentence on "Law of nature and human flesh".** The law of nature and human flesh is generated by the action of the conjugate base of the human forces and laws "with/man that it dominates" action that generates two processes: a process of ") compasses psychological" invisible and poorly identified which directs nature and human nature, and it works independent of human will and desire, creating relations between people; b) process of an invisible "nets" and hard "identified by the strap conjugated action between the human forces with/and laws of human it dominates", which "enchain psychologically" the man to evolve dialectic as kind and yarn of what is normal and should be used judiciously since it is packed with thought.

These two processes generated by the action of immunoglobulin of human forces and laws with which man/it dominates human thinking psychologically "pollute" and a "lock" in the "ecological" of pollutants generated by the action of the conjugate base of the human forces and laws with which man/it dominates. This "imagination" of the law of nature and human flesh, and those two processes generated by the action of immunoglobulin of human forces and laws with which man/it dominates is confirmed by the experience of the human species.

5) Sentence on the State of the world in time and space. For thousands of years, "State of the world" in time and space was perceived by herself. Big thinkers of the time, concerned about the "State of the world" of her time living, socio-economic "orders" that passed that humanity, in which humanity found, sensitive to what it characterizes the good and bad, and the relationships between people, and they imagine that by democracy and the right to think freely, by changing the nature of ownership of the means of production in the private property owned the life and work of the human species may enter into normality, in conformity with the laws of nature. Life experience has shown that these are necessary means which can lead to a change in his State of the world "'and that changing the State of the world may be known as" absolute truth ",", source and engine "which gave his State of the world and give form and content in time and space! This "absolute truth", "source and engine", which gave his State of the world and give form and content, it was discovered by the great thinkers of the time, thousands of years, and there is no known now, in the beginning of the Millennium III. Only this can explain why their efforts to devise theses and ways leading to the normalization of the life of the human species, have led only to the improvement of social injustice, the problem remains unknown. Regarded human society as "General" of a "private" and "particular" and perceived as a "cell" of the "General", "human society as a whole", "imagination" you can realize more than likely, that along with "absolute truth", "source and engine" which gave his State of the world and give form and content in time and space to be searched and "particular of General", and "the living cell" of General, which is "concrete man". "Concrete Man" is "particular of General" and "living cell" of the "General". Or, the man charged as: "a biological being with social thought, in possession of four forces and dominated by a series of laws", of the elements necessary to discover the "law of nature and nature's," which, once you know it, you can begin the process of image searches is what man is in his relations with his fellows; You can start the process as it searches forward what it characterized as a kind of human society and nature. And after many searches to get to the conclusion that what characterizes him as a kind man, and fire, shall be forwarded as a "magnetic wave" of human society through the work of the ORGANIZATION and MANAGEMENT at the LEVEL of STATE ADMINISTRATION. Hence the conclusion that changing the State of the world of what is in what you want to involve practicing business organization and management at the level of State administration always in line with the dialectic and the labor of man intellectual dialectic.

6. **Sentence on socio-economic system of capitalism.** The disposition of social-economic capitalist, once formed, evolved in time and space, always dialectic, but with many and diverse social wrongs. The disposition of social-economic development of capitalism has accumulated historical important intellectual force potential and benefit from many of the quantitative accumulation of human life experience that can and should be used, in the knowledge of the facts, the law of dialectic, which use it consciously, creator and rationally in order to ensure the evolution of the dialectic of capitalism to abundance and well-being in General, towards a social order "democracy and social justice dialectical opposition". It stand the harmonization of the factors of production: Labor, capital, accumulated with nature and ultimate aim of giving a human walking society in which social classes to join in a process beneficial to the whole revolutionary peaceful human species, to human, "dialectic as kind and fire". Particular man being "General" and "living cell" figure, "human society as a whole" by his dialectic, as kind and fire, will begin the process of dialectic human society, namely the socio-economic system of capitalism towards a social—economic order democracy and social justice dialectical opposition, order social-economic crisis without job seekers, without economic, social and political. Terrorism and unjust wars disappear from human life once and for all. Relations between the people take a new content both within the national-State and within the framework of universal-global. Human dialectic as nature and fire, and, through this process, the revolutionary dialectic of human society, namely the dialectic of social-economic and legal system of the opposition social democracy and justice, the peaceful opposition, the revolutionary process beneficial to each class, will be achieved by: dialectic of organizing and managing labor at the level of State administration, which will establish scientific research studies. They will be drawn up by the large intellectual personalities: philosophers, psychologists, theologians, economists, historians, and others, who will carry out an activity within the framework of scientific research institute profiled on knowledge and perception of man, the nature and organic yarn, unity between the particular concrete man, "", and "general", "human society as a whole", the perception of human society as a "universal" worksite in a continuous modernization. The modernization will be projects of tactics and strategies designed to institute of scientific research on the analysis and knowledge sections "law of nature and human flesh", the organic link between the perception of "the law of nature and human nature and social-economic law orders, General, special concrete man".

7. **Sentence on socio-economic system of socialism-communism.** The disposition of social-economic development of socialism-communism, prepared istoriceşte by many intellectuals, great thinkers of the time, was seen by Marx and Engels as a dialectical evolution of socio-economic orders the sense that after disposition of social-economic capitalism will follow a different socio-economic order upper capitalism which they called a Socialist Communist in first phase, in the end. This social economic order has been developed by Marx and Engels as feasible by a party of the working class, to organize and lead the process through the so-called

"revolutionary dictatorship of the proletariat". Lenin, the Russian philosopher and politician, a great intellectual and a great

Organizer, appropriating and phrases and points of view of Marx and Engels, initiated, organized and led the revolutionary process of 1917 in Russia, which was the world's first socialist State, and after the second world war, socialism-communism to take the form of social-economic order at world level.

Existence of socio-economic and legal system at the level of world-wide has revealed new information about the process of knowledge "absolute truth", "source and engine" which gave his State of the world and give form and content in time and space. He highlighted that socio-economic order is characterized not by itself but by its "particular", "concrete man", and "living cell" of "general human society as a whole". The existence of both social and economic orders, perceived as a "huge" laboratory of fundamental scientific research on knower truth absolute, source and engine that gives the form and content of the world in time and space, he had a particular historical importance, highlighting that the disposition of social-economic capitalist continues to evolve, that dialectic and the socialist-communist, once formed, evolved and she always dialectics. He highlighted that both capitalism and socialism are many and various advantages but also various disadvantages and especially important is that they have revealed that their dialectical evolution in line with the dialectic of human intellectual labor and with the experience of living collections of quantitative human species is dependent on the human dialectic as "nature and temperament", by human thinking "greening" of pollutants generated by the conjugate action between the human forces with/and laws which it dominates. This "giant laboratory" scientific research has revealed that occurred historical disposition of social-economic capitalist and socialist-communist have a common denominator: "concrete man", as nature and temperament. He, "the man", as a concrete and wires, "particular of General" and "living cell" figure, is one who, by his forces and laws, give form and content of a socio-economic orders in time and space. The dialectic of "human nature", as a concrete and wires, the common denominator of the two orders socio-economic historical, will lead to one upper both capitalism and socialism, cumulating to a maximum possible benefits. The process will be long duration and will be peaceful in nature, each beneficial groundbreaking social class, and each State national small or large, rich or poor. Violent social revolutions, which have generated historically dialectic of human society, social revolutions become dialectical, peaceful world in the process of moving and auto moving always dialectic and in line with the dialectic of human intellectual labor; "thinking" human "polluted" with many and various nuisances arising from co-operations between human action with/and forces laws of human whitch it dominates, it starts to get "auto perception"

The thinking of many great intellectuals of the time, big thinkers, across from the historical State of the world in time and space, enters a new stage, qualitatively superior, so scientific, by its leaders, unable to give politics theses and ways to govern the Organization and management of the human society with the objective of the human species as Supreme lives in normalcy, in conformity with the laws of nature.

8. **Sentence of human thinking**. The great German idealist philosopher Hegel said cognoscibility world, stating the thesis that things, phenomena and dialectical thinking evolves and progressively thinking that leads to the dialectic of the knowledge of the absolute truth. Marx and Engels, German philosophers, have extended the materialistic law of dialectic thinking, things and phenomena and human society by formulating dialectical materialism thesis and the historical materialism have stated thesis that the disposition of capitalist social-economic development and it is limited in terms of history and that it will follow the other superior, appointed by its socialist-communist. In the books "democracy and social justice—the future of humanity", "the dialectic of human and human society", "dude, let's change the world" and "Nature and human nature «compass»—targeting human society development", the author demonstrates that the dialectic thinking there are two sources: 1 the intellectual force) dialectic of human speech through the process, the accumulate and writing part, sometimes totally from human to human from generation to generation, with the trend of development potential to infinity ($\rightarrow \infty$) and 2) quantitative build-up of experience of life and work of the human species. The fact that human thinking for over 2,500 years, great thinkers of the time of historical and imagined "State of the world" by "the effect of the case" due to the lack of an intellectual labor potential of necessary size "perception" of the case which gives the State the world form and content in time and space. Due to the fact that collections and quantitative experience life and work of the human species would have been sufficient to generate the absolute truth "knowledge", "source and engine" which gave his State of the world and give form and content in time and space. The fact that the existence of n-set for major intellectual personalities, big thinkers, object of analysis, in order to verify that human thinking led to the knowledge of "absolute truth", "source and engine" which gave his State of the world and give form and content in time and space, is due to "psychological" thinking polluted with many and various nuisances generated by the action of immunoglobulin of human forces and laws with which man/it dominates. "Psychological" Thinking has been polluted to appear several trends in the way of thinking and acting of the intelligentsia, when there are "huge" laboratory of fundamental scientific research, which offered the possibility of checking what is done to ensure that the "State of the world" to enter into a process of dialectical evolution in line with the dialectic of human intellectual labor, namely the life of the human species to normalcy in line with the laws of nature: a group, that of the Socialist world, criticizing capitalism and socialism, and another idealize group, that of the capitalist world, defending capitalism and criticizing socialism . . . and what deserves much attention is that scientific through its leaders, "the collapse of communism" at world level, while remaining in their country's leadership, mentions the theses and points of view that "shadow" the way human society dialectics and endangering the very fate of human life on Earth".

This scientific, due to "psychological pollution of thinking", is not sensitive to the fact that after the dissolution of a military bloc, at Warsaw, the other block has continued to develop both intensive and extensive, and the history of the facts reveals that stimulates the concerns of many other countries of the Haganah with the means of mass destruction. Production of means of mass destruction with a single value of usage—destruction of lives and collections of forces of production, by means of a possible atomic war may lead to "ecological catastrophe", putting in danger the lives of the human species on Earth.

9. Sentence on how to work the politics, religious and scientific, forms of social consciousness. a) Politics. The leaders of the political class who hold power in the State, the practical work of the Organization and management of society on the basis of the so-called platform-program of the party. Platform aimed at improving program in his State of the nation, but that history facts reveal that although political parties are rotated periodically to power, State of the nation remains relatively the same, with many and diverse social wrongs. This state of affairs is due to the "law of nature and human flesh", which is the common denominator of all men, so leaders and political class. Alternation of political parties in the organization and management of the company has only a single character: moving, downsizing of power from one group to another, the fate of the majority of citizens of the country remained relatively the same, hence the conclusion that "the law of nature and human flesh" cancels the advantages of democracy periodical elections. The fight between parties loses at some point the meaning. The leaders of the political class out of date practice work and malevolent human society for dialectic. Election slogans of the leaders of the political class have one purpose and sense: to influence voters on whom to choose and no matter whom they choose, results "law converge to nature and the human natures". Why this situation? Because human society is a "universal" site designed to "build" the most "complex construction of the world", or, to organize and lead a "universal" site, "human society as a whole", in a continuous process of modernization, it is impossible to achieve on the basis of "political" program platforms. The construction of a human society is much more complicated than the construction of a combined steel plant, a chemical compound, or block "skyscraper", a cosmic ship etc. These structures shall be undertaken on the projects, which are based on the scientific research institute profiled on made in different areas, depending on the nature of the building, where works of high quality materials specialists connoisseurs of art and technology, the objective of the Organization and management, the objective and so on.

Construction of human society, the most complex construction on Earth, in a continuous process of modernization is based only platforms-political program made at random one or several members of a political party.

Thinking psychologically polluted "by pollutants generated by the action of the conjugate base of the human forces and laws with which man/it dominates, at the level of politics, social consciousness form, makes the leaders of the political class to practice such labor organization and management of human society, that, in addition to the fact that it does not lead to the dissolution of social injustice, but also ecological disasters and preparing" "particularly severe for a substantial segment of the human species in the form of wars and the size of their evil has the trend of evolution of the dialectical bad to worse, with the danger, God forbid!, to put human society to "deny" . . . Human life is in very great danger because of the arms race, and politics, form of social consciousness, does not escape because it is "psychological" handcuffed in a "mesh" invisible and perceptible, "hard strapped" by the action of human immunoglobulin with forces and laws of human/it dominates and acting independently of the will and desire of man. The man political leader should be aided by scientific form of social consciousness in order to make the work of organizing and leading to the construction site of the "universal" in order to enter into normality, in line with the work carried out in the building of things much simpler. To enter the legality! b) Religious, a form of social consciousness. Representatives of religious worship are no exception to the "law of nature and human flesh" but that their work is originally a force exterior to man: "divine strength", which he presented in chip and just inventing and "Heaven" and "Hell" in the world of man, the scarecrow then not to do bad things in relations with their peers, which makes the nature of human nature and of improvement in beneficial effect. If thinking of religious worship would not be polluted with pollutants generated by psychological action of the conjugate base of the human forces and laws with which man/it dominates, and it would show that both "Heaven" and "Hell", existing in the world here, are "opera man" generated by "the law of nature and human flesh", the law that you don't know and therefore cannot be charged anything. We think we say a fact stating that religious does not practice a dialectical work beneficial to humans only because of the "psychological" by thinking polluted pollutants generated by the action of the conjugate base of the human forces and laws with which man/it dominates, but also because religion is a dogma. The evil of the strenuous work of representatives of religious worship is to influence those sufferers not to act to remedy social wrongs, which means "Hell" in which survives a considerable potential of the human species. If the religious, a form of social consciousness, "psychological pollution of ecological thinking", representatives of religious worship, large recipients of a considerable potential of intellectual labor, would find the necessary change of tactics and strategies from a religion's dogma in a science whose content may influence the radical nature and human nature, which is one of the most important Sciences leading to the normalization of the life of the human species in line with the laws of nature. Religious, a form of social consciousness, would become, through its representatives, a great support for the political conditions under which their thinking would be "ecologist of psychological pollution". And at the level of religious, as at the level of politics, it is most needed the help of the form scientific, psyche, which through the specifics of their work is the generator of dialectic human intellectual labor, and to discover the secret, because the State of the world with many and diverse social wrongs, and to discover the secret, because of "Heaven" and "Hell" in the world here. c) Scientific, a form of social consciousness, under pressure from the "law of nature and human flesh", although it is the bearer of the highest potential of intellectual labor, however, his thinking has generated the process knowledge and perception of nature and human flesh, so for thousands of years "the law of nature and human flesh" remained unknown.

The action of immunoglobulin of human forces and laws with which man/it dominates it "psychological" on man compassing belonging to scientific from practical work of scientific research in a specific area of activity, which is very good for human society as a division of labor scientific on different areas of activity, facilitates and accelerates the discovery of many physical laws, chemical, biological, and mechanical, etc., experienced some implemented in technique and technology, leading to continuous progress in the life and work of the human species. The fact that scientific does not work "general welfare" galore and not his fault, the fault must be attributed to politics, which has the object of man's work and human society as a whole, and political, in turn, should be pardoned because he is not acting in bad faith to do what they do.

The leaders of the political class, almost without exception, I want to change for the better life history of the human species, that fail to work for the Organization and management of human society, such as to benefit from the technological and technical progress, in equal measure, the entire human species is due to the "law of nature and human flesh". However, this law was not and is not yet known, the political form of social consciousness, and what the surprise is that the scientific did not succeed, for thousands of years, to discover this law of nature and human flesh. He succeeded because "thinking" representatives "scientific is" psychological action of polluted conjugate of human forces and laws with which man/it dominates and the "psychological" compassing to be narrow and even lock in giving due research on finding the cause of State secrecy, the world in time and space, with many and diverse social wrongs.

Labor dialectics of human intellectual and quantitative build-up of experience of life and work of the human species, will form the basis of the guidelines of scientific and to the knowledge and perception of nature and human flesh '". And since that time scientific can and should influence the politics and even religious to practice a work which would lead to progress and general well-being.

With express emphasis that the role is to organize and lead the human society is the responsibility of "social" consciousness a triad»: politics, religious and scientific, and the Organization and management of the company, perceived as the most advanced building in the world, cease to be carried out after program-political platform. Leadership and organization of management to the construction site "universal" modernization of human society will be made on the basis of studies of scientific research and design of tactics and strategies designed to give a direction of development of the world's dialectical evolution in line with the dialectic of human intellectual force in the lead role with scientific.

Scientific, a form of social consciousness, it will be all the time concerned about the "greening" thinking psychological pollution generated by the action of the conjugate base of the human forces and laws with which man/it dominates and will even block brake and the emergence of theses and views of scientific generating confusion, noxious seeds in dialectic of human society, as it was, for example, and the condemnation of communism order because particular it has committed some mistakes and makes you look what he has done good "special-General", during the Socialist social-economic and legal system.

And what you need to give thought about scientific is that, in addition to the fact that it is "coregent" in discovery of truth, indeed, "the source and engine" which gives the State the world form and content in time and space, and invents all sorts of feedback concerning the advantages and disadvantages of a socio-economic order, summing up his experience another evil orders and denaturant in many cases the reality and on the other, a "splitting". Who serves such a tactic and strategy of some representatives of science?

My creed is that scientific, not in all cases, such a tactic and strategy with "bad faith", but more because of a psychological "polluted mentality" of pollutants generated by the action of the conjugate base of the human forces and laws with which man/it dominates.

10. **Sentence the draft charged.** The work is hence who created man; detach him from among the animals. The work is one that, through the dialectic, as the efficiency of the intellectual force of dialectic human generated process of dialectic human from the stage of "primitive man" the man always modernized, always perfected, always civilized, with peaks pyramid of people scholars.

The dialectic of human being "concrete man" and "living cell" of the "General" human society as a whole ", resulted in the emergence of forms of social organization—" race "," tribes "," national States "and, once raised, they have come a way always historical dialectics, passing through several forms of social organization: common primitive, Native American, feudalism, capitalism and the emergence of socialism-communism which has survived to level world-wide with capitalism for about 45 years in an atmosphere known as the "cold war" due to "psychological pollution of thinking".

The work is hence without which man and society cannot exist.

Economic and philosophical notion of work i was concerned about the many great intellectuals of the time, and the philosopher, Economist and German political man interpreted Marx and characterized the work complex and multilateral.

In the book "democracy and social justice—the future of mankind", the author of the work as it is in reality and so:

1) Physical workplace;
2) Intellectual work; and
3) Work organization and leadership

And demonstrates scientifically that the organizing and driving work is the most important side of work. It unites the intellectual and physical work, primary production factor and active, with production likely factor, a factor of primary production and passive and with inputs derived. Work organization and management is one which transforms the manpower physical and intellectual work force in a "child" live ", a premise of the creation of economic capital, in a live and functional.

Work organization and leadership at the level of State administration and the feature has to be generated by the process of social injustices, which, when raised, were maintained as a historic chain measured in thousands of years, due account being taken of the origin and nature of the Act "and human flesh". Work organization and leadership at the level of State Administration has generated and the process of the work (malefic human society), which, in addition to the fact that it requires a considerable workload for the concrete living of an amount of usage, is aimed at the destruction of economic goods accumulated, death and mutilation of many human lives and cause pollution of the environment. It directs the development of human society to a "ecological catastrophe", prepared step by step, through the modernization of weapons of mass destruction (chemical, and atomic weapons bacteriological), which, in the case of a war, can lead to the extinction of life on Earth. Avoiding a "deluge of fire" implies "greening polluted psychological thinking" of pollutants generated by the conjugate action between the human forces with/and laws which it dominates.

Greening the psychological pollution of human thinking of pollutants generated by the action of the conjugate base of the human forces and laws with which man/it dominates will generate the type of a concrete and abstract only beneficial human and human society as a whole, and the capital of living available to human society at a time will be fully exploited, rationally and creator for the benefit of every Member of the human species.

Superior recovery, rational and creative capital of the "living" human will generate the abolition of social injustice arising in the slave era, maintained as a historic chain whose length is for thousands of years and opens the perspective of historical life and activity of the human species would enter into normality, in conformity with the laws of nature, terrorism and wars will go into "the sunset "the national security of each State, will begin to be in total safety and without exceptions.

11. The Sentence. Harmonization of social class-level happiness. Happiness is a philosophical concept is to be levied complex and multidirectional. In the modern Romanian language dictionary ", Editura Academiei Republicii Populare Romania, 1958, happiness is characterized as" an intense and full of Thanksgiving, due mostly to satisfy an ambitions "(p. 299).

Seen at the level of the three social classes—poor and rich, middle—we can find that happiness is a philosophical concept that differs radically from one social class to social class. Thus, if the poor social class happiness consists essentially in primary needs: food, clothing, housing, at the level of middle class happiness takes whole other dimensions, and to the rich class is happiness and more diversified.

Viewed the three social classes through the "law of nature and human flesh", law common to all the people of the world, we can conclude that happiness is dependent on the level of wealth possessed, so that if the poor social class happiness begins with primary insurance needs—food, clothing and housing—the middle class and rich notion of happiness is quite another. However, it is Important to all social classes that happiness is determined by the nature and effectiveness of the work carried out. Or, at the level of poor social class, "capital live" available to families is always unable to exploit his rational, that factor of production nature (Earth) and factors of production, the accumulated capital, derivatives are privately owned Middle families and particularly of the rich, the poor are likely to capitalize "partly" live in the capital only if the private owners of capital accumulated Earth and offers them a job. However, the law of nature and human flesh "psychological" rich compassing and medium class to accumulate wealth/wealth without limit, the wealthy and the Middle does not concern the fate of the poor. At the level of State administration is sensitive to the fate of the class involved in part through various supporting leverages: unemployment benefits for those employed (the unemployed), aid for maintaining housing, allowances for young children and The improvement of the social status can be viewed and even bi-directional multidirectional. Thus, social aid, although partially improve the living conditions of impoverished social class members, however, they live each day unhappy, safety day tomorrow is always uncertain, the families of the impoverished social class, basically, not like any of the minor form of happiness: the possibility of ensuring that the necessities—food, clothing and housing at a decent level using even partially live up to their disposal.

The parade is made of so-called social aid, in some countries, in the sense that they provide a decent standard of living, reveals how "polluted the human thinking is psychological," which, in place to deal with the harmonization of the factors of production labor and capital accumulated, nature, and that harmonization to ensure the rational exploitation of living and creative capital available to human society at a time social aid, invents, besides the fact that the beneficiary does not bring happiness of families, social aid and "push" these families to how to be animals because, if the work was therefore

He broke away on the man from the animals, unlabored it coming man how to be. And what is very important and noteworthy is the fact that the factor of production, the production factor and passive, in order to be kept in operation to a higher quality level, requires a substantial amount of physical labor, intellectual work and work of the Organization and management, with much higher than is the potential 'existing capital live "not even partially, idle!

Harmonization of happiness social classes are an issue of essentials, it has many and various beneficial effects on the State of the world in time and space; it becomes beneficial to every social class and so also for human society as a whole.

The concerns of many great intellectuals of this on the economic growth and sustainable economic development are not possible without harmonization of factors of production—work, nature and capital accumulated. Harmonization of the factors of production can be achieved as long as "human psychological thinking remains polluted" by the action of immunoglobulin of human forces and laws with which man/ it dominates, where the findings conclude that: "the ecology of human thinking which pollute the psychological pollutants" is the priority of priorities, generating and the process of harmonizing the social classes happiness.

12. The Sentence on harnessing rational and creative living capital available to human society at a time.

Harmonization of the factors of production, work, nature and capital accumulated, prerequisite for bringing out the "live" capital, is a logical necessity generated by the law of dialectic thinking, things and phenomena. However, dialectic thought is most easily perceptible to humans, by two springs. A spring is the dialectic of human intellectual labor, which through the process of speaking and writing builds up partially, sometimes totally from human to human, from generation to generation, with the trend of development potential to infinity ($\rightarrow \infty$) attended, as a source, and collections of quantitative experience life and work of the human species, as a result, resulting in the "live" of human capital currently always dialectics.

Therefore, human thought evolves dialectic, as well as live, and the source of capital and their dialectic engine is common: the dialectic of human intellectual labor and collections of quantitative practical experience of life and work of the human species, hence the conclusion that the dialectic between thought and dialectics "live" human capital, there is an organic. Normal and reasonable would be to influence the "mutually beneficial", only that both "human thought", and "live" human capital, which is in the law of dialectic thinking things, phenomena, and highlights the existence and internal forces that find themselves in a continuous "war". No "thinking" or "human capital" cannot live in normality often, in conformity with the laws of nature, because the causes being generated by the "law of nature and human flesh" which rises and the engine in action by forces of man with man and the laws that/it dominates.

The exit of the "maze" means both "greening of human thinking which pollute the psychological pollutants", and the harmonization of the factors of production which are found in an internal contradiction arises from the nature of the dialectic of production factor, a factor of production work and active and productive factor, a factor of production nature primary, passive and static. Equation solving is the dialectic of Labor Organization and management in general, and at the level of State administration in line with the dialectic of human intellectual labor and with collections of quantitative practical experience of life and work of the human species. This is possible by practicing business organization and management based on scientific research studies developed in the institute of scientific research on the knowledge and perception of the profiled "law of nature and human flesh".

Harmonization of the production factors is being the secret which can lead to psychological pollution "greening" thinking and rational exploitation of living and creative human capital working always dialectics.

An ecologization of thinking "that pollute the psychological pollutants" can and must find the resources necessary for valorization rational and creative living capital available to human society, the burden of being awarded the "psyche a triad»: politics, religious and scientific", which, through the Supreme Forum of the human species and the institutes of scientific research on the knowledge and perception of the "law of nature and human flesh can act upon the dialectic at work organization and leadership at the level of State administration so that the dialectic to be in line with the dialectic of human intellectual labor. Where and how rational action must be taken for the upgrading and creative living capital available to human society at a time? The answer will give workers in scientific research institutes and got stuck into the knowledge of the law "perception of nature and human flesh" and how it is transmitted from the concrete to the man "particular of general human society as a whole".

Some considerations on exploitation of rational and creative living capital available to human society at a time are important.

Harmonization of the factors of production, work, nature (Earth) and the cumulative capital—is the key to resolving, bringing out the rational creative capital live available to human society in time and space. However, the harmonization of the factors of production means, necessarily, as the Earth, the main factor of production, in his majority to be public property. This need should be in the interests of reason: the Earth is a pre-existing human element and is the home town of the entire human species, and that it unfairly became the private property of some families, especially large and very large. You can accept as rational private property of families on Earth, only small and very small, to ensure the rational exploitation of living capital available to the family, that the family shall ensure primary needs from a work factor of production practiced on Earth. You may accept as rational, private property on land, very small size and for families who have other sources and other means to harness the capital live available: a House, a small garden . . .

The vast majority of areas of land: arable, pasture and forests, necessarily should be public property of the entire human species on the territory of a country.

Why this view? For my invested to organize and lead the country to act operatively in uniting factor production work by a factor of production nature (Earth).

The factor of production ", although it is limited by a good organization and leadership at the level of State administration," living "human capital, in the evolution of his dialectic, finds hundreds of years the possibility of turning to its rational and creative.

The Earth, the primary factor of production and, in addition to that liability is limited, and subject to the phenomenon is more of a qualitative degradation due to human activities and natural factors (Frost, thaw, torrential, etc.).

Maintaining production factor to land a higher quality level requires a workload of such a size as if the entire active population of a country's workforce-to work exclusively on Earth would still be insufficient.

The Earth, as well is unknown, form of arable land, grassland and forest, and its landscape is furrowed with permanent water leaks and intermittent. Torrential rains and melting snow raised water flow flowing valleys with permanent drainage and intermittent, and at certain times of the year, the flow of water is of such a size that causes flooding, causing compromising results, damage to roads, houses and even death of some families, the annual damage to the country, in the concrete case of Romania, is of the order of many billions. A thinking "ecologizată of pollutants generated by the action of the conjugate base of the human forces and laws with/, which pollute human psychological" could lead to a process of prevention of floods: the water-works with permanent drainage and intermittent; by storing water in Lakes dammed small, medium, large and very large, depending on the configuration of the relief, lakes to be built in series "over water", from source to drain into the Black Sea, in the case of Romania; parallel to the direction of drainage water, where the topography permits, you can build small miscellaneous collections of water-bearing different materials: ground eroded wood, leaf, etc. that, periodically, you can remove and use primarily to restore the quality of the soil.

Waters stored in Lakes reservoir can be used as sources of drinking water source of electrical energy by hydro constructed on water discharges from the Lakes of accumulation and of course the waters stored in accumulation Lakes may be reserve for irrigation of agricultural areas and even for pastures and forests suffering in times of drought.

Intervention on the factor of production, in order to be exploited, requires a higher workload of such a size as integer 'live' human capital in each country can be fully exploited, rational and creative and lasting, we could say to infinity.

Our credo is that the triad psyche: politics, religious and scientific, forms of social consciousness, can become what they are as normal and rational should be, when they will know and perceive nature and human nature as a legit ate generated by the action of the conjugate base of the human forces and laws with which man/it dominates. Informed, will be able to get your hands on the steering wheel movement "targeting" and auto movement of human society in time and space, worn by the waves of dialectic, thereby making step dialectical starting the process of "conveyance" of the wave of life and work of dialectical characteristic of the human species within the meaning of "master", organize and conduct the only beneficial in work and in line with the dialectic of human intellectual labor. However, this requires entry of a triad» psyche "purgatory" human thought "ecologizării" of pollutants generated by the action of the conjugate base of the human forces and laws with which man/it dominates, is feasible if the dialectic of human intellectual labor and life experience in quantitative collections practice of the human species will generate process of dialectic thinking. It is important that the man must know and perceive as kind and fire, so that by their own forces and by laws that it dominates and "imagination" will start to charge that the action by the human forces and laws with which man/it dominates, it generates the type and nature, becoming a legit ate. They, promote the induction of particular into general, like a magnetic is to provide general for human society as a whole, generating socio-economic orders laws.

"Greening" the psychological thinking at the level of human consciousness a triad»: social politics, religious and scientific is the "key" to resolving, recovery "capital live" of the entire human species, the only capitalization only rational and creative.

"Greening" of human psychological thinking of pollutants generated by the action of the conjugate base of the human forces and laws with which man/it dominates is because representatives of a triad»: the political and social consciousness religious and, in particular, scientific are beneficiaries of a considerable potential labor scientific. Thus, the leaders of the political class are in their great majority, intellectual personalities of great prestige, and representatives of religious, priests, turn out to be, almost without exception, the best philosophers and psychologists goodies. As regards scientific, his work is "fount" and the dialectic of human intellectual labor and recipient of the largest potential of human intellectual labor. Hence the conclusion that the representatives of a triad» psyche are the conditions necessary to know and to be charged, the nature and fire forces and laws which it dominates.

Triad psyche: politics, religious and scientific may be organizations summoned Moldovan authorities that man is "compass" in his "law of nature and nature's" law that works independently of human desire and the will, that because of this law were social-historical injustices in the life of the human species. Religiously may also be organizations summoned Moldovan authorities that "Heaven" and "Hell", imagined to be in the world then, actually exist in the world here, "Heaven" for some, and "Hell" for others, who are a majority. Politics, religious and scientific, taking knowledge of how to charge the man as a being in possession of four biological social forces and dominated by a series of laws ", will auto perceived that" the source and engine "which gave rise to social injustice is found in the" human brain "in the form of dualism of good and evil. Therefore, "greening the psychological human thinking" of pollutants generated by the action of the conjugate base of the forces of good and evil forces in existence as the dualism of good and evil human laws which it dominates, should start the process of a report by "R" between F.G. and E.F. of the form:

$$R= FG/EF = >1$$

that remains always the same, which means the beginning of a process of revolutionary change in the nature and the human flesh.

13. **The Sentence on the army.** One of the big problems for complexes and to be "a thinking ecologizată" pollutants that a psychological "pollutes" is the role of the joint army.

Triad psyche: politics, religious and scientific, once you know and perceive the "absolute truth", "source and engine" which gives the form and content of the world in time and space, and the law of things, phenomena and dialectic thinking, knowledgeable, begin a process of profound revolutionary dialectic, evolution, never to be worn by the waves of dialectic man but to "steer" for the benefit of dialectic human society without barriers and without the brakes. Human dialectic as nature and temperament is a profoundly revolutionary process which changes the role and the rationale behind the army no longer is what it was throughout history human species and first generating considerable destruction of all genres: of life, property gained, pollution of the environment, stimulating the hatred and vengeance of those losers etc.

The role of the army will evolve, in terms of a dialectical process, peaceful world revolutionary related human dialectic as kind and fire, to no longer be what it was thousands of years, to no longer be what it is today, beginning of the Millennium III, i.e.:

1) when: "man to man";
2) when: "man Fox likes and devious manipulation to man";
3) when: "man to man" crook;
4) when: "man versus man killer"

But by being always only "man versus man" man. Human dialectic as nature and fire, will generate a peaceful world revolutionary process of human society as a whole, in that it will always evolve, without brakes and dialectical indoors and in direct proportion to the dialectic of human intellectual labor. In this peaceful world revolutionary process is the role of the army and with considerably "beating eternal" because of the nature and human nature is generated by the action of immunoglobulin of human forces and laws with which man/it dominates and which operate independently of the desire and the will of man. However, the revolutionary world peacefully must be perceived in a dialectical evolution which directs the development of human society to a new historic epoch and without terrorism, without wars, mankind will enter into "the era of wisdom and reasoning". Only this process deeply revolutionary peaceful in nature and involves a lot of work, physical, intellectual and organizational leadership. The current army, equipped with means of mass destruction and with the technical means to carry their preconceived, at distances and she begins a process of radical change in the purpose and role of its historical, becoming what is normal and should be used judiciously, "right hand" of a triad» psyche: politics, religious and scientific, which, through a body created, called the "Supreme Forum of the human species", will organize and lead the world revolutionary process-with the support of the army and the dialectical evolution.

The army, outnumbered, will increase considerably, and the rationale behind her role being to ensure national security through individual security-state of each families, but also in relations between States, due to the fact that the world is peaceful and revolutionary. The link between the armies will be of help and support each other, as needed, and the army in time and space will be equipped exclusively with weapons not only to reach a level that they cannot cause harm to the adjacent areas, and over time will become organized and led by a central command.

One of the essential tasks of the army will be to oversee, organize and lead the burdening working with international and national importance both nationally and internationally. For example: water projects with permanent drainage that collects a series of water and that have different flows; and along the waters will build accumulation Lakes of various sizes and will provide the hydroelectric power stations with classical, etc. etc.

Within the army, probably it will be necessary to operate the specialized compartments, where many civilians to work, and youth . . .

Synthetic said the army becomes decisive revolutionary world peacefully as the process to be held in good conditions at all points of view . . .

Viewed through the army law of dialectic thinking, things and phenomena and it must evolve dialectical in size and facilities, as they can act on the "axis of evil" involved in biological body of each individual human. Located in the central nervous system—in the human brain—, when the "axis of evil" (greater than), > "axis of good", the man can generate processes its malefic Fellows of the human and the environment. For this reason, the size of the army must be of such magnitude that any movement of people who at times are in psychological crisis due to a report ("R") between the proportion of forces of good and evil forces in the form of share:

R= FG/EF = <1 respectively R= FG/EF = <1 to be stopped.

The army, the task force, able to act on any man for help cannot harm his neighbor.

Those people who still make various acts that bring them a life sentence, not even a day is imprisoned and deprived of freedom. They must be sent in the yards of municipal, County, national and even international so that the work to pay for the mistakes and any construction site work with prisoners, of every kind, to be under severe control of the army.

Synthetic said, the army must be the means of action of a triad» psyche in organizing and leading a revolutionary process—national and global levels to ensure peaceful human dialectic as kind and threads, to become what is normal and should be used judiciously. The army must be the "guardian angel" of organic unity: "man, human society and the environment". As a wave magnetic must operate army because of the safety of each particular concrete General and General to be ensured; as a safety which protects different objectives, you must run the army.

14. The Sentence concerning the future of the youth. Youth and world peaceful revolution. Peaceful world revolution, which was beneficial to each class, to be seen in a moving and auto moving dialectic, which means that the youth of today will become tomorrow's manufacturer of human society, a society "ecologizată of many and diverse social wrongs".

Children from the kindergarten, play must be educated by, to begin to perceive that the man still at birth possess "buds" of four forces: physical strength, intellectual force, the force of good and evil force, and the elementary school, one of the basic disciplines, in the formulation of the nature and the human flesh must be human perception, as "a being biologic-social, language, equipped with thought and articulated the four forces, possession and dominated by a series of law ". Gradually, starting from class I to class VIII-X, learn of human action together with forces and laws of human/it dominates, as it teaches arithmetic: Add, subtract, multiply, and divide.

In high school, the course takes another dimension, making it the student to perceive what "healthy mind is in a healthy body", i.e. they need to do man, from the point of view of its forces and laws, as they may benefit from "healthy mind in a healthy body".

The institutes of higher education, students will philosophy about the law of human nature and temperament and, under the guidance of teachers, with the profile of human cognition and perception of the nature and temperament, will present reports on the ways and means that may lead to human dialectic as "nature and temperament".

Important is to create the environment necessary for informed, the man all his lifetime, to be concerned about the State of nature and his flesh.

Because the young man to become a man of work with "healthy mind in a healthy body", from the elementary school will create the conditions necessary for the physical and intellectual force of human force, constituted as a "living capital" of humans, can be developed, used rationally and creator. To this end, in addition to educational institutions, labs will be organized in the practice of initiatory work when physical, intellectual, and when there are conditions where, near schools, of whatever degree, is recommended to create private profile the different activities: gardening, experimental batches of various cereal products, grassland, poultry and other livestock, horticulture, etc. etc.

Orphans and homeless children are accommodated in dormitories, built on the outskirts of modern cities, where they will have all the necessary conditions for their comprehensive training; where they will be able to learn and will be able to qualify in the different professions of their choice . . .

In addition to the schools in all towns and municipalities of the country will be created nuclei, scientific research groups, in various fields of activity, which will be linked vertically with various scientific research institutes, whereby a significant proportion will handle scientific research on the rational exploitation of living and creative capital available to human society.

At a local level, for example, the scientific research group will be composed of teachers, the priest, Mayor of the commune, the students of classes V to VIII-X and the peasants who are passionate in practice various activities and connoisseurs of production factor of land in the commune. Some considerations on the scientific research level: based on the topography and climate of the commune is the commune will investigate and experience what priority activities are required to live so that the capital was available to the village can be exploited rationally and creator in all year long. In the municipalities were exist enough arable land, favored by climate, will perform works of irrigation and drainage so production at hectare to be the maximum possible, and where fattening took the Earth to be made a priority, with natural fertilizers. To this end, the livestock will be given priority attention. In municipalities with hilly relief will be given priority attention to agriculture, and so Important is that the Group of scientific research to focus on finding ways and means necessary to harness the rational and creative capital live available. It can be harmonically related to the factor of production, land for this purpose, through the scientific research group, will organize and cooperation with various other adjacent municipalities or even removed that have different climate, relief and in order to facilitate the possibility of reconciling work, primary production factor and active and nature (Earth), primary production factor and liability.

15. Sentence on retirees, but, in general, on upon those of the third age, who must watch both in individual and concretely in terms of the general interest of society.

Many people in the third age, many years, enjoyed a considerable capital live ", which sometimes gets lost in part due to the total, how they continue life, in particular those living in different cities of the country.

To imagine what the socio-economic effects would have to build dorms mixed homes and orphans and homeless children, to be placed on the outskirts of towns, where there are areas of land that could be considered superior by the "old-children families". These mixed dorms and children's homes are equipped with a cafeteria, a dining hall, a library, an ambulance, a dental surgery, a pharmacy, where work on skilled and paid money and some pensioners and older children, and besides these mixed dorms, be small parcels of arable land, livestock management growth rate and so on many of these mixed dorms would company, a large proportion, the products obtained in the household of the annex. Of special importance and high perspective would be the formation of a youth with many opportunities to achieve and practice of the creative work of economic goods, and for old people, life would be easier and more gratifying lived, etc., etc.

For retirees who do not inhabit the mixed dorms, on the outskirts of cities will build houses for rest and leisure, with small areas for gardening and other activities, equipped with drinking water and electricity, so that the people of the third age to continue their lives more enjoyable . . .

This way of thinking is preparing in many ways the future of human society's tomorrow with fewer, or no, social wrongs. And what is of special importance that any past, present future-nothing is lost from the practical experience of the past history, so that what was good and it may take in the future, and what was and is bad you can remove it from the life and work of the human species.

Caring for homeless children and towards those who are the beneficiaries of a life in the age of three, with a thinking ecologizată psychological pollution generated by the action of the conjugate base of the human forces and laws with which man/it dominates human society development may give a new direction for the benefit of all.

16. **The Sentence on "Law of nature and human flesh".** The law of nature and human flesh is the conjugate base of the human forces and laws with which man/it dominates. The law of nature and human flesh Act throughout the life of a man and works independent of human will and desire. The law of nature and human flesh, and the engine is "fount" which gives form and content of the world in time and space.

The law of nature and human flesh, the man being "particular" of "General" and "living cell" of General are transmitted from private to general induction forming law of general human society, i.e. the law as a whole, the process taking place through the work of the Organization and management at the level of State administration. Socio-economic order laws, which are General-special, are generated by the law of nature and human flesh.

The conjugate action between the human forces with/and laws of man, which it dominates, "pollute the human psychological thinking" with many and various nuisances and so size as man, unwittingly, becomes its own enemy.

The law of nature and human flesh is hardly perceptible to humans, thousands of years this law was unknown and not collected. "Historical times, some of whom great thinkers, sensitive to what they characterize human society of her time lived with many and diverse social wrongs and explain" the effect of the case ", the cause remains an unknown thousands of years. Their attempts to make theses and ways leading to the normalization of life and work of the human species in line with the laws of nature, aimed at "the effect of the case", have generated from almost nearly, just some enhancements to social injustices so that social and economic injustices, once in the slavery, remained in some form of improvement in the form of a "chain historian" whose length is for thousands of years and, unfortunately, "the chain" is the snake grows further.

"Psychological Pollution of human thinking" with pollutants generated by the action of the conjugate base of the human forces and laws with which man/it dominates, making him the man to be a foe, is not limited only to the emergence of social injustices, which, when raised, remain as a historical "chain" whose length is for thousands of years. Harder is that this gift of man: "thinking", although it is dialectal, leading progressively to the knowledge of the absolute truth (Hegel), however, in terms of "psychological" pollutant, thinking human fails to "ecologizeze", the consequences are particularly serious. The man, regarded as kind and fire, by law of dialectic, negation auto direct to "denial", unwittingly and without realizing that "psychological" thinking his polluted generates the phenomenon known as terrorism, which, when released, evolve, unfortunately all dialectics, the nuisance, the challenge to generate some kind of "Hell" in the world here, hardly bearable for the human species. How to fight against terrorism, all due to "psychological pollution of modern thinking" with arms: cars, tanks, planes, rockets . . . create the optimum environment to develop and diversify forms of terrorism because through this way to the fight against terrorism cause death and mutilation of innocent people and who, through their close relatives or their friends, is over. Who is over? Innocent people all . . .

The fight against terrorism with modern weapons: tanks, cars, airplanes, missiles, bombs, etc. is that the "effect" as if you look for a "needle" in a car with hay with a backhoe and of course with much more serious consequences.

Be charged that terrorism as a phenomenon is "fount and engine" in the central nervous system in the human brain in the form of "force of evil" in the dualism of good and evil, dualism which is found in a continuous process of internal fighting, beating when one when another imaginary thinking and which, in this fight, I get an internal report ("R") of the form:

$$R = FG/EF = 1; >1; <1. \text{ where:}$$

F.G = % of forces of good.
E.F. = % of evil forces.

Causing many and sundry suffering of innocent people by way of the fight against terrorism, promote growth of evil forces so that F.G. > E.F., which creates the optimum environment for the development and diversification.

You are looking for a terrorist "x" or "y" with tanks, planes, etc. or "fount" terrorism is found in the central nervous system in the human brain, in the form of "axis of evil", generated by F.G., which, through a "psychological" thinking polluted and lead to terrorism. What is even more serious is that "Man, the greatest enemy of man", "psychological" thinking his polluted, prepare step by step, unwittingly and without realizing, by arms race with the means of mass destruction from becoming a "more modern, eco-catastrophe", identical to the "deluge of fire" predicts some prophets of time historical or wisdom or by chance, "ecological catastrophe" which put in danger the lives of the human species on Earth.

The fight against terrorism and avoid a war by means of mass destruction requires "greening the psychological pollution of human thinking" of pollutants generated by the action of the conjugate base of the human forces and laws with which man/it dominates.

"Greening the psychological pollution of human thinking" of pollutants generated by the action of the conjugate base of the human forces and laws with which man/ it dominates is "KEY" that will generate process as terrorism would enter into "the zone" sunset and a possible "bed of fire" to be avoided.

Greening the psychological pollution of human thinking is a very complicated process and requires the first perception of the phenomenon (process) of pollution of human psychological thinking. Or scientific demonstration, "the law of nature and human flesh" as being generated by the action of the conjugate base of the human forces and laws with which man/it dominates is based on human perception as "a being with societal biologic-thinking and articulated language holder of four forces: natural force located in the intellectual force behind the muscular system, located in the central nervous system in the human brain and the force of good and evil force located in the central nervous system "and dominated by a series of laws:" the law of accumulation of wealth (wealth) at any cost and by any means, without limitation, law regulations appetite, thirst for power, law no limit the law of selfishness "and many others (see the books" democracy and social justice—the future of humanity "; "The dialectic of human and human society").

Force of good and evil force, existing in the human brain as a dualism of good and evil, by the action of their conjugated with human laws which it dominates generates psychological process "pollution of human thinking". However, the action of immunoglobulin of human forces and laws with which man/it dominates acts throughout the life of a man and works independently of the will and desire of man, which means that "psychological pollution of human thinking is a process that occurs and persists throughout the life of a man. These considerations are confirmed by our own practical experience, which appears in the life and work of the human species. There is a whole family on Earth the "thinking" is not affected by the "psychological pollution". The fact that to some people the degree of pollution is either smaller or larger is explained scientifically by the existence of the report ("R") between the forces of good weight (F.G.) and share of evil forces (E.F.), report to be imagined by the form:

$$R= FG/EF = 1; >1; <1.$$

The question to ask is how can "ecologiza thinking polluted psychologically" generated by the action of pollutants between the forces of human immunoglobulin with/and the laws of man who dominates?

Before we say, it is necessary to do a brackets that influence the perception of action to that end: to imagine how it feels the man following a bath temperature, well prepared as the biological human body is washed by the sludge accumulated by different physical efforts made in a certain period of time; Let us imagine why every morning, after the man getup, wash hands and cheeks and how are the consequences of benefic . . .

Psychological pollution of thinking, being generated by the action of the conjugate base of the human forces and laws with which man/it dominates and which operate independently of the will and desire of man, lead us to the conclusion that we need to act on "the spring" and the engine that generates pollution psychological thinking. Accordingly, the action must be taken on the report 'R' of the weighting of the forces of good (F.G.) and share of evil forces (E.F.) so that the "R" is always of the form:

$$R= FG/EF = >1$$

Influencing the report ("R") to be the only form it always involves the same practice generated by humans, to wash away daily on the hands and face and the body periodically so that his body be kept always biologically in a form. Only this process by influencing the relationship ("R") of F.G. and E.F. to be in the form of the aforementioned, it is very hard achievable because of human action together with forces and laws of human/it dominates, in addition to the fact that acts throughout the life of a man must also be borne in mind that it works and is independent of human desire and the will. Or scientific demonstration, submitted following a fundamental scientific research on the State of the world in time and space, whither Mankind? "," underscored that human society and auto movement in time and space has its source engine "and" to "his" cell, in the man, whose nature and threads are a legalities generated by the action of immunoglobulin of human forces and laws with which man/it dominates and which generates both psychological pollution "process thinking "and the two threaded processes. These processes of formation of a "psychological" imaginary compasses, invisible and hardly noticeable, that directs how to be human, as a kind and threads, and process of formation of an "imaginary invisible nets" and hardly discernible, which "enchain psychologically" how to be human nature, as it stifles and fire, and even blocks to evolve dialectics from what is normal and should be used judiciously.

The man, the kind and nature, although it is equipped with "thinking", who plays always dialectic, however, due to "psychological pollution of thinking" and thanks to the two threaded processes, is caught in a "trap" from which it cannot auto free due to its own laws, "the law of nature and human flesh".

And because I said that the man is the biggest "enemy" of man, the law of nature and human flesh, according to the law it directs towards negation "denial of dialectic", perceived denial of human nature, like negation and bi-directional yarn:

1. If the work was that it had stripped the man from the animals, all work that may be due to psychological pollution process, thinking can result in "denial", the process being generated by the work of the Organization and management at the level of State administration, practiced by those of my invested it do so. They, due to "psychological pollution of the environment promote thinking" dialectical evolution of terrorism and preparing "deluge of fire" by the arms race with the means of mass destruction, which has the value of the single "use": "ecological catastrophe" for the life of the human species on Earth to be "denied"!

2. If the work was that it had stripped the man from the animals, all work can be one which, through a process of "greening" of psychological thinking polluted, can lead man to be as kind and fire, the largest of the "friend" and "human shield" protection of the environment.

The dialectic of human thinking generates this process of perception of nature and human, as fire, knowing and charge State of the world in time and space, with all that characterize good or bad, as a result of the action of the law of nature and human flesh. The man has thought can act on them was a "psychological" greening of pollution generated by the action of the law of nature and his flesh. Man with a "ecologist thinking" may, by a labor organization and management at the level of State administration, to put his hand on the steering wheel "targeting" walking human society and was a "direct", knowingly, to "negation" in denying the beneficial human and human society as a whole and, of course, in the protection of the environment. The process becomes profoundly revolutionary and the peaceful and beneficial to the whole human species environment. The role of organize and lead this process at the national and global peaceful revolutionary is the responsibility of a triad» psyche: politics, religious and scientific who, knowingly, he formed the Committee of organization and management of the world revolutionary process peacefully. As part of a triad» psyche role with scientific.

There is only one variant of the beneficial influence of the law of nature and function of human flesh for the benefit of organic unity between humans, human society and the environment: 'modernization of work organization and management of human society. "Necessarily have to be based on fundamental scientific research studies developed in the institute of scientific research on the knowledge of the phenomenon of profiled induction law of nature and human flesh from the concrete to hold particular man and leads the human society from what characterizes the General. Human society no longer needs to be organized and led by the political program of platforms-political parties because the leaders of the political class, regardless of what party they belong, have a "common denominator" that i do is, ultimately, their own and enemy of the human society as a whole, by generalizing the three processes: 1) compassing, as the human psychological nature and fire; 2) enchaining of man as a kind of psychological and threads and 3) psychological pollution of man as kind and threads. Human society is able to enter the normality of function in conformity with the laws of nature, only if scientific, a form of social consciousness, make up the dialectics to influence the political and spiritual religious to work-based studies of fundamental scientific research on the knowledge and perception of the "world" status in time and space through what characterized his concrete particular, man as kind and threads. The problem has no solution other than sacrificing some pleasure to organize and lead after lust . . . and start to organize and lead the Organization and management of projects developed in the institute of scientific research on the knowledge of General profiled by his particular.

CHAPTER XIX
EARTH "EDEN GARDEN"

Through a fundamental scientific research on the State of the world in time and space, whither Mankind? "," I discovered the secret of enigma, the cause, the State of the world in time and space was as it was and why it is now, at the beginning of the Millennium III, in a State so confusing.

Tactics and strategy practiced in finding the way and means that the entire human species on Earth can live in "the GARDEN of EDEN", imagination by some thinkers historical times that would have been sometime in the making of the world, was multidirectional.

I watched the human society as "General" of a "private"; I meditated on the "General", "human society as a whole", in its historical evolution: race, tribes, States, and still I meditated on the socio-economic orders known historical: common primitive, Native American, feudalism, capitalism and the emergence of socialism which, after World War II, became the order social-economic development worldwide cohabited with capitalist socio-economic order in an atmosphere known as the "cold war". Towards the end of the Millennium II, socialism is entering a process historically called revolutionary, in which several countries of the former Socialist and have chosen the road of transition to capitalism, which had been, hence the question: "Humankind," Whither?

Regarded human society as "General" of a "private", "practical man" who is "living" cell and of general human society as a whole, I began to imagine that what characterized it in time and space as the form and content must be "Spring" and the engine in its particular.

The problem to which I sought an answer was: why human society, in his history, along the road has seen such changes in form and content as the existing relations between people, in the commune of primitive, with normal and rational "relations", both between people and between people and nature, i.e. cooperation relations and mutual benefit, work in common, egalitarian distribution of goods produced, etc. With the passing of the slavery, became "abnormal and irrational" (I don't call them of exploitation and oppression!). These relationships between people, "abnormal and irrational", once raised, remained in the form of a chain of length which is thousands of years and continues the historical chain of lengthy relations between people, called me "abnormal and irrational".

The secret, the cause, enigma of these relations between people have begun to perceive it as a "special" legit, who is also and "living cell" of the General, shall by induction from particular to general, which characterizes the good and evil 'legality of particular'.

I was sensitized by the advent of history some great thinkers of the time, sensitive to the historical emergence of relationships between people, "abnormal and irrational", and have formulated these views to change, from what they were during their lifetime, and imagine it would be normal and rational to be.

Some examples: 1) Lao-tzi, sec. VI BC, great Chinese thinker, living in an age of historic slave where relationships between people "abnormal and irrational", proposing a return to the primitive commune, where relationships between people were "normal and rational"; 2) Socrates, Pythagoras and Greek philosophers, great thinkers of the 20th century VI BC, living in the era of the historical relations between the slave, where people were "abnormal and irrational", believed that through democracy and freedom of thinking you can normalize the relations between people; 3) Winstanly (1609-1659), English, French ideologue in his paper, "the law of liberty ', supported the idea that private property on land is the fount of all evil and social disasters and called for the establishment of common property on Earth and on the products; 4) Mably (1709-1785), French philosopher, regarded as private property, of any kind would be "she", as "source" of all social evils and social organization based on it unjust and averse to the laws of nature; 5) Morelly, 18th century French, French Communist, believed that private property is the source of the moral and addictions of social uprisings and envisage building a compliant order social "reason and the laws of nature", based on collective property and the obligation of all people of the society to work; 6) Babeuf (1760-1797), French revolutionist, was a French training of company "equal" by means of a provisional revolutionary dictatorship which would lead to the dissolution of private property and to the introduction "equalizes society"; 7) Illuminist 17th century-XVIII, ideological movement of emergent bourgeoisie anti-feudal conducted during the preparation for and the exercise of the bourgeoisie revolutions of the 17th-18TH, considered irrational rules as "feudal", campaigning for the replacement of feudal socio-economic and legal system with an order social-economic "rational"; 8) Marx (1818-1883), German philosopher, materialist, economist and politician, considered historical "tenses philosophers have done nothing other than to interpret the world in different ways, important is to change it!" Marx makes historical materialism thesis and dialectical materialism and, on this basis, and the disposition of sentence that mentions the social economic capitalist is limited in terms of history and that after she is another top Socialist, nominated him in the first stage, the Communist finally; 9) Engels (1820-1895), German philosopher, materialist, Marx's contemporary, Marx's theses are associated; 10) Lenin (1870-1924) materialist philosopher and politician, great advocate of Marxist thinking organizes and leads a revolutionary process in a Marxian conception in which, in 1917 in Russia, the world's first socialist State, and after the second world war socialism expands as the social economic order in many countries, becoming world-wide level. Will living with capitalist socio-economic organization in an atmosphere of "cold war".

Towards the end of the Millennium II, 20th century, socialism is entering a crisis, a result of which a number of socialist countries entering a process of transition to capitalism, where they had been. Beyond by of the many and diverse views with regarding the form and content of the two socio-economic orders existing about 45 years at the level the world-wide, important is that human society is evolving in time and space, even if dialectical and some periods of stagnation. The history of the occurrence, and then winding up the socio-economic and legal system of Socialist world-wide level reveals that thousands of years, many great thinkers of humanity, concerned about the influence of walking the world in time and space, through theses and points of view, from what was in their time to something higher, resulted in the almost close to the many and diverse social and economic changes But however, relationships between men remained continuously "abnormal and irrational".

Cause, secret, the enigma of these relationships between people, historical times "abnormal and irrational relations", encountered in the slave era, it remained historically the form of a "chain" historian whose length is for thousands of years and, unfortunately, is still the snake grows, is because it has a "source" engine and capable of "logical" unknown and forgone thousands of years of human mind.

The theses and the views of many great intellectuals of the time, big thinkers, concerned about the changing state of the world, focused on "the effect of the case", the cause remains an unknown thousands of years and continues to be unknown and now, at the beginning of the Millennium III.

The existence of the two orders socio-economic world-wide level, perceived as a "huge" laboratory of fundamental scientific research on the knowledge and perception of absolute truth "," Spring "and" engine which gives the State the world form and content in time and space, "revealed a socio-economic order is characterized not by itself", it being a private "General". Evident that 'particular of General", "nature and nature's law", gives the form and content of the world in time and space.

Knowing the absolute truth "—source and engine" which gives shape and content walking the world in time and space can and should influence the human thinking, her spokesmen, in finding ways and means necessary to ensure that relationships between people to become 'normal and rational' and in line with the laws of nature.

The emergence of socialism as the socio-economic order at world level, and the events that took place on end of the Millennium II, Millennium III highlights that human society always walking, dialectic, cannot continue, if not human society is organized and managed, informed choices, those of my invested do so, unless there is significant work to organize and manage the knowledge to stand absolutely truth "and" spring-engine that gives shape and content walking the world in time and space.

"Absolute truth"—spring motor that gives the State the world form and content in time and space "is located in the particular of General" in "concrete man", and "living cell" of general human society as a whole.

I arrived at this conclusion after a fundamental scientific research on the knowledge and perception of the case which resulted in transforming relations between people, the normal and rational "relations" existing customer "originally in abnormal and irrational".

Tactics and strategy practiced during the fundamental scientific research made of passion, was based on the sentence sought by the German idealist philosopher Hegel, who had the wisdom to support the "cognoscibility world" through the imagination and by contemplation on the practice, stating the thesis that "the things and phenomena and dialectical thinking evolves and progressively thinking that leads to the dialectic of knowing the truth absolutely . . ." The problem that caused me to do a scientific research was fundamental, secrecy of the search which generated the process of relationships between people "abnormal and irrational".

In the process of fundamental scientific research about the knowledge of radical transformation in the secret of the relationship between people in normal and rational "relations" in "abnormal and irrational relations" have been influenced by the famous maximum sought by the philosopher Socrates about the process of knowledge: "you know you!" . . ., prompting me to consider on my and on many of my fellow men that i have known, seeing what they do and how it changes radically depending on certain circumstances in their way of being. On this basis I have made a characterization of human knowledge that provides the necessary elements and perception of him as kind and fire: "man is a being biologic-social thinking and language provided with articulated, in possession of four forces and dominated by a series of laws ". Through imagination and contemplation on me and on many of my fellow men, I deduced (I found) that human forces acting shared human laws, which it dominates, throughout his life, independent of his will and desire, generating process of nature and his flesh, as a "legal". The law of nature and human flesh generates three processes: 1) the process of "psychological" compasses, invisible, imaginary and hardly noticeable, that directs how to be human, nature and fire in its relations with his fellows and in relation to the environment; 2) the process of "imaginary invisible nets" and hardly discernible, "mesh" by the conjugate actions between of the human forces with/and laws which it dominates, "net" that it "psychological" on enchain, as a kind man and threads, braked and even stranding him evolve dialectal, beneficial, as kind and wires, from what is normal and should be used judiciously since it is equipped with the less thinking and dialectical evolves; 3 pollution process) "psychological thinking" with many and various nuisances arising, imaginary thinking, action by the human forces of the laws of man which it dominates, makes man became, unwittingly and without realizing, "his own" and "enemy of the human species."

The law of nature and human flesh, the man being "particular" of General and "living cell" of human society "Maj., as a whole" is transmitted as a magnetic wave, from private to general, giving it the form and content in time and space.

This way of thinking is identified with a "discovery of the law", which seems to be one of the greatest scientific discoveries of mankind and not excluded to the greatest scientific discovery of the life and work of the human species, it has a special importance in many ways: political-economic, social and environmental protection.

The discovery of this law: the law of nature and human nature is a prerequisite for a change in the history of life and work of the human species. Mankind in the threshold, as a start of a peaceful world revolutionary process, will benefit from this law for the benefit of all social classes, each national State, regardless of the disposition of social-economic development that is found. Mankind, irrespective of ethnic, religious, race and sex, will enter into a new historical stage: "the ERA of WISDOM and RATION's", in which the entire human species on Earth, begins a new life, abundance and general well-being. Earth is transformed into the Garden of Eden, imagination to have been the genesis of the world.

These considerations seem to be a utopia for some people this, be they large and scholars in various fields of activity, but for other great thinkers, may be considered achievable because it relies on knowledge of the absolute truth, "the source and engine" which gave and gives shape and content walking the world in time and space.

History of the facts reveals that thousands of years, many great intellectuals of the time, big thinkers, sensitive to the occurrence in the life and work of the human species has many and various social wrongs, generating relationships between people "abnormal and irrational" have made great efforts to ensure that the intellectual relationship between the people of Earth to join in a process of radical transformation, to be rational and normal relations. The fact that relations between people have left thousands of years "abnormal and irrational", with all the efforts made by many intellectuals of the time, big thinkers, who have opposing theses to change the world of what was in their time in what is hoped to be, to enter into normality, in conformity with the laws of nature, is due to an unknown cause, a secret and forgone.

The theses and their points of view have seen "the effect of the case"; the cause remains unknown thousands of years.

"Absolute truth-ignorance of the fountainhead and engine" which gave shape and content walking the world in time and space is because this spring and "engine" is a legal hardly perceptible, that, contrary to the laws of physics and chemistry, are "born" with the man and becomes a sort of "perpetual mobile" as long as there are people on Earth, living and working in a certain system of relationships between them and the environment. Hence the conclusion in order to normalize the relations between people should be acted on "system of relations", so that the internal contradictions of the inputs are continuously balance.

The process can be achieved through the work of the Organization and management at the level of State administration, which requires an evolution always dialectic and directly proportional to the human dialectic as kind and threads. Nature and human nature is a legal generated by the action of the conjugate base of the human forces and laws with which man/it dominates and which operate independently of the will and desire, and what is particularly important to note is that the "law of nature and human flesh" is a common denominator of the whole human species on Earth. The common denominator of the whole human species, "the law of nature and human flesh", the man being "particular of General" and "living cell" of general human society as a whole, are transmitted from private to general by induction, magnetic waves, like a, hence the conclusion that it is "fount" and in his engine, which is particular and cell vineyards. General special, human society as a whole, historical has evolved and, as I pointed out several times, dialectics: from race, tribes, the national States. In parallel, the company has evolved from primitive to stage commune, slavery and the emergence of socialism capitalism arrived after World War II at the level of world-wide. The disposition of social-economic Socialist appeared after many searches of historical great intellectuals of the time, thinkers, who, sensitive to the existence of relationships between people, they sought ways and means to get into normality, in conformity with the laws of nature. With all the intellectual efforts made by some great thinkers of the time of history, in a period of thousands of years, the relations between people remained historical "abnormal and irrational". The emergence of social-economic socialist legal system may be considered a peak search of normalization of relations between people in social and economic. But the phenomenon that took place at the end of the Millennium II, Millennium III, in which a series of socialist countries in the world socialist system have entered into a "revolutionary" process of transition from socialism to capitalism, which had been about. 45 years ago, raises many and various question marks, one of which is the same: "Humankind," Whither?

Beyond the many and diverse views expressed including some intellectuals of this making theses and ways which have no connection with dialectic thinking things, phenomena and sometimes unwittingly do and a great disservice to the society of human movement and auto movement, polluted psychological thinking human such that those of my invested to organize and lead the human society, rather than the practical work of organizing and driving always negative dialectic, determined action, serious. A psychological thinking human pollution is far more serious than alcohol consumption with and without as many degrees. It affects the progress of human society with not only by maintaining social injustices but also through the generation of historical processes that endanger the destiny of mankind on Earth.

The law of nature and human flesh works very variable and it makes the man, in many cases, to be his own enemy and a great enemy of his fellow men, and the man who is made to the organize and lead the company might encounter such situations that the decisions taken by some leaders to generate world wars, and collections of means of mass destruction can lead to such "environmental disaster" that human life on Earth is in a perspective historic: "to be or not to be"!

Man cannot be, in many cases, human rational and normal due to the nature and his flesh, and the law of nature and the flesh of others. There is only one escape: "protection" that shield to protect him against the law of nature and his flesh and against the law of nature and the flesh of others.

Why the brackets and why this comparison? To raise awareness on my fellows at the level of "simple man" at the level of "scholar" man that can make the law of nature and of man's flesh, and to be well and properly understood, I have to make a comparison with global resonance point: George Bush, former President of the United States, often spoke of "missile defense shield" and "Star Wars "and the new President of the United States, Barack Obama, in his speech on the occasion of the investiture, said among others that "peace and tranquility" would be one of the concerns of his reign as President of the United States, a critical point of a high moral obligation towards the people who elected and that, I was impressed on me and some members of my family in front of the TV. As an explosion tears began to flow. Wife asks me: "yeah you, why you crying?"—so that you will flow the tears and on the cheek. And, without any break, I pronounced the word: he (Barack Obama) is not only the President of the Executive Board of the United States, but and the President of the entire human species moral on Earth through his way of thinking.

I could give many and various other examples at the national level, but they were made, some of this work, therefore not repeat them. My family's way of seeing things, it seems that all planetary level like this occurs. Here's what they write in an article in the newspaper the truth from 26 January 2009, page. 14 and 15. I Quote:

"THE OVERALL MISSION," YES WE CAN"

Team. Obama needs to use the enormous global sympathy and ask people to be part of the solutions you expect from him.

Hopes legate by the charismatic man of 47 years are the same as so diverse like the countries from which they come-environment, peace, aid, trade, etc.

A new president of US does never receive a «welcome» so resounding from throughout of the world. The sun burned streets of Africa and Asia to the snow covered offices of the European Commission in Brussels, the electoral slogan of Barack Obama, "Yes, we can!" rang out as a cry that promised a stubbornly in front of the increasing global function.

Obama's ability to inspire and unite people with different origins has impressed European politicians that feeling still reject shown recently by the voters, have made, with a mixture of envy and admiration, in remarks on the use of force of the Internet by Obama in his campaign. "The political class has ignored the growing importance of the Internet. We must learn some lessons from the United States ", said Margot Wallström, Chief of communications in the EU, which has a blog, part of its efforts to bring the EU closer to the people.

At 7,000 km of Brussels, the person of Uganda thinks the same thing, which they have learned from the new President of the United States. Politicians say that Obama's victory over racial barriers should be an example for the establishment of a country such as Uganda, deeply divided along tribal faults. In neighboring Kenya, the largest Economics of East Africa and the scene of violent ethnic clashes last year, has hopes and higher. Young Kenyans I see in Obama a model. Kenyans hope to farmer's easier access of their exports on the U.S.A. Market in Kenya counts Doctors on American help in the fight against HIV/AIDS and malaria. Human rights activists will ask Obama to moderate on African dictators.

COMPETITION OF PRIORITIES

Realistic or not, there is a sense of urgency that encompassed the entire world. The EU is pleased that, after years of opposition and even threats of lawsuits by the US against European policies on climate change, one of the first calls Obama's was by the President of the European Commission, José Manuel Barroso, to repair relations on the climate front. Indeed, the list of energy and environmental priorities of the Obama looks almost like one: European emissions trading scheme as the EU, improving energy efficiency, reduction of oil consumption and reduce emissions of greenhouse gases by 80% by 2050.

Rising sea levels and flooding, dry season and cyclones already threatens the vast expanses of coastal areas in developing countries such as Bangladesh, which receives much of its food aid from the United States.

At 12 hour circle, in Latin America, Peru relies heavily on trade with the United States just like the people of Bangladesh, The Peru population fear that internal pressures on Obama might turn into disadvantages for them.

In the last weeks of the Bush administration have appeared new hot spots of major importance that will require immediate attention to Obama's. The EU hopes that the new President of the United States to come to Brussels in the coming weeks to outline an urgent strategy on the Middle East, Afghanistan, Pakistan and Russia.

«Middle East must be the priority ", says Benita Ferrero-Waldner, EU Chief of foreign relations. «In past U.S. Presidents, all have neglected this issue until the end of the first term or even have postponed it until the second term». It takes a "productive dialogue" with Obama's America, she says, not only on the topic of the Middle East, but also with regard to Afghanistan and Pakistan, to solve problems the US on "sharing" in the battle counter. Pakistan, whose border region with Afghanistan has been transformed into a war zone, where Al-Qaida fighters trying to escape the war on terror, America's hope for a significant change in American policy.

"HUGE CHALLENGES"

On top of all these problems is hung the financial crisis. Given that unemployment is increasing worldwide, tens of thousands of people lose their homes and dissatisfaction among the items increase college graduates without jobs, the traditional reward for working hard is in doubt, increasingly more.

«2009 won't bring much relief», says Joaquín Almunia, EU Commissioner for economic and financial affairs. "We will hit big problems as you try to do with the effects of the crisis".

In Western Europe, young people took to the streets in Greece, France and other countries, protesting against the fact that, they say, do not have a future, which reminds me of street disturbance clashes in the 1960s and 1970s. According to Dr. Azaveli Rwaitama, Associate Professor of philosophy at the University of Dar es Salaam, Tanzania, East Africa, this represents the fall of the Western capitalism. "The world needs more urgent than ever, to win the minds and hearts of many people and groups with ethnic origins and socioeconomic increasingly more diverse and broader," he says.

In Brussels, European Commission President agrees that the mere magnitude of the problem require fundamental reconsideration of some of the most-held convictions of political and economic principles which have governed the world over the past 60 years. «Truly feel that we live historical moments ", says Barroso «We are at a turning point in human history. There are issues related to large macroeconomic imbalances. There are fundamental problems in the relations of the most important parts of the world. Our citizens will not accept excuses, if their leaders fail to take the right decisions ".

Andrea Thalemann—Ardyatmo—Brussels, Agung Jakarta, Steve Mbogo—Noiribi, Jeff Mbanga-Kampala, Kamran Reza Chowdhury—Dhaka, Haq Nawaz Khan Islamabad, Juan Vargas—Piura City and Mnaku Mbani—Dar es Salaam.

USA: A SMARTER POWER

Joseph S. Nye Jr.

Adapted from Gulf News

Whereas it is easier for a country to change their policies than culture, Barack Obama will have to choose the policies to assist in the recovery of 'soft power' of America.

Hearings to become Secretary of State, Hillary Clinton said: "America is not able to solve their most pressing one, and the world cannot solve without America . . . must use what has been called" smart power ", the full range of tools that we provide."

"Smart power" is a combination of "hard power" and "soft power". The latter defines the empowerment to get the results you want through attraction rather than coercion or payment. Public opinion polls reveal a serious decline of the attractiveness of us in Europe, Latin America and, most dramatically throughout the Muslim world.

LIMITS OF 'SOFT POWER'

Resources that produce "soft power" include the culture of a country (the attractiveness to others), values (they are not undermined by practices inconsistent) and policies (as they are perceived to be comprehensive and legitimate).

Ask why have reported a decline in soft power of America, respondents indicated more American than policies or culture values. Whereas it is easier for a country to change their policies than culture, Barack Obama will be able to choose policies to assist in the recovery of 'soft power' of the USA.

SOFT + HARD = SMART

Of course, the "soft power" is not the solution to all problems. The fact that the dictator of North-Korea Kim Jong II likes movies and 1976 is unlikely to impair in any way on the nuclear weapons program. And 'soft power' does not helped atoll distracting of Taliban Government to the medium on which it offered the group Al-Qaeda in the 1990s. It took the military "hard power" in 2001 to bring to an end. But other purposes, such as the promotion of democracy and human rights can be better achieved just by using 'soft power'.

With just over a year ago, a Commission of "smart power" bipartisan came to the conclusion that America's image and influence has diminished in recent years and that the US should move from export optimism and fear to inspiration of hope. And it was not the only one that has come to this conclusion. The Chief of Defense, Robert Gates, appealed to the U.S.A. Government to commit more money and more effort in tools 'soft power', including diplomacy, economic assistance and military communication, because one cannot defend the interests of America into the wide world. Gates has spotlighted that total military spending reached almost half a trillion dollars annually, compared with the budget Department of the State which has only 36 billion dollars.

The Pentagon is best prepared arm of the Government and has the best resources, but there are limits to what "hard power" can achieve on its own. The promotion of democracy, human rights and civil society is not done with the gun. It is true that the U.S.A. military has an impressive operational capacity, but the practice of calling the Pentagon always leads eventually to the picture of supra-military policy.

The effects of the terrorist attacks of 11 September have derailed America. Terrorism is a real threat and it's likely to accompany the decades, but exaggerated response to challenges, then we do more harm than they could ever the terrorists themselves. The success of the fight against terrorism means finding a new premise central to American foreign policy, which will replace the current theme of "war on terror".

THE GLOBAL WAR FOR GLOBAL GOOD

A commitment to participate in the good of global can deliver that premise.

United States can become a "smart" power by investing back in providing global public goods—things that people and Governments from all over the world, but they cannot obtain in the absence of the leadership of the strongest countries.

Development, health and climate change are good examples. By expanding military power and economic investment in ' soft power ' and focusing on global public goods, the United States can rebuild the framework they need to figure it out with tough global challenges.

Style matters too, even when global public goods are substance policy. In 2001, ' Charles Krauthammer has called for what he called "a new unilateralism", which recognizes that the USA was the only superpower and were so powerful that they could decide what was good and expect others to follow, with few options. However, this style has proved to be counterproductive in achieving the objectives of America.

The Obama administration will have to generate ' soft power ' and to correlate with the power of "hard" by "smart" strategy—smart. The bad news is that Obama and Clinton are faced with a difficult international environment. The good news is that previous Presidents failed to enlist "soft power", "hard" and "smart" in contexts as difficult, and Clinton has shown through his testimony that understands this.

OBAMA, SEENING IN RUSSIA

Comment

Giodor Lukianov

Adapted from Moscow Times

Many observers believe the change of leadership in the USA will open new opportunities for relations with Russia. It is difficult to argue this for the simple reason that it is unlikely that the bilateral relations to go worse than now. First, there is an extremely high level of mistrust between the two countries. Both sides have lost almost any wish to understand the other. Secondly, relations between Russia and the USA are completely unbalanced. Even in areas where the interests of both sides coincide clearly there is a real breakthrough, as each side tries to "sell" more expensive than the other cooperation. Thirdly, the mechanisms for maintaining good relations were thinned out. Communication in multiple parts between Russia and the UNITED STATES during the Soviet era and in the 1990s has been reduced today to formal contacts and exchanges demagogic.

If tensions between the two sides will fall, not because the Obama administration will make this a top priority, but because they will see that Moscow helps resolve some issues on which Washington considers being priorities.

WHAT ARE THESE PRIORITIES?

Overcoming the economic crisis is at the forefront of the list. Russia's influence on the global economy and the USA is much smaller than that of China and Europe, and even the price of oil is less than Moscow. More likely, it will be happen the opposite: in an effort to overcome the crisis, the United States will implement certain measures which may prove to be difficult for other countries, increasing tensions. The Middle East will be another priority for the Obama administration. Moscow holds some leverage because of his Council have UN Security, but rather will defend the initiative of States other than to take the leadership in this issue. Over Iraq, the situation is similar. Moscow will not do anything to create the conditions that cause Washington to withdraw its troops faster, but neither will complicate the process. The UNITED STATES cannot solve the problem of Iran but without the participation of Russia. There is a possibility that Russia may use its levers on Iran in order to make it more willing to accept a compromise. Similarly, the problem of Afghanistan cannot be solved without close cooperation between all the powers of the region: India, China, Russia and Iran.

The area that causes the greatest friction between Moscow and Washington, the former Soviet republics will remain a source of tension.

It is unlikely that Obama opposing a future enlargement of NATO, but the events in Georgia and Ukraine demonstrates clearly that the accession process should be done in a hurry.

It is clear that no country meets the primary criteria for membership.

PLANETARY PRESIDENT

Obama is claimed by countries at a great distance from each other: Kenya, where he was born his father, and Indonesia, where the new President of the United States spent four years of his childhood, along with his mother and Indonesian stepfather father.

In Indonesia, the country with the largest and most diverse Muslim population, the only unifying hope is that Obama's victory will lead to a rapprochement between the US and the Islamic world. Expectations are high given that the new American leader made the early school years in Indonesia.

Question asked of a triad» psyche—politics, religious and scientific: What is the cause, the secret and enigma that leaders of politics, religious and science are not acting under the "flag of wisdom and reasoning" for placing the State of the world to "orbit" of social justice?

We put this question because I demonstrated scientifically that the intellectual force of humans through speech and writing process is partially, sometimes accumulates a total of man-to-man, from generation to generation, with the trend of development potential to infinity ($\rightarrow \infty$).

We put this question because the representatives of the social consciousness a triad»: politics, religious and scientific have a common denominator: "the dialectic of intellectual labor" and the law of nature and human flesh.

Ask this question because human intellectual dialectic of force generates process of dialectic thinking, and dialectic thinking leads to knowledge of the absolute truth. Hence the question: which one as "absolute truth" that representatives of a triad» pyramid tops psyche does not act knowingly, unitary and specifically, under "flag of wisdom and reasoning" to place mankind on "social justice" orbit?

Our view is that: the secret of enigma, case, is that "human thinking is polluted by pollutants generated by the action of the conjugate base of the human forces and laws with which man/it dominates!"

With the way in which the new President of the United States begins its activity on the occasion of the investiture of the President, I feel morally obliged to repeat some of my conclusions made in the books in question and, in particular, point out that the good intentions of President Barack Obama must mobilize international intellectuals to formulate sentences and points of view in line with the said of his reign on the occasion of the investiture of the President of the United States. However, this is possible with one condition: the intelligentsia does not leave worn by waves of motion and auto movement "the law of nature and human flesh" but to make the intellectual effort of a steer into knowledgeable, organic unity "for the good of man, human society as a whole and its environment".

Any sentence and point of view expressed by the scientific, social consciousness, to direct the work of politics to work for the Organization and management with rational and creative evolution always dialectic.

At the level of social consciousness a triad»: politics, religious and scientific must be practiced assiduously convergent and in line with the progress of the human mind whose supreme objective to be: "initiating, organizing and directing a revolutionary process

World peaceful and beneficial social beneficial to each class, each State national small or large, rich or poor, regardless of the disposition of social-economic development in which they are located; This work will bring "peace and tranquility of all".

Triad psyche, informed, must act convergent for dialectic of human society to a new historic epoch: ERA WISDOM and REASONING ", this is possible only through a process of peaceful world revolutionary beneficial social beneficial to each class, the whole human species regardless of race, ethnicity, gender and religious worship. Only that the man, regardless of who would have it, is carried by the wave motion and auto moving "the law of nature and human flesh", which works independently of the will and desire. Without realizing, acting through work they practice under the pressure of "the law of nature and human flesh" without protection with protective shield "live". The live shield of protection will be recovered from those who organize and conduct the human society, but also at religious and scientific, forms of social consciousness. All politics is undergoing a process of many action figures from the political, religious and scientific acting worn by waves of motion and auto moving of the law of nature and human flesh. No Barack Obama can't expect mild days because the coming avalanche views and actions that it may determine not to differ radically from its predecessor, George Bush. Already such trends have emerged: Obama's "Bush", article in the newspaper the truth of 2 February 2009, and page. 15:

«BUSHNESS» of OBAMA

ANALYSIS. Following a period in which many will try to explain that there is a big difference between the George w. Bush and Barack Hussein Obama.

It's not easy to have someone so popular at the White House. For many, such international admiration towards the head of the American Empire is a big problem. Molsés Naim.

For some Governments, it is absolutely imperative that the UNITED STATES to be enemy. And we know the people for which Anti-American is a primary instinct and the determining factor of their political opinions. This is why you will soon be fashionable to turn on Obama in Bush.

Bush-ification of Barack Obama is the next chapter in the story that inevitably began with the belief that it is impossible that the United States to elect a black President and continued with the surprising victory of Barack Obama, with emotions that broke out during his investiture and with extraordinary expectations regarding its ability to solve problems that we inherited.

It will follow a period in which many will try to explain that at the base there is a big difference between the George w. Bush and Barack Hussein Obama. Or, in the words of gabby President of Venezuela, "they come from the same miasma", which means that both are malign or toxic waste, Chavez is not the only one. We will attend the Bush-Obama's ification around the world. The regime in Iran will do everything possible to show that Obama, like its predecessor, is the representation of land of the great Satan.

THE FIRST ACCUSATIONS

Three days after the investiture of the Obama Government, armed forces of the UNITED STATES bombed a group of Taliban fighters legitimize, in North-eastern Pakistan, killing and injuring 14 people. The Pakistani Government has protested against the recent incursions into its territory and said he now realizes that the hope that Obama not to continue Bush's policies was a dream after Timothy Geithner, the new Secretary of the Treasury, has accused China that is trying to destabilize the dollar on international currency markets, Beijing responded angrily through a communiqué which said: "China's Prosecution in connection with the exchange rate of the dollar just to help American protectionism and will not contribute to finding a real solution to this problem ".

In his speech, Obama i was warned "those leaders around the globe who seek to sow discord or who blame the West for all the ills of their societies", saying: "to know that your people will judge you based on what you are able to build, not what you destroy. For the ones witch is clinging by the power through corruption, deception and suppression of the opposition, they must to know that they are at the wrong side of history ".

OBAMA'S CHARACTERISTIC IS THAT IT HAS ALWAYS SURPRISED AND SKEPTICAL CRITICS ON

«But that we will extend a hand if you are willing to break out his fist ". Who sent this invitation: Syria's Assad, Cuban President Raúl Castro, Vladimir Putin? All the leaders that witch don't see any difference between Bush and Obama.

We also know that Obama believes that the war in Afghanistan should be increased, that will not allow Iran to develop atomic weapons and that supports Israel's right to defend themselves against Hamas. "If someone would launch missiles against my house where I sleep my kids, I'd do whatever I can in its power to stop it", he said during a visit to Israel last year. Therefore, it is a little surprising that many in the Arab world perceive the Obama administration as a continuation of the Bush Government; the only difference that there are more Jews in the cabinet.

THE FIRST CONTINUITY

In some cases, the Bush-Obama's ification will bring forth from reality that it will continue some of the policies of his predecessor. But the majority of comparisons will be determined by the propaganda of those who will always need an enemy to the White House. But will not be easy. One of the characteristics of the political rise of Barack Obama is that i was always surprised the critics and skeptics. There will be hard to continue to do that—if only for one reason: it is not George w. Bush ".

I made this bracket to awaken the man whatever he, worn by auto moving "waves of motion and law of nature and human flesh and confessed that I and my family, I watched on television the emergence of Barack Obama during his investiture as President of the United States. Influenced by how he was received a new President of the United States, a "Welcome" so resounding throughout the world, deeply of the electoral slogan of sensitized Barack.

Obama on the global mission: "Yes, we can", we lachrymal deep. With reading at some considerations of many intellectual personalities of this from different countries of the world, and the quotes from the newspaper Adevarul, i. 2009, and page. 14-15, relating to the historic role that Barack Obama should have, I began to meditate and new: "If Obama's ability to inspire and unite people of different origins, you may or may not be completed?" Basing on those offered by human history, as they appeared and appear many intellectuals of the time, big thinkers, sensitive to the State of the world of her time lived, as formulated theses and points of view aimed at changing the world, I have concluded that many of the theses and points to "the effect of the case" led only to improve the State of the world, the cause remains unknown. The problem remained the same, economic crises; social and political organizations have evolved and continue to evolve with the dialectic society and human environment.

If Barack Obama, the new US President will be able to focus the work of this great responsibility, based on the knowledge of "absolute truth", "source and engine" which gave and gives shape and content walking the world, when good intentions will materialize in the "change history".

CHAPTER XX
THE CONTEMPORAN EPOCA

Understanding the contemporary era, now at the beginning of the Millennium III, XXI century, when mankind knows political and governmental changes of historical proportions is made on the basis of many searches of a considerably large number of intellectuals, thinkers of the time, historical, sensitive to the State of the world, at the time lived by them, have formulated theses and points of view aimed at normalization of life and work of the human species in line with the laws of nature.

Great intellectuals of the time they discovered historical and law of dialectic thinking, things and phenomena, and the great German idealist philosopher Hegel, dialectic has modernized the law on the basis of which the alleged cognoscibility of the world. He formulated the laws of dialectic: quantitative collections lead to a new quality; fight the internal forces (the source and the dialectic), denying negation.

In an idealistic conception, Hegel formulated the thesis that: things, phenomena and dialectical thinking evolve and progressively thinking that leads to the dialectic of the knowledge of the absolute truth. Hegel made the absolute spirit "process". Marx and Engels, German philosophers, extend the law materialist of dialectic thinking, things and phenomena and human society by formulating dialectical materialism thesis of historical materialism and the orders sentence mentions a new socio-economic situation, made by her, bigger than the capitalist.

Historical experience has confirmed the dialectic of socio-economic orders, humanity through several forms of State Organization: common primitive, Native American (upper village primitives), feudalism (superior slavery), capitalism (superior feudalism); socialism in Russia appears and in 1917, and after the second world war, socialism, expands into a large number of countries, becoming world-wide level. For about 45 years, humankind is organized into two socio-economic orders: one capitalist, based on private property over the means of production, another socialist-communist based on common ownership of the means of production. These two socio-economic orders, the level of world-wide, were live in an atmosphere known as the "cold war", and at the end of the Millennium II, 20th century, socialism is entering a crisis in which a series of socialist countries entering a process of transition from socialism to capitalism, where they had been. Hence the natural question: where did humankind?

Beyond the many and diverse views on the appearance of this historic process, in accordance with the principles and laws of dialectic, appears the question: was the thinking of many intellectual personalities, great thinkers of the time of history, founded on knowledge of the absolute truth? Order is a high socio-economic system based on common ownership against an order social-economic development based on private property over the means of production? Or the existence of socialism at the world level has highlighted that the human society as the social economic order is characterized not by itself, that the forms of ownership of the means of production are "effects", not "concerned", are "means" action figure walking human society a certain direction. Who gives the direction of movement of human society in time and space? As a fundamental scientific research on the State of the world in time and space, made in the books social justice and Democracy-the future of humanity, the dialectic of human society, man, let's change the world, nature and human nature-"the compass" targeting human society development it was discovered that the secret, because, "the source and engine" that prints the status of the world a direction of movement, which gives the State the world form and content in time and space, and directs the development of human society is the "Law of nature and human flesh", regulations generated by the action of immunoglobulin of human forces and laws with which man/it dominates, which operates independently of the will and desire of man throughout his life.

Knowing this spring and "engine" that directs the development of human society in time and space and the form and content of the world, you start to perceive that the world is "General" of a "private". This "particular" owns "the fount and engine" which gives the State the world form and content, which directs the development of human society. "Particular" of "General" is "concrete man" which is "living cell" of the "General", "human" society as a whole. Specifically, as a kind man and fire, is highly variable, due to the case giving rise to the nature and human nature, a joint action between forces of man with man and the laws that/it dominates. Times, we have demonstrated scientifically that man is a being "biologic-social thinking and language provided with articulated, owner of four forces: physical strength, intellectual force, the force of good and evil force and dominated by a number of objective and subjective laws: the law of accumulation of wealth (riches) at any cost and by any means, without limitation, law regulations appetite, thirst for power, law no limit law of selfishness, and many others (human Dialectic and society, p. 12)."

Human's physical strength is relatively constant, instead it is radically different from intellectual force from man to man and is characterized by the fact that dialectical always evolves. Force of good and evil are in force throughout the life of a man in a process of internal fighting, beating when one when the other, what makes this fight forces show a relation "R", which, through imagination, is of the form:

P.F.B.

R = 1; > 1; < 1

P.F.R.

The action of immunoglobulin of human forces and laws with which man/it dominates generates "law of nature and human flesh," which directs the development of the world in time and space, giving it the form and content.

I argued that the law of nature and human flesh generates three processes:

1. The process of formation of "imaginary" compasses psychological, invisible and hardly noticeable, that directs how to be human as kind and fire;

2. the process of formation of an "imaginary invisible nets" and hardly discernible, "strapped" by the action of immunoglobulin of human forces and laws with which man/it dominates, "net" that "enchain psychologically" how to be human, it and even stranding it in dialectic, to evolve as kind and threads.

3. I also inferred, I concluded that the action through imagination, conjugate of human forces and laws with which man/it dominates generates and the "psychological pollution of thinking".

These three processes generated by the action of immunoglobulin of human forces and laws with which man/it dominates, led to the emergence of many socio-economic wrongs in life and work of the human species and the historical be imagined as a "historic" chain whose length is for thousands of years; more serious is that the action of immunoglobulin of human forces and laws with which man/it dominates causes him to become his own "enemy".

The facts of life experience and activity of man, in his history, along the road reveals that the man, the kind and nature, in relations with his fellows, is:

When "man Fox devious manipulation and likes to man";

When "man versus man" crook;

When "man versus man killer" not only become: "man to man" as normal and rational should be since it is packed with thought. Cannot be made to be always only by "man to man" because "the psychological thinking is polluted," with many and various nuisances generated by the conjugate actions between human forces with/ and human laws which it dominates.

In the process of fundamental scientific research on the State of the world in time and space, Humanity, Whither?, I used several points of support:

1) I pondered over my flesh and nature starting from early childhood to old age, now deep when I write these lines I 83 years;

2) I pondered on how to be of many of my fellow men the whole time of life;

3) we watched the evolution of thinking of many intellectual personalities, big thinkers, across from the historic time as perceived state of the world, time lived them and I reflected on the theses and their points of view on the change in status of the world with many and various socio-economic wrongs;

4) I meditated on some historical writings on the social uprisings, revolutions and their social consequences;

5) I reflected on the consequences of the second world war, knowing the consequences for a child in training, at the age of 20 years;

6) I was psychologically "injected" how to be of my parents, who in getting up said a prayer at any meal would say a prayer, both before and after mass, and before bedtime would say a prayer;

7) I was psychologically "injected" additional way in which the priest of the village, through songs and sermons, urge people to do only good things;

8) I lived in a capitalist socio-economic order until the age of 20 years and I met on my own life its advantages and disadvantages;

9) I lived and I contributed a lot of work in the Socialist construction in Romania;

10) I participated passively, retired as the process of Romania's transition from socialism to capitalism, where we were by about 50 years ago;

11) throughout my life I was sensitive to the way of being human: "the good man, when the bad man";

12) impressed me deeply how changing human, based on the circumstances. Particularly bothered me how to be of people during the construction of socialism, when they sentenced the disposition of the capitalist and social-economic, and beneficial, have exaggerated the Socialist, and during the transition period from

socialism to capitalism where we were, the same people or, more exactly said, some of whom have changed radically.

These "points of reflection" helped me to perceive that the man, described as "kind and fire", "the source" is in itself.

I reflected on the consequences of the second world war, organized and led by Hitler and his family and friends, against which the United States with different orders, and after the war he rallied the forces guarding the two systems worldwide—capitalist and Socialist. Then some of the enemies of Germany Italian joined in action with their former enemies and against those who have suffered the heaviest impact of the second world war and who fought against Germany.

And again I am starting to perceive at a larger scale and that the man, the nature and source of the fire, he has in himself.

These points of support, reflection and meditation they took me to the conclusion that the man, the kind and nature, must have a "question", a "source". So we concluded to give a characterization of human form and content that can be used in order to perceive the nature and human nature.

Knowing the law and dialectic thinking things, phenomena, I began to perceive the perfect man dialectic in law from the viewpoint of nature and his flesh. The problem that I have put it out was how to imagine the evolution of his dialectic "like kind and fire", since he is the good man, you evil man. Meditating over and over and over some of my closest friends, I began to perceive the man with the trend of dialectical evolution: beneficial and two-way malevolent.

Using my characterization of human time, confirmed by the experience of life characterize the human species, I began to perceive that the man, the kind and nature, and is "fount" engine in its biological body. And I began to perceive the nature and human nature as a legally hardly perceptible.

Legality of nature and human flesh is generated by the action of the conjugate base of the human forces and laws with which man/it dominates and which operate independently of the will and desire of man, hence the conclusion that the man is likely to develop dialectal, as kind and fire, when beneficial, when mischievous in relations with his fellows and in relation to the environment.

Using I mode of being of many people who were on their way between historic reports generated by the nature of the known people in slavery, feudalism and capitalism and given the historical spent after the World War II, I started the conclusion that "the law of nature and human flesh", viewed through the prism of dialectic, law directs how to be human to be "the greatest enemy of man", which may result, in accordance with the laws of dialectic, and the "negation man" and denying the right of the human society as a whole. Unfortunately, the man does not perceive himself as kind and fire and leave worn by waves of dialectic, and terrorism, the development and modernization of means of mass destruction are signs that human society is moving towards the "denial of negation". What to do for the human dialectic as kind and threads, to evolve dialectal beneficial?

Perceived source and engine that gives the form and content of the world in time and space in his "living cell", "concrete man", which is headed by particular of General and human nature and temperament as being generated by the action of human immunoglobulin and human laws forces which it dominates, lead us to conclude that a "thinking" cleaning ecological the psychological pollution generated by the action of the conjugate base of the human forces and laws with which man/it dominates could change the direction of movement of human society from that in the looming in a new direction for human benefit and human society as a whole.

The events that occurred after the second world war confirms that development of human society is directed towards an ecological "disaster" which endangers human life on Earth.

The dissolution of a military bloc (Warsaw) and further development of the NATO military bloc stimulates other means of mass destruction, and a "polluted" psychological thinking of building a "protective shield" stimulates anti-racket and more general preparation for an "ecological catastrophe". There is only one escape: "peaceful Revolution" beneficial world of each social classes, each State national small or large, rich or poor, regardless of the disposition of the social.

"Peaceful" World Revolution, which was beneficial to the whole human species, is aimed at changing the nature and human flesh from what is normal and should be used judiciously.

A ecologic cleaning of thinking that a psychological pollutants will give pollute the perception that it is not a "protective shield" missile, not the development and improvement of means of mass destruction are ways of ensuring the security of the State, on the contrary, these means preparing a "ecological catastrophe" which, in fact, be identified with the "deluge of fire", "predicts" the prophets of time historical or wisdom, either by chance.

Saving humanity supposed perception "live" protection shield that would protect man against nature "law enforcement action and human flesh" that generate and process "ecologic cleaning of psychologically thinking" polluted with pollutants generated by the action of the conjugate base of the human forces and laws with which man/it dominates.

Representatives of a triad» psyche, large beneficiaries of a considerable potential of intellectual labor, pyramid, their tips may be organizations summoned Moldovan authorities that their historical role is something other than that which it practiced now work-wear of the waves, "the law of nature and human flesh".

Our view is that although the leaders of the political class are generally intellectual personalities of great prestige, however, they are the worst of the "law of nature and human flesh". Normal and rational would like them to learn from the mistakes of the past history, but it may be because "the law of nature and human flesh", at the level of politics, acting so powerful that makes the leaders of the political class "immune" from the mistakes of former rulers of States which have done much harm in the lives of the human species.

Religious, regardless of the religious cult, its representatives also are major beneficiaries of a considerable potential labor intellectual and practical work, however, towards the object of their work, the man, in contradiction with the law of dialectic thinking, things and phenomena. Representatives of religious worship "handles" too much heaven and hell "in the world that are made and then not perceive that in fact Heaven and hell" exists only in the world from here ".

Scientific, which, by the very specifics of, is standing as Builder one form or another, of dialectic thinking, is nevertheless "coregent" in providing theses and political points of view as religious and can be influenced spiritually by the practice a dialectical work always and in line with the dialectic of human intellectual labor.

Historical experience is so generous in offering human species many concrete examples and what to do as the way of the human species would enter into normality, in conformity with the laws of nature and the evolution of events, however, reveals that the man is "locked" by the "law of nature and nature 's" in the paths of history favorable as the way the human species to be directed towards the normalization of life and work of the human species in line with the laws of nature and in the light of changing potential human intellectual labor.

In order to protect man against the action of the law of nature and his flesh, it is necessary to "making up" urgent "live protection shield" to protect its harm of others and the environment, urgent, until it's too late.

And because "the shield of protection live" can work more effectively, apart from the imagined, as should be organized and what to think it would be very useful to show the organizational "inspired the Academy ' to deal exclusively with the offer of a triad» psyche: politics, religious and scientific—a platform-program of work.

Historical, the level of a triad» psyche, democracy, freedom of thinking and human rights must be the joint work with "debt". Thus, the "debt" of leaders of the political class is to organize and lead the human society such that each Member of the society of human labor apt to capitalize "capital live" available (physical and intellectual strength). This principle became the principal indicator of human political leader job description with power in the State.

Why this view? Because democracy, freedom of thinking and human rights at the level of poor social class is a "fruit", that is what unfavorable uses democracy, freedom of thinking and human rights to those people who do not have private property, by any means, not have a job, many live together with their families in a white-knuckle, and social aid they receive confirms the existence of a polluted psychological thinking from those who organize and lead the company, and some do and great parade that aid offices are at such a level that ensures a decent living. Very pernicious this thinking, scientific hypothesis is the emergence of man on Earth by the factor work and non-perceived that non-work is a way of approaching human mode of being of the animals, which is very serious.

The common denominator of all States of the world, regardless of the disposition of social-economic development in the history, is: "the law of nature and human flesh".

Knowing the absolute truth "source and engine" which gives shape and content walking the world in time and space, "the law of nature and human flesh" means for all States of the world "the key" normalization of life and activity of the entire human species on Earth, in line with the laws of nature.

For thousands of years, many great thinkers of the time, sensitive to the historical State of the world of her time lived with many and diverse social wrongs, have formulated theses and points of view aimed at normalization of life and work of the human species in line with the laws of nature. The theses and their points of view, generally focused on "the effect of the case", the cause is not known as an absolute truth, the effect of the theses and the views formulated led to some improvement of the socio-economic injustices, the problem remains the same.

The law of nature and human flesh, the man being General and cell particular of general human society as a whole, was and is "fount" and which gave the engine and give form and content walking the world in time and space.

The discovery of this law, the common denominator of the whole human species on Earth, is the premise of the normalization of life and work of the human species on Earth, in line with the laws of nature. Relationships between people and between people and nature both within the boundaries of a country in any way, and between all States of the world is entering a process of "greening" in which man and human society as a whole is "washed" by what is "harmful" and "wearing a coat" which benefit both special and General.

Man endowed with thought, once "purgatory" and "ecologic cleaning of thinking" it washed "what is harmful" auto-sense it is absolutely necessary to "think". To "think with the mind's ecologic" of pollutants generated by the action of the conjugate base of the human forces and laws with which man/it dominates and begin a process of meditation upon him and his fellows, on what is to be done, what worked as his role and purpose in this world here in the world of Terra, to be a mediator at the maximum possible between human activities and the law of nature.

Politics, religious and scientific, forms of social consciousness, holders, beneficiaries of a "huge potential of his intellectual labor, begin to meditate on the philosophical concept of the" axis of good "and" axis of evil "," thrown "philosophical notions of great political attire as a psychological serum ". The purpose would be to "inject" human thinking to perceive that the "axis of evil" and is where a he imagines in country x "or" y "or" z ", imagination not to be perceived that it would be made in" bad faith ", even if that would be in some cases, but to be seen as a form of manifestation of the" law of nature and human flesh ".

To be seen "axis of good" and "axis of evil" where she in reality, in the central nervous system in the human brain, so everywhere where there are people and "axis of good" and "axis of evil". "Axis of good" and "axis of evil" are found in the form of dualism of good and evil in every human brain. However, I have demonstrated scientifically that man being biologic-social, is packed with thought and articulated language, owner of four forces: physical strength, intellectual force, the force of good and evil force and dominated by a series of laws: the law of accumulation of wealth, riches, at any price and by any means, without limitation, the Regulations Act of selfishness, as biological human nature and fire. Accordingly, the man being what it is and that makes him to be his own enemy.

We want to demonstrate the scientific imaginary leads to the idea that nature and human nature, generated by the action of the conjugate base of the human forces and laws with which man/it dominates work and independent of the will and desire of man there is a huge warning signal. The man with the power of decision in the State can act at any time, due to the three processes generated by the action of immunoglobulin of human forces and laws with which man/it dominates with the potential for mass destruction, whose value usage is unique: "ecological catastrophe" identical "deluge of temperament".

Historical events from the end of the Millennium II, Millennium III, be levied, from our point of view, as a big warning that humanity no longer mutate dialectic by ways and means of its history: social uprisings, violent social revolution organized by a social class against other social classes; that class struggle, according to the law of dialectic, is located on the border "denial negation". To give a new direction of quantitative accumulation and the practical experience of life and work of the human species, a "new quality" concrete and beneficial human society as a whole, at the same time and the environment, human thinking "ecologic cleaning of pollutants which pollute the psychological" will offer a triad» psyche of politics, religious and scientific ways and means necessary to ensure that development of human society in time and space to be always dialectics in human society and beneficial environment in direct proportion to the dialectic of human intellectual labor.

History facts reveal that periodically appear political personalities that make great intellectual effort to print walking human society a motion direction from what is something higher quality: a new leap forward.

Any attempt to do so it seems to be welcomed only if it is not based on knowledge and perception of absolute truth, "the source and engine" which gives shape and content walking the world in time and space, the consequences can be something other than those intended by the originator. Let me explain why this view: the advent of Gorbachev's political scene has given many hope of mankind, including the system of social and economic order both Socialist and capitalist, reason for which was awarded the Nobel Peace Prize.

The dissolution of the Warsaw Pact military bloc, creating the environment necessary for German unification, the Elimination of the consequences of the "cold war" between the two warring order socio-economic world-wide level are seen as beneficial, a great achievement of world peace.

CHAPTER XXI
THINKING AT CONTROL

Knowledge and perception of "thinking" is an issue that must preoccupy the pyramid tops of a social perception triad.

Through a fundamental scientific research, made by the chance and then by passion, I began a process of perception of law and dialectic thinking things, phenomena, law discovered by the great German idealist philosopher Hegel, who formulated the thesis that "things, phenomena and dialectical thinking evolves" and that "the dialectic of progressive thinking leads to knowing truth absolutely", hence the conclusion that the "cognoscibility of the world" is possible.

Passionate about knowing and perceiving the menticultural, this "but" enjoyed by the human species, I began to perceive that the dialectic thinking has two "streams": 1. dialectic of human intellectual force human and 2. quantitative collections by life experience and work of the human species. However, I have demonstrated scientifically, in the book democracy and social justice—the future of humanity, that man's intellectual force differs radically from man to man and is characterized in that it builds up in part, sometimes totally from human to human, from generation to generation, with the trend of development potential to infinity ($\rightarrow \infty$). Collections of quantitative experience life and work of the human species also grow continuously, hence the conclusion that "dialectic thinking, potential, are evolving towards infinity ($\rightarrow \infty$)" and that, at some point, cognoscibility of the world is possible.

The scale of a perception social triad: politics, religious and scientific, dialectic of human intellectual force is easily perceptible, as well as collections of quantitative the experience and the work of the human species. And then thinking of politics, religious and scientific do not converge to know and perceive the "ultimate truth" concerning the cause, secret, enigma? Why man, human society and its environment, such as "organic unity", outside the normality of function in conformity with the laws of nature? For the person thinking, "man", the definitely does not know himself, like nature and its forces by fire, and the laws that it dominates; because of its forces and laws which it dominates acting shared throughout the life of a man, independently of his will and desire, generating a process logic, common denominator, the entire human species: "the law of nature and human flesh", unknown and not levied by Bill humans thousands of years!

The law of nature and human flesh, unknown law generates three processes that define the nature and human nature:

1. the process of "compass psychological" man as nature and temperament,

2. the process of "enchain psychological" man as nature and temperament, and

3. the process of "pollution psychological" human thinking.

The law of human nature and flesh, through these three processes that define the nature and the temperament, causes him to become, unwittingly and without charge, "his own enemy and of the entire human species".

Through a fundamental scientific research, made of passion, on knowing the truth absolutely why man, human society and the environment, organic unit, does not work in line with the laws of nature, I began to perceive that man, because the law of nature and his flesh, becomes a harmful factor of "organic unity—man, human society and the environment", imperceptible process for him. I managed to do this scientific discover, it seems to be "the key" change the history of the human species, based on the characterization of human data that provides the necessary elements of knowledge and perception of human as nature and temperament.

Taking as a foothold for considering time as a human being "biologic-social, language, equipped with thought and articulated", owner of four forces: physical strength, intellectual force, the force of good and evil force, and dominated by a series of laws: the law of accumulation of wealth (wealth) at any cost and by any means, without the law, the law duly suitability, to force the star power, law no limit, law selfishness and so on, through imagination and contemplation of things and phenomena of life and work of the human species, I made a series of theses. By their content, they define the secret, because the State of the world in time and space, "the source and engine" that give form and content of riding the world and outlines why social and economic injustices, once in the slave era, remained in the form of a chain, whose length is for thousands of years and, unfortunately, is extended continuously. These highlights and that the fate of mankind, thanks to the law of nature and human flesh, is in great danger: "to be or not to be"; that the conclusions and views expressed by many intellectuals, great thinkers of the time of historical change, aiming at a State of the world, have led to what is wanted, because they have targeted "the effect of the case", the cause remains an unknown thousands of years. The theses cover ways and means necessary to ensure that the life and work of the human species would enter into normality, in conformity with the laws of nature; concerning changes history so that the condition of humanity to change their course by motion and auto moving of the "orbit" the social and economic injustices in the "orbit" the socio-economic equity, humanity is entering a new historical era: "the ERA of WISDOM and REASONING", epoch without unemployment and economic crisis, without wars, without terrorism, the general well-being of the entire human species . . .

It is a noble goal, not a utopia, but the consequence of the action of the law of dialectic thinking, things and phenomena. It is possible thanks to the absolute truth "knowledge—spring and engine", which gave his State of the world and give form and content in time and space. This noble objective is the consequence of dialectic thinking that, through the two sources of its: 1. dialectics of human intellectual labor and 2. quantitative accumulation from the life and the work of the human species, has led to the knowledge of the "absolute truth—spring and engine, which gave and gives shape and content walking the world in time and space.

These considerations have a "scientific "support, have "concrete steel "support, resulting of a fundamental scientific research, made of passion, regarding the knowledge and perception causes of the world state in time and space . . .

Synthetic, scientific support consists of:

1. Characterization datum of humanvvv which provides the necessary elements of human perception and cognition as nature and temperament;
2. The discovery of the "law of human nature and temperament" as an conjugate action between human forces with/and laws of man which it dominates; conjugate action that works independently of the will and desire of man;
3. Discovery, through imagination and contemplation on me and many of my fellow men on my way to be/the way of being of some of my fellow men that i have known, of the three processes that define the nature and human nature:
   a) process of made a "compass psychological" invisible, imaginary and hardly discernible, which directs the way of being human and its relations with his fellows and in dealing with the environment;
   b) process of made a "lace" imaginary invisible and hardly discernible, "strapped" by the conjugate action between human forces with/and man laws which it dominates, "lace" witch "enchaining him psychological" as nature and temperament, breaking and even stranding him evolve dialectics from what is normal and should be used judiciously since it is packed with thought;
   c) psychological pollution process of "thinking" with many and various nuisances arising from co-operations between the forces of human action, constituted as a dualism of good and evil, with/and the laws of man it dominates;
4. Human perception as "particular" of General "and" living cell "of general human society as a whole, hence the perception of the" law of nature and human flesh "as a" compass "imaginary directs human society development in time and space, the" compassing "channel of human society development taking

place through the work of the Organization and management at the level of State administration;

5. Design and formulation of a sentence which to generate a process of radical change in the way of the work of a social perception triad» representatives: politics, religious and scientific, whose work to be in the knowledge of the facts, subordinate of the control, and conveyance of "law of nature and human flesh", so that their work is always dialectic as efficiency, always rational and creative, directly proportional with the dialectic intellectual force of human and in line with the laws of nature;

6. Design and formulation of the thesis of a peaceful world revolutionary process, beneficial to each class, each national State, great or small, rich or poor, regardless of the disposition social and economic in the historical; the world peacefully revolutionary aimed at human dialectic as kind and fire in direct proportion to the dialectic of human intellectual labor;

7. To formulate thesis of human organization and management of the company by triad psyche: politics, religious and scientific, by an organization which I've called the "Supreme Forum of the human species", consisting of great intellectuals, big thinkers, philosophers, psychologists, theologians, historians, economists, and so on, the writers of all genres, which, in turn, have a platform-work program, on the basis of which will be made in the scientific research institute of scientific research on the knowledge and perception profiled drive organic between man human society and the environment. Here will work great intellectual personalities, connoisseurs and skilled in the evolution of human society, dialectic of goodies in the tactics and strategies aimed at changing the action of the law of dialectic in the sense of no longer being worn as a kind man, and fire, by the waves of the law of nature and human flesh, but to a steer to operate in conformity with the laws of nature and in direct proportion to the dialectic of human intellectual labor;

8. Organic unity between sentence inputs: work, nature and capital accumulated and the role of a triad» psyche: politics, religious and scientific in continuous production factors approximate, based on the dialectic of "human capital" live, the premise of the factor of production work.

Apart from these few examples, which forms the basis of the "scientific" placement on the State of the world "orbit" social injustice on "social right" orbit with historical perspective as humanity enters into a new HISTORICAL ERA, the ERA of "WISDOM and REASONING", in the books: democracy and social justice—the future of humanity, the dialectic of human society, man, let's change the world, nature and human nature-"the compass" targeting human society and in this book there are over 25 theses formulated.

They relate to the contents of the start of a process scientifically revolutionary world peacefully, beneficial social beneficial to each class, each national State, small or large, rich or poor, regardless of the disposition of social-economic development in the works.

In closing, the bequest by the one who reads the books above or at least the gist of these books, it is not to pronounce the "pro" or "against" until they make a small break in which to meditate upon himself as kind and threads, using the characterization of human time and trying to characterize the "law of nature and human nature" and by the three processes generated by the law of nature and human flesh.

This appeal is justified by the fact that many of those who read books on democracy and social justice—the future of humanity, the dialectic of human society, man, let's change the world and Nature and human nature, the compass of human society development targeting fail to organizations summoned Moldovan authorities that man is immune to everything they do many large historical intellectuals of the time on how the work of politics form of social consciousness, and, in this respect, I quote the following three articles that appeared in the newspaper "Jurnalul Național", February 9, 2009 in articles, which is typified by human society in Romania after 1989 to the present day:

"Ion Cristoiu: Fooling Top without anesthesia

Emil Boc would have had to realize that another one before him, Calin Popescu Tariceanu, he shared the same illusion, giving to Sorin Ovidiu Vantu (SOV) the Danube Delta and uranium ore from Budureasa.

1. Appointment by Emil Boc of a man's SOV in as Chairman of the National Agency for mineral resources. Much the world has asked what lies in front of diversion made about media trust of the FNI's parent exploitation of gas because of the so-called revelations of deontologists by cost from Reality and Cotidianul, some have been tempted to believe that it is a gesture of servility from Traian Basescu. A minimum knowledge of SOV—hyena, who has managed not only to escape unpunished for abjection called the NFI (National Found for Investment), but, more, and become the owner of a media empire, ought to be saying that SOV does not follow only self-interest. In the present case, the interest was a man of his at the forefront of key agencies in relation to financial blows. A man put on his face, of course, because, from a simple investigation, you discover that father FNI has many other dignitaries, leaders of parties and PARLAMENTARIES lists his payout. Emil Boc hastened to please his SOV. With the consent of the Chief of his Cotroceni, is assumed. Imberbul premier counted perhaps Sov, as gratitude, will assist the media with his empire.

2. The belief that the electorate's Mircea Geoană PSD will be shooting for his statements diddle that by participating in the governance of right-wing party and fulfilled its electoral promises. According to a speech given during a working visit to Romania, Mircea Geoană said that "If the PSD would not have been in Government,

today there had been an increase in the pension would not have guaranteed minimum pension was introduced, which I have promised those who have worked at the head, and the rise of wages had been frozen throughout the crisis". These so-called measures of social protection, in fact some crumbs thrown the poor so as not to starve, they would have taken any Government in Romania today.

3. Elena Udrea Declaration whereby the Ministry Tourism restore function will get involved heavily in promoting international Program-system restore function "Easter in Bukovina". As far as is known, promoted to the post of Chief of the County Council, a post he still approached one of the local landlord's son, Gheorghe Flutur announced a program to mark the fast of Easter this year that PDL wants to spend money on County gambol type his paint the largest egg in the world or bringing a match from the Holy Flame from Jerusalem with the plane is, ultimately, the job of Suceava, Serb at Baron Aktuelt. But that Elena Udrea wants to throw the money throughout the country bringing the majority of Orthodox pilgrims from countries to see Romanian traditions of Easter is a matter of stupidity on behalf of the State. In its view, protected the presidential phantasmagorical believes that the Russians, for example, will leave their country in churches to listen to the service of the churches of Romania at Easter. Not only Russian or Greek congregation will not be boarding planes to take the sacred flame from Traian Băsescu, but Romanians will jostle to go in Bukovina. First, because the true believers prefer for the night of Easter churches that frequency and the rest of the year and, later, because all other Romanians see in Easter holidays a pretext to give Calico. What we could offer the monasteries in northern Moldavia?

"Adrian Păunescu: pamphlets cordial

I captured a defeat

By not knowing when, with the exception of periods when I scattered between us, we, our, us, riches Romanians do devastating endeavor losing everything. I came with patriotic pride justified, in the long historical periods, birr from the Turks. I have given many fortunes, soil and subsoil, the Germans, as if to conquer hearts, that they might support us to lose support if Ardealul can call bluffing Ribbentrop.

I paid massive debts of war the Soviet Union, which has victimized over extent in relationship to a raving statist not demanded damages for ruthless Stalinist terror exerted over Bessarabia and Northern Bukovina.

They came and some years of peace, dignity, independence and more or less proper resource management. In recent decades we have range. National efforts with the supernatural, I managed during these years to give everything of our others.

A recent historical victory of Romania in the Hague, in the matter of Continental Highland of the Black Sea, is about to become a bitter defeat, since we are given to know, here, that our great conquest, logical and fair, is already sold by various nomenclaturists of Romania. We, on this occasion, that all that is heard and not be heard, the sea, not only the bottom of the HARLOTS, high space, not only the high the mountains, all and all were sold. Guys we have alienated their fountains and springs, and their crosses, cemeteries, horses from households and large horses, shoulders and arms, to nail. The tricks up more yesterday, with land and borders, with grandchildren and mistresses, with licenses and royalties, pale in the face of this impressive stories, sold to the firms that do not exist, the gas and oil from the depths of the Black Sea, which had, after long and after so many efforts facing us.

For a football match or handball, won an international competition, said Romanian people in the street, could come to revenge repeated absence of joy. For victoria, against Ukraine, on the pitch at the Hague could spend a unifying people's celebration. But it was not possible.

These two intellectuals of this, and many others in Romania, now in the beginning of the Millennium III, make great efforts to influence the intellectual, spiritual and political form of the psyche, to stop to give Romania a walking direction so harmful life and activity of citizens.

Allow me to say that any intellectual efforts will continue the great intellectual figures of Romania, unless it manages to get to know and to collect the secret, because that gives shape and content walking the world in time and space, this nation, not only to remain in a State of depression, social and political situation, but they will also worsen. Generalized, the very life and activity of the human species is in great danger and may point out that the phenomenon is common to the whole human species on Earth.

So it is of very great importance to the introduction of a new way to work at all levels, to perceive human thinking in the light of the law of nature and human flesh which pollute the psychologically with many and various nuisances generated by the action of immunoglobulin of human forces and laws with which man/it dominates and informed both by politics, religious and scientific to focus on the cause that makes him the man to be what it is for deciphering and elimination they, like the fate of the human species to come to work in line with the laws of nature.

Scientific, a form of social consciousness, the peaks of his pyramid is, in my view, the role of the history of the spiritual influence of mode of thinking and work of politics, but also religious (scientific), so that "thinking", at the level of a triad» psyche can work "untainted" unpolluted "with both" generated by the action of immunoglobulin of human forces and laws with which man/it dominates.

Scientific, a form of social consciousness, the tips of his pyramid, particularly those personalities who work in the field of free press, free broadcasting organizations summoned Moldovan authorities may be that their way of thinking and to work depends on the change history of the human species. Only scientific can do this "giant step" before knowing himself as kind and threads. This is why the order of psychological influence of the way of thinking and work of a triad» psyche must start with scientific. He, scientific, must know and perceive as kind and fire, "the law of nature and human nature" and by the three processes generated by the law of nature and human flesh and only after that will start influencing psychological of a triad» psyche to initiate, organize and lead a peaceful world revolutionary process, beneficial to each social classes at the level of world-wide the result of which the history of the human species will change!

SUMMARY

By means of a study which can be considered as a fundamental "imaginary" scientific research regarding the state of the world in time and space, "Mankind, whereto?", I have discovered the secret, the cause which led the man, endowed with the thinking ability—the common nominator of the entire human species—generated the historical process of the organization of life and activity—of the human species in an "unjust" world, in which some people cannot benefit from what the nature has to offer. The secret, the cause of the state of the world in time and space in an "unjust world", which once it appeared in the slavery epoch, Continued its existence historically under the form of a "historic chain", having a length of thousands of years and, unfortunately, continues to lengthen, it is "the law of nature and humanity", which has its own course, regardless of the man's will and wish.

It is not a real man, it is not a social class the cause of the secret which gave the world the form and content of an "unjust world", the source and the engine, which gave the world a shape and content of "unjust world", it is the law of nature and mankind".

The attempts of many intellectuals throughout the history to influence the common thinking in finding the necessary paths and means to change the world from an "unjust world" into a "just world", in which the life and activity of the human species develop in consensus with the laws of nature, could not be accomplished, for: since thousands of years, the intellectuals of historical times, the great thinkers imagined the state of the world through the "effect of the cause", the cause remaining unknown for thousands of years.

The absolute truth—source and engine—which gave and continues to give the world its shape and content in time and space is the law of nature and mankind.

I have discovered this law, which seems to be the most important law from the history of life and activities of the human species, by using the manner of thinking of many intellectuals of the historical times, by making use of the historical events during my life time, by analyzing my way of being and of many others fellows of mine whom I met, discovering the way they think, the way they work and how do they change depending on certain circumstances.

On such grounds, I gave a characterization of the man, which offers suffice elements in order to discover and perceive the nature and interior of the man, and the three processes that generate these, which define the man's nature and interior.

The discovery of the law of nature and of the mankind, knowing it and perceiving it as a conjugated action of the man's forces with/and the laws of the man who dominates him, action which function independently of the man's will and desire, I have come to the conclusion that the law of nature and of mankind leads the man, without wanting it and without even realizing it, on the "waves" of its motion and self-motion.

The real man cannot influence the action of the law of nature and of mankind, out of his own biological organism, not even in the moment when he knows and understands the law, but he can control it by means of the "mechanism" through which it operates: the organization and labor work at the level of state administration. This work should be given the necessary shape and content for the law of nature and mankind to operate only to the benefit of man, of human society and of environment. To this purpose I have invented "THE LIVE PROTECTION SHIELD", to give to the work of organization and management at the level of state administration the necessary content, so that the life and activity of the human species function in consensus with the laws of nature.

The triad of the social consciousness—the politics, the religion and science—taking into account the characterization given to man, which offers sufficient elements of knowledge and perception of nature and of human kind; of knowing the law of nature and mankind and of the three processes which the nature and interior of man generate; of the live protection shield, invention which offers the organic unity man, society, and environment, an evolution which is always dialectic and a consensus with the dialect of the man's intellectual force, it has the necessary "ammunition" to practice a not only rational work but also creative, beneficial to the organic unit: man, society and environment, giving to the world's course a direction to be place from the social injustices "orb" on the social rights "orb".

The law of nature and of mankind, the common denominator of the entire human species, acts differently from man to man and determines the consciousness of the self, of certain given men, from the general mass of the human species, to be out of ordinary: some of them "beneficial", others "maleficent", in the relationships that are established, logically, between men and between men and nature. And when, historically, these two processes appear in great political personalities, the faith of the citizens of the country is radically influenced either in a good or bad way, depending on how does the "axis of the good" acts or the "axis of the bad" from the central nervous system, from the man's brain, in certain moments, stating that with certain great political rulers the axis of good dominates the axis of the bad, while in others, the axis of the bad dominates the axis of the good. Sometimes such cases may appear as well, when the action of nature and of humankind has a positive or negative influence over the entire human species from Earth. A real case is Hitler in the Second World War, in which the axis of the bad had a range of action on a great potential of the human species. Another example is the great contemporary political man, Barack Obama, who seems to be dominated by the axis of the good, by means of the noble thinking of "peace and tranquility" and a world "without" nuclear bombs". Nevertheless, a great political leader may be influenced by the people close to him, either in a positive or negative way. These are my considerations for which I claim that the faith of the world should not depend on a certain person, either if this person is a great genius, even if this person is dominated by the axis of the good, because, from time to time, the report between the axis of the good and the axis of the bad shifts without the knowledge of the person in question, being unable to influence the report between the axis of good and the axis of the bad, because I have scientifically proven that the law of nature and of mankind functions regardless of the man's will and wish. And what it is very important to remember is that the law of nature and of mankind protects itself by means of one of the three processes that generates it and it cannot be influenced in its operation, but it may be guided by means of the organism which acts from particular to general: "the work of organization and leadership at the level of the state administration". The work of organization and leadership at the level of state administration needs to be given the necessary shape and content, so that the axis of the good be always predominant, which implies that the work of organization and of leadership at the level of state administration should have at its grounds tactics and strategies elaborated by great intellectual personalities: philosophers, psychologists, churchmen, historians, economists, biologists, writers of all genres, to work with the fundamental scientific research units, based on the knowledge and perception of man, as nature and temper, of the self-knowledge and on the perception of human society as a "universal site" in continuous modernization, on the organic perception between man, society and environment, on the man's perception as the particular and vivid cell of the general of the human society as a frame; on the perception that the man and the human society perfectly frames as a particularity, in the law of the dialectics of things, of phenomena and thinking and through the perception that the "law of nature and mankind", through its content, is in most of the cases, in contradiction with the dialectics in general, generating also the process of the becoming of man as nature and interiority, into a great enemy of man, human society and of the environment.

The law of the dialectics of things, of phenomena and thinking implies the dialectics of the work of organization and leadership of the society from platform programs which have at their basis personal ideas of a ruler and of the cooperation group, towards a platform program having at its basis the scientific research in the field.

The novelties, scientifically funded, as theses and points of view; the discovery of the laws of nature and humankind, which directs the people's way of being and which represents "the source and the engine" which gives the course of the world shape and content in time and space; the invention of the "live protection shield", which ensures the dialectics of the work of organization and leadership at the level of state administration directly proportional with the dialectics of the man's intellectual force, make sensitive the human thinking in perceiving that the state of the world in time and space is the piece of work of the human being, generated by the "law of nature and mankind", which functions regardless of the man's will and wish, it makes sensible the human thinking which is blocked and polluted by the conjugated action between the forces of man with/and the laws of man which dominate him. They make sensible the human thinking, that the work, regardless of whom practices it, starting with the level of the ones practicing the simple work, until the level of the ones practicing the complex work, be they scientists, is under the influence of the action of the law of nature and man temper, which generates also the process of wearing out and self-wearing out of a considerable potential of the energetic basis and not only. At all levels of the work provided, it must be ensured the necessary environment for the work to be not only rational and creative, beneficial to the organic unit: ",man, society and environment".

At the level of the triad of social consciousness—the politics, the religion and the science—the law of nature and human temper, which lead the man on the waves of his motion and self-motion, depending on the report (R) that took place between the weight of the forces of the good "the axis of the good" and the weight of the forces of the bad (the axis of the bad), is created the environment of the apparition of an "unjust" world, which once appeared continues to exist historically under the shape of a historical chain, with a length of thousands of years, and which, unfortunately extends. Attention: in this manner of the work of the triad of social consciousness is created the environment, by the law of nature and the human temper, so that the life and activity of the human species to be directed also towards "denying the denial", which can be visible by the modernization of the mass destruction means and by the accumulation of the potential of mass destruction (atomic and chemical bombs, which in case of being used will generate an ecological catastrophe of such dimensions that the life of the human species will be "denied").

Within the triad of social consciousness, the politics is the most gravely influenced by the psychological pollution of thinking by the action of the law of nature and human temper. At this level, the work is poor and a "Perpetua mobile" is practiced: insults and mutual offences between the leaders of the political class, mutual accusation as to the bad things in life and the activity of human species from the given country. Any intellectual efforts the representatives of the free press would make, their pyramidal peaks, the representatives of the free mass media, endlessly criticizing the political class, even if the criticism is justified and well-intended, as long as the cause is not known and perceived, the secret that makes the free man to work as he works, his work being an "effect of a cause", the work at the level of the mass media will be inefficient as well. And we have to take into consideration as well that the representatives of the free press and the free mass media are under the action of the law of nature and human nature.

We can draw thus the conclusion that the human species ought to know and perceive the law of nature and human nature and most of all the intellectuals, regardless of the field they work in. From here the thesis results: know yourself, as nature through the lens of nature and of man, change yourself as manner of work, for your work to be always rational and creative. Man, wherever you may be, whoever you may be, act until it is not too late, because the good, as well as the bad from the life of the human species is the consequence of the work of any of us, the people, under the influence of the law of nature and of the human nature, the common denominator of the entire human species. By knowing and perceiving the law above mentioned, you can make much better than harm your fellows and the environment.

When we succeed in knowing the law of nature and the nature of man, but we cannot influence radically in the beneficial way, you can participate as well, whoever you are, in influencing it and you can even guide it through the "mechanism" by means of which from particular becomes general: the organization work and leadership at the level of state administration.

The science, a form of the social consciousness, has the decisive role in influencing the politics and the religion in perceiving the necessity of the active and direct participation in the perfection of the "mechanism" by means of which the law of nature and of mankind is transmitted from particular to general: the work of organization and leadership at the level of state administration.

The leaders of the political class, the representatives of the religious cults, by means of certain intellectual personalities, may be aware that by means of a new method of work, the action of the law of nature and of mankind may be influenced in such a way that the man may take the dialectical leap as nature and temper, as to avoid being carried by the waves of motion and self-motion of the law of nature and of mankind, but to direct, in complete awareness, through the mechanism that takes place—the passing from particular to general—organization and management work at the level of state administration.

Making use of the characterization given to man: "The man is a biological-social being, endowed with thinking and articulate language, holder of four forces: the physical force, the intellectual force, the force of good (the axis of the good), the force of the evil (the axis of evil) and dominated by a series of laws: the law of accumulation of fortune (wealth) with any price and through any means, law without limit; the law of craving, the law of power craving, limitless law; the law of selfishness and individualism a.s.o. (see the books "Democracy and Social Justice", "The Dialectics of Man and Human Society") through contemplation over myself and over may of my fellows, and by means of imagination (abstract thinking) I have discovered the law of nature and of mankind, as being the conjugated force between the forces of man with/and the laws of man which dominate him, law which functions conjugated between the forces of man and/with the laws of man who dominate him, law which functions independently of the man's will and wish; a law which carries the man on the waves of his motion and self-motion.

Based on practical experience and imagination (abstract thinking) I have drawn the conclusion that the law of nature and of mankind generates three processes that define its nature and temper:

1. the process of creating a "psychological compass", invisible imaginarily and hardly perceivable, which directs the man's way of being in his reports with his fellows;
2. the process of "psychological enchainment" of the man as nature and temper, in an imaginary "net", an invisible and hardly perceivable net, woven by the conjugated action between the forces of man with/and the laws of man which dominate him, restraining him and even blocking him to evaluate dialectically, as nature and temper;
3. the process of the "psychological pollution of thinking", with many and diverse masses generated by the conjugated action between the forces of man with/ and the laws of man which dominate him.

From the practical experience, by means of contemplation, firstly upon myself, but also upon many of my fellows, and through imagination (abstract thinking), I have drawn the conclusion that the law of nature and of mankind functions independently of the man's will and wish, and it cannot be influenced by the man, but it can be influenced and even directed by means of the "mechanism" by means of which the process of transmitting form particular to general takes place: the organization and leadership work at the level of state administration. To this purpose I have invented the "live protection shield" which has to be imagined as a "selective psychological radar".

"The live protection shield" I invented, which needs to be imagined as a "selective psychological radar", is the key of life and the activity of human species in consensus with the laws of nature. "The life protection shield—selective psychological radar" cumulates and controls the laws of physics, chemistry, biology, knows and directs the law of the dialectics of things, of phenomena and of thinking, knows and perceives the man, the human society and the environment as an "organic thinking", in which the internal forces fights continuously each other, conquering one or the other. The source and the engine that puts into motion the internal forces is "the law of nature and humankind", or the man is the particular element and the "live cell" of the general of the human society in its whole, which makes the law of nature and human kind to become the "compass" of directing the course of the human society in time and space.

The man is also the holder of the primary and active production factor, "the work", which acts over the primary and passive production factor, the "nature" (the environment).

The law of nature and of mankind generated, from the historical point of view, a process of apparition of an "unjust world" in which the organic unit man, human society and environment, entered in a suffering living regime! "The live protection shield", with its multiple beneficial directions over the organic unity between man, the human society in its whole and the environment acts in consensus with the law of the dialectics of things, phenomena and thinking, and becomes thus a "protection shield": psychologically pollutant anti-thinking with the emission wastes generated by the conjugated action between the forces of man with/and the laws of man which dominate him by the fact that they act through the "mechanism" through which the nature and mankind become the "compass" of directing the course of the human society in time and space. He who is invested to organize and lead the human society, thus "universal site", does it based on tactics and strategies designed by great intellectual personalities—philosophers, psychologists, churchman, historians, economists, biologists, artists, writers of all types—who fundament their organization tactics and strategies and of leadership of the society which needs to be perceived as a "universal site" of continuous modernization of all chains of economical and socio-cultural nature, the characteristics of life and activity of human species in a dialectical motion and self-motion, on specialized scientific research study, that takes into consideration the human being, the human society and the environment as organic unit. The human being avoids thus the law of nature and of mankind vested to organize and lead the human society, this "universal site" to be able to influence the directing of the course of the "sinusoidal" human society; practically, the human society, this "universal site" begins to be led based on the common thinking of several great intellectuals, great thinkers, who, under full awareness, build the fundaments of the leading of the human society, this "universal site", the wisdom and rationality in the dialectic evolution proportionally with the dialectics of the intellectual force of man and of a thinking ecologization by the psychological pollution generated by the conjugated action between the forces of the human being with / and the laws of man which dominate him. "The live protection shield" needs to be imagined as "SELECTIVE AND MULTIDIRECTIONAL PSYCHOLOGICAL RADAR, BENEFICIAL TO MAN, TO THE HUMAN SOCIETY AND TO THE ENVIRONMENT". It screens "like a perfect sieve", what is bad in our life and in the activity of the human species and withholds only what is beneficial to the organic unity between man, society and environment. Thus the life and activity of the entire human species cross the border from an "unfair world" into a "fair world", in which the entire human species may benefit from what nature has to offer.

Why can the "live protection shield" be imagined as a SELECTIVE psychological RADAR? Because it provides the economic growth and the sustainable economic development, it avoids the level of unemployment and the economic crises from the life and activity of the human species, it ensures the rational and creative capitalization of the entire "live capital" that the society is provided with in time and spaces, it avoids the terrorism and the wars in the life and activity of the human species.

The mass destruction means (the atomic and chemical bombs), and their means of transportation to predetermined distances become wastes which will enter in the "waste damp of history", and the anti-missile protection shield becomes an artifact which can easily join the world historical museum.

It is important to notice as well the fact that the raw matter for the "live protection shield—the selective psychological radar", exists in most of the country on Earth, remaining to be organization only its operation, task of the TRIAD OF SOCIAL CONSCIOUSNESS: THE POLITICS, THE RELIGION AND SCIENCE.

There is also a need of political, religious and scientific will. This consciousness effort of the triad is worth for the general good of the entire human species and the protection of the environment!

My belief is that the representatives of the social consciousness triad, their pyramidal peaks, with power of decision, will become aware of the beneficial consequences of the "live protection shield—the selective psychological radar" and will make a comparison between a "psychologically polluted thinking" with many different toxins generated by the conjugated action between the forces of man with/or the laws of man who dominate and directs the course of the human society towards the maintenance of the social injustices, under the form of a historical chain, having a length of thousands of years and the worst of all, is preparing an "ecological catastrophe", which endangers the organic unity between the human being, the society and the environment, and this preparation to trigger the "ecological catastrophe" is also very expensive. Billiards of dollars are invested annually in nuclear bombs and in their transportation means at predetermined distances and all these have a single value of use: the destruction of human lives and the mutilation of many people that survive enduring pains and sufferings of all kinds, and a considerable destruction of economic goods. A "thinking cleaned of the toxins which pollute it psychologically" directs the course of the human society towards the healing of the organic unity between man, society and environment, and this process takes place in the conditions of reducing the huge financial efforts for the development and perfection of the mass destruction means, namely in the preparation of the environment of a truly generalized "Hell" on Earth. "The live protection shield—the selective psychologically radar", consequence of the colorization of the human thinking of the toxins that pollutes it psychologically, directs the course of mankind towards a true "Heaven" on Earth, generalized for the entire human species.

What must be done for this "millenary dream", desired by many intellectuals of the historical times to become a vivid reality? The human society must be organized and led through reason and collective wisdom by great intellectual personalities: philosophers, churchmen, historians, economists, biologists, artists, writers who should be more partisans of the dialectics of things, of phenomena and thinking, with great knowledge of the human society's history in time and space, with the express highlight that these are organized in a Supreme Forum of the Human Species, which approves the tactics and the strategies, designed in the institutes of scientific research institutes, specialized on the knowledge and perception of nature and of mankind, names the executant of the designed tactics and strategies, and follows during the entire course the manner of involvement of the tactics and strategies designed in the life and activity of the species.

The key issue is: will the leaders of the social consciousness triad succeed in making the dialectic self over step, in the sense of not letting themselves carried on by the "waves" of motion and self-motion of the law of nature and of mankind, and informed by it, to catch the "steering wheel" of directing the action of the law of nature and of mankind in operating only in a beneficial way for the organic unity between the man, the human society and the environment? My belief is "yes", because the law of the dialectics of things, of phenomena and of thinking, sooner or later, logically, rationally imposes this dialectical leap.

"The life protection shield—selective psychological radar" has two component groups:

1. a group of organization and leadership;
2. another of fundamental scientific research and design and tactics and strategies of organization and management of the human society.

These two components of the "live protection shield—selective psychological radar" are composed of the same "live material"—with great intellectual properties: philosophers, psychologists, churchmen, historians, economists, biologists, artists, writers of all kinds. The group from the scientific research institution researches and designs strategies of organization and leadership of the human society, a "universal site", so that the motion and self-motion of the human society in time and space be always in concordance with the dialectics of the human intellectual force of man and with the accumulations constituted from the experience of life and activity of the human species.

The group of organization and management of the human society approves and selects the order of implementation in practice of the tactics and strategies designed by the scientific research group, names the manager for organization and management of the "universal site", follows through supervisors the way the actions of the manager vested with the organization, leadership and management of the society, and intervenes when appropriate.

The discovery of the "law of nature and mankind", the invention of the "live protection shield—the selective psychological radar" and the formulation of a number of over 50 theses with reference to the "mechanism" of the change of nature and mankind, the healing of the human society and the ecologization of the environment from different forms of degradation, is the "key for a normal life and activity of the human species in consensus with the laws of nature": Nobody loses, the entire human species stands to gain.

The hate and revenge between people start with a process of "setting" for the future historical times of the human lives and activity. The man endowed with thinking starts a historical process of "self-revolution", the democracy, the freedom of thinking, the man's rights and liabilities become a beneficial "fruit" for the entire human species, the differentiation between people will be only in function of how will the man capitalize the "live capital" he has. For the requirements of capitalizing the live capital enter an optimal environment created through scientific research accomplished in the scientific research institute and of tactics and strategies design which ensure, from a dialectic evolution, the harmonization of the factor of production the work, the primary and active factor of production, with the nature factor of production, which is a primary and passive production factor, and with the derived production factors. The work protection factor enter into an ecologization factor, so that the rational labors and the ones which create economic and spiritual goods begin to operate dialectically, and the detrimental labors begin to slowly disappear, for good (production departments for the mass destruction weapons and their means of transportation to the predetermined distances, etc.).

Each member of the human society, within the social division of work, starts to practice a concrete or abstract work which will direct the course of the company towards general welfare, the mankind being placed from the orbit of an "unjust world", to the orbit of a "just world", in which every single unique and particular element of the human species starts to live in an environment in which his/her life will depend on how does he/she capitalizes the available live capital.

Synthetically said, the human species enters in a "self-revolutionary" process, following a "cleaning of the human thinking" of the toxins generated by the conjugated action between the forces of man with/and the laws of the man which dominate him. The humanity begins to evolve always dialectically by means of a peaceful world revolutionary process, benefic to each social class, to each small or big national state, rich or poor, regardless of its social-economical organization.

The organizer and leader of the world peaceful revolutionary process being the "leaders of the social consciousness triad: the politics, the religion and the science", the faith of humanity begins with not depending anymore or a person or a group of persons, the human society, "a universal site", begins to enter into normality and lawfulness, to be led by a collective wisdom, by the greatest thinkers of humanity organized in two parties (in two groups): a group of people who researches and designs tactics and strategies for organization and leadership, and the other approving and following them as they are implemented in the practical life of the human species.

The leaders of the social consciousness triad—the politics, the religion and science—from all countries of the world, please meditate on the substantiated scientific novelties, over the discovery of the law of nature and of mankind, and over the invention of the "live protection shield—the selective psychological radar" of life and activity of the human species and you will find the necessary "ammunition" to become the "source and engine" of the change of the state of the world from an "unjust world", suffering from a chronic disease—unemployment, economic, social and political crises, terrorism and wars—in a "just", healthy world, with a dialectical evolution.

For the passing of the border from an "unjust", suffering world into a "just", healthy one, is needed only the political, religious and scientific will to start the process of the "ecologization of thinking" of the toxins generated by the conjugated action between the forces of man with/and the laws of "the man who dominate him.

The organization and management of the human societies based on scientific research and design of tactics and strategies, which should lie at the base of the "modernization of the universal site", in consensus with the dialectics of the intellectual force of man and with the quantitative accumulations from the experience of life and activity of human species, is the "key of normalization of life and activity of the human species in consensus with the laws of nature".